D1566462

TONY KUSHNER

TONY KUSHNER

New Essays on the Art and Politics of the Plays

Edited by James Fisher

McFarland & Company, Inc., Publishers
Jefferson, North Carolina, and London

LIBRARY OF CONGRESS CATALOGUING-IN-PUBLICATION DATA

Tony Kushner : new essays on the art and politics of the plays /
edited by James Fisher
    p.   cm.
Includes bibliographical references and index.

ISBN 0-7864-2536-9 (softcover : 50# alkaline paper)

1. Kushner, Tony — Criticism and interpretation. 2. Kushner,
Tony — Political and social views. I. Fisher, James, 1950–
PS3561.U778Z92   2006
812'.54 — dc22   2006008760

British Library cataloguing data are available

On the cover: Bethesda Fountain in Central Park in New York City
photographed by Rachelle Bowden (rachelleb.com)

Manufactured in the United States of America

McFarland & Company, Inc., Publishers
  Box 611, Jefferson, North Carolina 28640
  www.mcfarlandpub.com

To Dana

Contents

Preface   1

1 "The Angels of Fructification": Tennessee Williams,
   Tony Kushner, and Images of Homosexuality on the
   American Stage
   — JAMES FISHER   5

2 Kushner, Inge and "Little Sheba": Strange Bedfellows
   — JEFF JOHNSON   28

3 Blood Relations: Adrienne Kennedy and Tony Kushner
   — ROBERT VORLICKY   41

4 Then and Now: W.H. Auden, Christopher Isherwood,
   Tony Kushner, and Fascist Creep
   — DAVID GARRETT IZZO   56

5 Stonewall, "Constant Historical Progress," and *Angels
   in America*: The Neo-Hegelian Positivist Sense
   — DAVID KRASNER   98

6 Queer Politics to Fabulous Politics in *Angels in America*:
   Pinklisting and Forgiving Roy Cohn
   — ATSUSHI FUJITA   112

7 Two Illusions: Cultural Borrowings and Transcendence
   — FELICIA HARDISON LONDRÉ   127

8 Reading Corneille with Brecht: *The Comedy of Illusion*
   and the Illusions of Citizenship
   — STEFKA MIHAYLOVA   135

9 When Worlds Collide: The Kushner-Lamos *A Dybbuk*
   at Hartford Stage
   — PAULA T. ALEKSON   149

vii

10   Repairing Reality: The Media and *Homebody/Kabul* in
     New York, 2001
          — *JACOB JUNTUNEN*   172

11   "Succumbing to Luxury": History, Language, and Hope
     in *Homebody/Kabul*
          — *JAMES FISHER*   190

12   The Therapy of Desire
          — *BERT STERN*   201

Contributors   215
Index   219

Preface

In an interview with Jane Edwardes, Tony Kushner stated his formula for navigating the complexities of contemporary life. "Pessimism of the intellect, optimism of the will," he said, is "still the formula. The planet may cease to exist over the next 100 years, but I can't be a gay man living in 1999, even given all that's still wrong all over the world for lesbians and gay men, and be blind to the fact that so much has changed in such an incredibly short time" ("Kabul's Eye," *Time Out*, 30 June–7 July 1999). Disaster looms, but change and progress are the means of avoiding or surviving it, Kushner insists. The job of the dramatist, as he explains in the introduction to the libretto for his 2003 musical drama *Caroline, or Change*, is to express that belief. "Words can say what words can't say; the apt description can describe the indescribable," Kushner writes of his lifelong desire to "move audiences with words alone." This apt description of the fundamentally human search for means by which to communicate the joys and sufferings of existence, for articulating the struggle to survive what cannot be survived, and for developing strategies to move forward into an unknown and often frightening future, offers a way of thinking about the essence of Kushner's dramatic works. His love of voluptuous, fiery, lyrical, hilarious, and heart-wrenching language provides his audience with a linguistic feast at which he serves up the complexities, contradictions, joys, and terrors of contemporary life, even when his unforgettable characters find themselves in period dress.

The first productions of Kushner's two-play epic *Angels in America* launched the career of a playwright that has had few parallels. Kushner, at the early midpoint of a working life from which will surely emerge many more intriguing achievements, has already secured a prominent position among America's most iconic dramatists— Eugene O'Neill, Tennessee Williams, Arthur Miller, Edward Albee. The essays in this collection place Kushner in the context of these and other essential U.S. playwrights, as well as international titans of modern drama and literature. Without a doubt, Kushner has emerged as a dramatic force to be reckoned with. The collisions of history, literature, art, spirituality, race and ethnicity, gender and sexuality, and, most significantly, politics that are found in his plays ensure that virtually any collection of responses to his work offers its readers a challenging journey through not only millennial American life, but also the vast corridors of world culture that have shaped it.

Of the many things that might be said of Kushner's work, foremost among these would be to acknowledge its range in theme and style. Although readers and theatre-goers know him mostly from *Angels in America* on stage and screen, Kushner's theatrical achievement thus far is more virtuosic and versatile than even its ambitious nightmare journey through Reagan's America would suggest. He has written libretti for musical dramas (*Caroline, or Change*) and operas (the as-yet unproduced *St. Cecilia, or The Power of Music*), vaudeville-style political farces (*Slavs! Thinking About the Longstanding Problems of Virtue and Happiness*), grim Brechtian dramas (*A Bright Room Called Day*), and visionary political epics (*Homebody/Kabul* and the forthcoming *Henry Box Brown*), along with a plethora of one-act plays on a wide range of subjects and the work-in-progess, *Only We Who Guard the Mystery Shall Be Unhappy*, the first scene of which has inspired strong reactions for its depiction of First Lady Laura Bush's heavenly encounter with a classroom full of dead Iraqi children killed by American bombs. Kushner's screenplay for the six-hour HBO film version of *Angels* has won him Emmy Awards and Golden Globes, and his screenplay for *Munich*, directed by Steven Spielberg, about Israel's response to the murder of its athletes at the 1972 Munich Olympics, was a contender for a 2006 Academy Award.

The exploration of millennial political dynamics is the heart of Kushner's art, and his political activism is a central focus of his life. It remains one of the more fascinating phenomena of his emergence that Kushner's plays seem in direct counterpoint to the neo-conservative slant of late twentieth and early twenty-first century American life. From the midst of Reagan's presidency to the divisive fifty-fifty, conservative-versus-liberal split in contemporary blue state–red state American politics, Kushner's neo-socialist, gay activist internationalism has surprisingly drawn audiences back to a declining American theatre through the confluences of its bracing intellectualism, political outrage, scalding humor, and heartfelt and redemptive compassion. At least two of his major works, *Angels* and *Homebody/Kabul*, have so fully tapped into the intensely emotional public debate as to generate a brand of controversy and attention extraordinary for any dramatist. *Angels* took its audiences into the profound personal suffering masked by Reagan's "morning in America" and the anti-gay rhetoric of the AIDS pandemic, while *Homebody/Kabul* anticipated the horrors of 9/11, the resultant "war on terror," and the ongoing quagmire resulting from the U.S. military invasion of Iraq. Kushner proved with these works the deep-seated need for a humanizing exploration of our values and the hope that theatre can provide in the most dire circumstances.

The essays in this collection span Kushner's oeuvre to date, from his early success with a lively adaptation of Pierre Corneille's seventeenth-century comedy *The Illusion* through *Angels in America*, and on to more recent works, including his adaptation of the early twentieth century Yiddish theatre classic *A Dybbuk, or Between Two Worlds*, the harrowing and prescient drama of confronting the "other" in *Homebody/Kabul*, and the convergence of race and history in the musical *Caroline, or Change*. Previous studies of Kushner have focused attention nearly exclusively on the *Angels* plays; in this collection of essays, the goal is to provide a broader exploration of Kushner's dramatic achievement to date, approaching his plays as both literature and texts for performance.

It should be noted that the able contributors to this volume offer views as diverse as Kushner's plays. Some are emerging scholars; others are among the most distinguished in the field. Paula T. Alekson's thorough examination of Kushner's free adaptation of Ansky's *A Dybbuk* in Mark Lamos's premiere staging of it stresses the performance component and production history, while distinguished theatre historian Felicia Hardison Londré contrasts Pierre Corneille's classic play *L'Illusion comique* with Kushner's celebrated adaptation of it, *The Illusion*. Young scholar Stefka Mihaylova vividly explores Kushner's Brechtian approach to his adaptation of this same Corneille classic, while simultaneously illuminating the significance of Brecht to all of Kushner's work. Atsushi Fujita investigates queer politics through *Angels in America's* memorable historical antagonist, the rapacious Roy Cohn, while Jacob Juntunen sheds light on diverse media responses to *Homebody/Kabul*. The juxtapositions of history and language are the focus of my exploration of the same play, while the raw personal tensions of race and ethnicity are illuminated in poet Bert Stern's study of *Caroline, or Change*. The prolific scholar David Krasner examines the phrase "neo–Hegelian postivist sense," spoken by *Angels in America's* Louis Ironson, to illuminate *Angels* and the gay revolution inspired to a great extent by the 1969 Stonewall riot. Convergences with other writers (as in Stefka Mihaylova's essay) are probed in some of the essays, including my own on Tennessee Williams and Kushner as central figures in the evolution of American gay drama. Jeff Johnson offers an analysis of the parallels he finds in the plays of Kushner and William Inge, while Robert Vorlicky, editor of the essential *Tony Kushner in Conversation* (Ann

Arbor: University of Michigan Press, 1997), explores the convergences in the works of Adrienne Kennedy and Kushner. Finally, David Garrett Izzo explores the work of literary giants W. H. Auden and Christopher Isherwood in a formidable essay in which he sees Kushner's neo-socialism as the logical descendant of the "fascist creep" the Auden-Isherwood plays identified in the 1930s.

To this collection's contributors, I offer my sincere thanks for their fine essays, good will, and infinite patience. Some "friendly ghosts" are also to be acknowledged: my late father, Clarkson S. Fisher, from whom I learned the value of a strong work ethic, and four dear friends: Erminie Leonardis, who gave me loving support and introduced me to the fine arts; Kenneth W. Kloth, who taught me about collaboration and loyal friendship; Lauren K. "Woody" Woods, whose passionate love of the theatre permanently infected me; and John C. Swan, who encouraged my scholarly pretensions. My mother, Mae Hoffmann Fisher, continues to encourage me, as do my brothers Dan, Scott, and Biff, along with Biff's wife, Carolyn, and their children Duke, Caylan, and Cilloran, and my in-laws, Dan and Kathleen Warner. Wabash College Theater Department faculty and students challenge me on a daily basis, and other supportive and inspiring friends to whom I am continually grateful include my brother-in-law Daniel Warner and sister-in-law Mary Russo and their daughter Karen, Peter Frederick, David Garrett Izzo, Kaizaad Navroze Kotwal, Philip C. Kolin, Felicia Hardison Londré, Diane and Jamey Norton, Warren Rosenberg, Tom Stokes, and Bert Stern. Above all, I express my sincere appreciation to Tony Kushner.

Most of all, I wish to express my love and gratitude to my two beautiful children, Daniel and Anna, and my amazing wife, Dana, to whom this volume is dedicated.

James Fisher
Spring 2006

1

"The Angels of Fructification"

Tennessee Williams, Tony Kushner,
and Images of Homosexuality
on the American Stage

JAMES FISHER

*Who, if I were to cry out, would hear me among the angelic
orders? [Rilke 244–245].* — Rainer Maria Rilke

*Still obscured by glistening exhaltations,
the angels of fructification had now begun
to meet the tumescent phallus of the sun.
Vastly the wheels of the earth sang Allelulia!
And the seven foaming oceans bellowed Oh! [In the Winter of
Cities, 32–34].* — Tennessee Williams

Angels have traditionally been viewed as symbols of spiritual significance. Residing in a realm somewhere between the Deity and His creations, they watch over humanity as unspeakably beautiful harbingers of
hope and of death. These simultaneously comforting and unsettling icons
are central to Tennessee Williams's poem, "The Angels of Fructification,"
in which his angels also provide a vision of homosexual eroticism comparatively rare in his dramas, despite the frequent emphasis on sexuality
and gender in Williams's plays.

To a great extent, Williams was the theatre's angel of sexuality, the
dramatist most responsible for forcefully introducing sexual issues, both
gay and straight, to the American stage. The fruit of his labor is particularly evident in subsequent generations of playwrights who present gay
characters and situations with similar (and increasing) frankness, depth,
and lyricism. Such works bloom most particularly after the 1960s, and
most richly in Tony Kushner's epic two-play drama, *Angels in America*, a

work recognized as one of the most important American plays of the past fifty years.

There are revealing parallels to be found in Kushner's *Angels* plays, *Millennium Approaches* and *Perestroika*, and the dramas of Williams. Their plays feature epic passions in their characters; both depict dark and poetic images of the beautiful and horrifying aspects of existence; both create a stage language that is at once naturalistic and lyrical; both ponder the distance between illusion and reality; both explore the nature of spirituality from a grounding in modern thought; and, both deal centrally and compassionately with complex issues of sexuality from a gay sensibility. Alfred Kazin writes of homosexuality that "'The love that dare not speak its name' (in the nineteenth century) cannot, in the twentieth, shut up" (Kazin 38), but the emergence of Williams, and those dramatists like Kushner following in his footsteps, prove there is much to say on a subject about which the stage was too long silent.

In reflecting on the history of homosexuals in American theatre, Kushner points to "a natural proclivity for gay people — who historically have often spent their lives hiding — to feel an affinity for the extended make-believe and donning of roles that is part of theatre. It's reverberant with some of the central facts of our lives" (Blanchard 42). It is not surprising that in a society in which homosexuals were firmly closeted before the 1960s, that the illusions of the stage provided a safe haven for gays. Williams could not be as open about his sexuality in his era as Kushner can be now and, as such, Williams often worked in overtly heterosexual situations and characters. Williams's creative achievements grow out of a guarded self-awareness and desire for self-preservation, as well as the constraints of the prevailing values of his day, although there is an increasing frankness about homosexuality in his work from the late 1960s until his death.

Donald Windham believes that Williams "loved being homosexual. I think he loved it more than he loved anybody, more than he loved anything except writing" (*Tennessee Williams. Orpheus of the American Stage*), and Edward A. Sklepowich seems to agree when he writes that "Williams treats homosexuality with a reverence that at times approaches chauvinism" (Sklepowich 541). In fact, as far as his writings go, Williams was ambivalent about homosexuality — his own or anyone else's. Williams's sexual preferences were well known in the theatrical community from the beginning of his career and it is unclear exactly when Williams first "came out" publicly. His 1970 appearance on David Frost's television program seems one of the earliest declarations on record. When Frost asked him about homosexuality, Williams replied that "I don't want to be involved in some sort of a scandal, but I've covered the waterfront" (Frost 40). Williams also told Frost that "everybody has some elements of homosexuality in him, even the most heterosexual of us" (Frost 40), but a few years later he wrote that "I have never found the subject of homosexuality a satisfactory theme for a full-length play, despite the fact that it appears as frequently as it does in my short fiction. Yet never even in my short fiction does the sexual activity of a person provide the story with its true inner substance" ("Let Me Hang It All Out" 1). A couple of years later, in an interview in the *Village Voice*, Williams made the point bluntly: "I've nothing to conceal. Homosexuality isn't the theme of my plays. They're about all human relationships. I've never faked it" (Bell), and in 1975 he explained that "Sexuality is part of my work, of course, because sexuality is a part of my life and everyone's life. I see no essential difference between the love of two men for each other and the love of a man for a woman; no essential difference, and that's why I've examined both" (Berkvist). In his fiction, *One Arm* (1945), recently (2004) adapted into dramatic form by Moisés Kaufman, and *Moise and the World of Reason* (1975), Williams is franker in his depiction of homosexuality than in any of his plays. However, more important than issues of homosexuality, the characters in his novels and short stories feel the absence of love and a need for connection, themes that recur more guardedly in Williams's dramatic work. There is no question that, as a rule, Williams was writing about love not gender and Williams criticized sexual promiscuity as "a distortion of the love impulse" ("The Lively Arts"). For him, this impulse, in whatever form, was sacred.

In retrospect, Williams's guarded exploration of homosexuality, or at least his unwillingness to be more overt about it in his plays, pales by comparison with the defiant openness of Kushner and other millennial gay dramatists. Williams balked at writing what he called gay plays, but Kushner feels "very proud that *Angels* is identified as a gay play. I want it to be thought of as being part of gay culture, and I certainly want people to think of me as a gay writer. It does also seem to speak very powerfully to straight people" (Raymond 17). For Kushner, a significant parallel with Williams is that the characters of *Angels* are "basic components of who I am and the people that I love" (Raymond 17). To understand, in part, why Williams obscured homosexuality in his plays, Gore Vidal explains that Williams "had the most vicious press of almost any American writer I can think of. Fag-baiting was at its peak in the fifties when he was at his peak and it has never given up, actually" (*Tennessee Williams. Orpheus of the American Stage*). Donald Spoto believes that Williams's ambivalence had to do, in part, with the fact that he wanted "to be controversial — the hard-drinking, openly homosexual writer with nothing to hide — and at the same time, a man of *his own time*, a Southern gentleman from a politer era who would never abandon propriety and privacy" (Spoto 292). This view may indicate why Williams seemed uncomfortable with public displays of drag or camp, which he wrote are

> imposed upon homosexuals by our society. The obnoxious forms of it will rapidly disappear as Gay Lib begins to succeed in its serious crusade to assert, for its genuinely misunderstood and persecuted minority, a free position in society which will permit them to respect themselves, at least to the extent that, individually, they deserve respect — and I think that degree is likely to be much higher than commonly supposed [*Memoirs* 63].

And it was in the area of the arts, Williams felt, that the gay sensibility was most likely to first engender such respect. In his *Memoirs* he writes that "There is no doubt in my mind that there is more sensibility — which is equivalent to more talent — among the 'gays' of both sexes than among the 'norms'" (63). At the same time, Williams wished to attract a broader audience than gays for his work and seems to have believed that a so-called gay play might limit his access to universal acceptance.

Williams's concern about acceptance was not without some justice. He did not have to look back too far into the preceding decades of American drama to see that the audience was, at best, uncertain about its willingness to accept homosexual characters and gay-related issues. The first known American play to deal openly with homosexuality is believed to be Mae West's *The Drag* (1927), which generated so much controversy over a scene depicting a drag ball that it closed before completing a tumultuous pre–Broadway tour. A few other curiosities appeared in subsequent decades, most notably Lillian Hellman's *The Children's Hour* (1934), in which the question of a lesbian relationship is at the center of the play, although, as Hellman herself frequently explained, the play is really about the power of a lie. The fact that the lie in question is about a supposed lesbian relationship is, for Hellman, incidental. Secondary homosexual characters appear in a few plays of the 1930s and 1940s, but they are rarely identified as such. Simon Stimson, the alcoholic choir master of Thornton Wilder's *Our Town* (1938), is a possible example of such types, typical in that he is comparatively unimportant to the plot and that he is seen mostly as a tragic victim (although the argument could be made that he is not, in fact, a closeted gay man, that his tragedy may stem from an unexplained source). The tragic victim or, as in most other cases, a comic sissy or stern spinster were the only dramatic evocations of gay life in mid–twentieth century America. With the appearance of Robert Anderson's *Tea and Sympathy* (1953), in which a sensitive young man is thought by his peers to be a homosexual (even though it later becomes clear that he is not), gay issues and characters slowly begin to come out of the shadows, even if within a level of ignorance and mendacity reflected in popular boulevard plays like *Tea and Sympathy*.

During the 1950s, other playwrights introduced gay characters and themes, but often not in their most visible work. William Inge, inspired to become a playwright by Williams, did not feature openly homosexual characters in his major plays, but in a few lesser-known one-acts he introduces some centrally in plays that are pleas for tolerance. Inge's *The Tiny Closet* (1959), for example, features a man boarding in a rooming house where a nosy landlady has attempted to break into a padlocked closet in his room. When the man goes out, the landlady and a friend manage to break in and discover an array of elegant women's hats. The landlady's violation of his privacy — and the presumption that she will cause him public disgrace — leaves the man's fate in question. Inge's blunt attack on anti-gay prejudice (his 1962 one-act, *The Boy in the Basement*, makes a similar tolerance plea) was written in the aftermath of the McCarthy era, and is a forerunner of later gay plays, particularly those written after the late 1960s as arguments for greater acceptance for homosexuals.

Mid–twentieth century dramatists employ varied techniques to present gay characters and situations. One device frequently discussed since the 1960s is "transference," the act of hiding gay viewpoints and situations behind a mask of heterosexuality. Edward Albee, often accused of using transference in the writing of such plays as *Who's Afraid of Virginia Woolf?* (1962), is a gay dramatist who, like Inge, emerged in the 1950s. With the homosexual triumvirate of Williams, Inge, and Albee dominating the non-musical Broadway stage — and despite the fact that none of them had publicly acknowledged their own sexuality at the time — *New York Times* drama critic Stanley Kauffmann "outed" them in 1966. Although he does not name names, there is no doubt to whom he is referring in his article "Homosexual Drama and Its Disguises." Kauffmann implies that homosexual writers ought not write about anything but gay characters, an attitude which, if carried into other areas, would logically imply that men are unable to write about women (and vice versa). The absurdity and inherent homophobia of this view becomes all too clear. Kauffmann's notion, undoubtedly prevalent in the mid–1960s, emerges fully when he writes that

> Conventions and puritanisms in the Western world have forced them [homosexuals] to wear masks for generations, to hate themselves, and thus to hate those who make them hate themselves. Now that they have a certain

relative freedom, they vent their feelings in camouflaged form. [...] They emphasize manner and style because these elements of art, at which they are often adept, are legal tender in their transactions with the world. These elements are, or can be, esthetically divorced from such other considerations as character and idea [Kauffmann 1].

Albee firmly refutes the idea that he, or Williams, employed transference in the writing of their plays: "Tennessee never did that, and I can't think of any self-respecting worthwhile writer who would do that sort of thing. It's beneath contempt to suggest it, and it's beneath contempt to do it" (Bryer 21). Gore Vidal's explanation of the centrality of women characters in Williams's plays seems a valid alternative to understanding his work and the reasons critics see transference in his characters. Vidal believes that for Williams, "The woman to him was always more interesting as she was apt to be the victim of a society" (*Tennessee Williams. Orpheus of the American Stage*). Williams believed that there are many aspects of the female in the male and vice versa as Strindberg did. And, again like Strindberg, Williams's pained, driven, poetic, and passionate characters are unquestionably extensions of his own persona, regardless of their gender.

Williams believed that "romanticism is absolutely essential" and felt that the "ability to feel tenderness toward another human being. The ability to love" was paramount and that people must not let themselves "become brutalized by the brutalizing experiences that we do encounter on the *Camino Real*" (Frost 35). Romanticism, however, must co-exist with self-awareness and a clear sense of the differences between illusion and reality. The characters who suffer most in Williams's plays do so less because of any deviance from accepted norms than because they are, somehow, self-deluded. There is no doubt that constraints on sexuality in the American society in his time meant that Williams's sexually-driven characters were often outlaws who could only be fulfilled through acts of transgression. His characters can often be shocking to audiences and certainly to the world in which they live. Aggressive in their pursuit of fulfillment, they can destroy and be destroyed as Williams undoubtedly hoped to destroy constraints and mores that prevented the survival of a romantic attitude and the ability to love. Reflecting on Williams's plays, Albee suggests that the drama itself is "an act of aggression. It's an act of aggression against the status quo, against people's smugness. At his best, Tennessee was not content with leaving people when they left a play of his the way they were when they came in to see a play of his" (*Tennessee Williams. Orpheus of the American Stage*).

Williams's first Broadway success, *The Glass Menagerie* (1944), is rare among his works in that the sexuality of his characters is not a central factor. However, beginning with his subsequent early plays such as *Summer and Smoke* (1947), the sexual personas of his characters become central and visible — and they would remain so for the rest of his career. In *Summer and Smoke*, Alma Winemiller fears and rejects sexuality, which she equates with bestiality, and places a high value on spiritual love. However, despite her attitude she is physically drawn to young Dr. John Buchanan, her neighbor, whose view of sexuality is purely biological. "I reject your opinion of where love is," she tells John, "and the kind of truth you believe the brain to be seeking!— There is something not shown on the chart" (Williams *Volume 2*: 221). She is stuck with a very unsatisfying form of love, given her attraction to John. He is similarly trapped behind his awe of Alma's spiritual and physical purity. He admits to her that "The night at the casino— I wouldn't have made love to you.... I'm more afraid of your soul than you're afraid of my body. You'd have been as safe as the angel of the fountain — because I wouldn't feel decent enough to touch you..." (Williams *Volume 2*: 222). Alma hides behind her propriety and the safe haven of her weak suitor, Roger Doremus, an unacknowledged gay man who, she instinctively understands, poses no sexual threat. Ultimately, Alma's despair leads her to abandon resistance to sexuality. As the play ends, she is discovered near the same angel of the fountain John mentioned, picking up a traveling salesman who refers to her as "angel." Williams acknowledges that Alma's startling liberation mirrors his own move "from puritanical shackles to, well, complete profligacy" (Gaines 27). Profligacy, as Williams describes it, represents "Liberation from taboos"; sex is a welcome release, and as a playwright he endeavored not to "make any kind of sex dirty except sadism" (Gaines 27).

Roger Doremus is one of several shadowy gay characters Williams includes in his earliest plays; in fact, often this sort of character would not even appear on stage. *A Streetcar Named Desire* (1947) was a seismic event in American theatre, but particularly so in the area of sexuality. Blanche Du Bois, raised in a genteel family of the Old South, faces so many burdens of physical and emotional death that she begins to believe its opposite is sexual desire, which she seeks promiscuously. The most harrowing death in Blanche's past is the suicide of her young husband, Allan Grey, many years before. Allan's repressed homosexuality can only be read as weakness by the immature and frustrated Blanche, as she recounts to her lumpish suitor, Mitch:

> There was something different about the boy, a nervousness, a softness and tenderness which wasn't like a man's, although he wasn't the least bit

effeminate looking — still — that thing was there.... He came to me for help. I didn't know that. I didn't find out anything until after our marriage when we'd run away and come back and all I knew was I'd failed him in some mysterious way and wasn't able to give the help he needed but couldn't speak of! He was in the quicksands and clutching at me — but I wasn't holding him out, I was slipping in with him! I didn't know that. I didn't know anything except I loved him unendurably but without being able to help him or myself. Then I found out. In the worst of all possible ways. By coming suddenly into a room that I thought was empty — which wasn't empty, but had two people in it ... the boy I had married and an older man who had been his friend for years ... [*A Streetcar Named Desire* 114].

Blanche also recounts the events of the same evening at the Moon Lake Casino, after Allan has killed himself: "It was because — on the dance-floor — unable to stop myself — I'd suddenly said — 'I saw! I know! You disgust me....' And then the searchlight which had been turned on the world was turned off again and never for one moment since has there been any light that's stronger than this — kitchen — candle..." (*A Streetcar Named Desire* 115). Blanche's deeply-rooted sexual dysfunction can be found in this moment, in Allan's homosexuality and her inability to understand or accept it. Despite her desperate dalliances with countless other men, mostly too young, she is unable to reignite the light of love snuffed out by her harsh treatment of Allan.

The issue of transference consistently emerges in critical discussions of *A Streetcar Named Desire* and Blanche's character. Among others, Robert Emmet Jones describes the play's remaking Blanche as a homosexual male, but he finally states that it is not the femininity of Blanche, but the masculinity of Stanley Kowalski that ultimately provides *Streetcar* with a "very homoerotic element [...] in a convincing heterosexual situation" (Jones 554). Before Williams, the male body was not depicted in the drama as erotically appealing, but Stanley, particularly as embodied by the young Marlon Brando who first played him, is a sexual catalyst for both sexes. Stanley, a character defined by his appetites, ultimately uses his sexual power as a weapon against Blanche, but learns, as Blanche has, that sex for its own sake is inevitably destructive — only when it is mixed with love and compassion can it redeem, a view Kushner would certainly share.

In terms of Williams's homosexual characters, *Camino Real* (1953), a drama that failed to attract an audience in its original production more for its startling theatrical innovations than for subject matter, is of significance. *Camino Real*, a play of fanciful metaphysics pleading for a romantic attitude about life, depicts the crosscurrents of history as described by a particularly literary sensibility, again pointing to another parallel with Kushner, whose plays are fueled by literary references drawn from his vast knowledge of world literature. In *Camino Real*, Williams intermingles literary icons Don Quixote, Kilroy, Camille, Casanova, and Lord Byron in a phantasmagoric world inspired by elements of Spanish folklore and Christian imagery. Although relatively unimportant in the main context of the play, the character of Baron de Charlus, borrowed from Proust, is an avowed homosexual and pointedly effeminate, a trait Williams claimed to deplore. When such types appear in his plays they are often objects of ridicule. Jones believes that in such portrayals, Williams "ironically shows less compassion than he does for his other males who, even though they may be homosexual, are at least masculine in appearance and action" (Jones 555). Such masculine characters of ambiguous sexuality appear more frequently in Williams's plays of the mid-to-late 1950s, although they appear in his early fiction, as in the case of Olly, the one-armed boxer turned street hustler in *One Arm*. In *Orpheus Descending* (1957) Williams makes use of the myth of Orpheus who descends into the underworld to rescue his lover Eurydice from the King of the Dead. Val Xavier is Williams's Orpheus, a sensual and poetic hero inarticulately yearning for some vaguely understood form of transcendence, either through art or sex. A somewhat less poetic version of this type can be found in Chance Wayne, the young male hustler of *Sweet Bird of Youth* (1959), but it is with Brick Pollitt, the alcoholic ex-athlete of *Cat on a Hot Tin Roof* (1955) that Williams takes another important step in the depiction of homosexuality.

Brick shares Williams's repugnance at what he calls "fairies," mocking the deceased former owners of the family estate who were two gay men. Brick's past successes in sports are taken by all as a sign of unquestioned masculinity, but his family, particularly his sexually frustrated wife, Maggie, are distressed by his reckless and relentless drinking. He does not drink, however, because his athletic career is over, as all but Maggie think, but because he fears that his confused feelings for his deceased best friend, Skipper, who he now knows was a homosexual, haunt him. In this inner turmoil, a parallel can be seen with Mormon lawyer Joe Pitt, in Kushner's *Angels in America*, a character brought up to be a heterosexual family man, but who is in fact a closet gay man. In response to questions about Brick's dilemma, Williams explains that Brick "went no further in physical expression than clasping Skipper's hand across the space between their twin beds in hotel rooms— and yet his sexual nature was not innately 'normal'" (*Where I Live* 72). Brick is also digusted by the "mendacity" he sees around him, and finally recognizes in himself. Here character and author meet, for certainly Williams understood as a gay man in 1950s America that mendacity, as Brick explains, is "a system that we live in" (Williams *Volume 3*: 127). Hellbent on destroying himself, Brick drinks to oblivion, but learns in the final scenes that the act of love is more important than anything — including the gender of those involved. Maggie becomes an angel of salvation for Brick and, as the play concludes, she succeeds in drawing him back to her bed through her love and wish to create an heir, a son of Brick's, to whom a dying Big Daddy can leave his vast fortune and estate. His sexual identity may not be a resolved issue, but the illusion of heterosexuality is maintained.

There are no such saving angels to be found in *Suddenly Last Summer* (1958), in which Williams sketches a vision of a predatory erotic universe. Following the violent and mysterious death of her son Sebastian, the imperious Violet Venable tries to convince young Dr. Cukrowicz to perform a lobotomy on her disturbed niece Catherine, who has witnessed Sebastian's death. Mrs. Venable does not want Catherine's version of Sebastian's death to prevail, but Cukrowicz encourages Catherine, who painfully recounts the final hours of the voraciously homosexual Sebastian, who died at the hands of a mob of predatory youths he had used sexually. In a sense, Sebastian is devoured by his own promiscuous appetites, he is caught up in a frightening cosmos in which only the most efficient predators survive.

The last stages of Williams's depiction of homosexuality is the most significant in his dramatic canon. Walter Kerr described *Small Craft Warnings* (1972), which is set in a down-and-out bar, as a play of "Talkers, drinkers, losers getting ready for one or another kind of death" (Kerr 8). Frequently considered by critics to be a lesser play in the Williams canon, it is, in fact, a highly significant work in appreciating Williams's dramatic depiction of homosexuality. Critics have generally claimed that Williams offers a dark and embittered view of homosexuality through the character of Quentin, a middle-aged, second-rate screenwriter and avowed homosexual. The play, which is written in a series of connected confessional arias for the major characters, permits Quentin, in a speech Williams himself considered the best in the play, to reflect on his way of life:

> There's a coarseness, a deadening coarseness, in the experience of most homosexuals. The experiences are quick, and hard, and brutal, and the pattern of them is practically unchanging. Their act of love is like the jabbing of a hypodermic needle to which they're addicted but which is more and more empty of real interest and surprise [Williams *Volume 5*: 260].

Quentin expresses his amazement at Bobby, the young hustler from Iowa he has recently picked up. Williams describes Bobby as having "a quality of sexlessness, not effeminacy" (Williams *Volume 5*: 240), and Quentin is amazed that Bobby has "the capacity for being surprised by what he sees, hears and feels in this kingdom of earth," and painfully acknowledges that he himself has "lost the ability to say: 'My God!' instead of just: 'Oh, well'" (Williams *Volume 5*: 261). Bobby presents an image of youthful wonder and a joy in his sexuality that balances Williams's portrayal of Quentin's dulled, cynical sexual sensibility. Another angle is supplied by Leona, the self-described "faggot's moll," a drunk and habitué of the bar, who recalls the experiences of her deceased brother to Quentin:

> I know the gay scene and I know the language of it and I know how full it is of sickness and sadness; it's so full of sadness and sickness, I could almost be glad that my little brother died before he had time to be infected with all that sadness and sickness in the heart of a gay boy. This kid from Iowa, here, reminds me a little of how my brother was, and you, you remind me of how he might have become if he'd lived [Williams *Volume 5*: 254].

At the time *Small Craft Warnings* was first produced, critics seem eager to believe that Williams was condemning homosexuality — or regretting his own — in this play, and that Quentin's bitterness and disillusionment were some sort of final statement on the subject by Williams (in the 1990s, critics would similarly suggest that the self-loathing Louis Ironson of Kushner's *Angels in America* might be an autobiographical portrait of Kushner himself.) In fact, Williams shows several faces of homosexuality in the play (as Kushner does in *Angels*). Quentin's and Leona's views, if indeed they are speaking for Williams, may well have more to do with the author's personal unhappiness and addictions than serving as a universal statement on homosexuality. Williams, who played the role of Doc in the off–Broadway production of *Small Craft Warnings* for part of its run, believed that Quentin was close to his own persona because he, too, had

> quite lost the capacity for astonishment.... I'm not a typical homosexual. I can identify completely with Blanche — we are both hysterics— with Alma and even with Stanley.... If you understand schizophrenia, I am not really a *dual* creature; but I can understand the tenderness of women and the lust and libido of the male, which are, unfortunately, too seldom combined in women [Jennings].

Williams's interest in androgyny also becomes clear in his depiction of Bobby's exuberant love life in *Small Craft Warnings*. Bobby has lost none of his capacity for astonishment, and at one point in the play he describes an experience that literally caught him between the sexes:

> On the plains of Nebraska I passed a night with a group of runaway kids
> my age and it got cold after sunset. A lovely wild young girl invited me
> under a blanket with just a smile, and then a boy, me between, and both
> of them kept saying "love," one of 'em in one ear and one in the other, till
> I didn't know which was which "love" in which ear or which ... touch....
> The plain was high and the night air ... exhilarating and the touches not
> heavy [Williams Volume 5: 264].

In his letters and *Memoirs*, which written at the time he was working on *Small Craft Warnings*, Williams writes with similar eroticism about his own sex life. Perhaps his ultimate public stance is best expressed by Monk, the owner of the bar in *Small Craft Warnings*, who opines of gays that "I've got no moral objections to them as a part of humanity, but I don't encourage them in here" (Williams *Volume 5*, 264). Williams's final explorations of homosexuality come in his free adaptation of Anton Chekhov's *The Seagull*, which he called *The Notebook of Trigorin* (1981), in which he imagines the world-weary writer Boris Trigorin as a bisexual, and, more significantly, in his autobiographical drama, *Something Cloudy, Something Clear* (1981), in which he returns to his dramatic alter-ego, Tom Wingfield of *The Glass Menagerie*, now called August, who is discovering himself as a dramatist and as a homosexual. Williams's view is less ambivalent than in his previous depictions of gay characters, but as always with Williams the complexities of character obscure, to some extent, the notion that any individual viewpoint may be a final statement on any human topic.

The theatre in general was catching up with Williams's depictions of homosexuality in the late 1960s. With the appearance of Mart Crowley's *The Boys in the Band* (1968), gay theatre, and the inclusion of homosexual characters and issues in mainstream American drama, increased significantly. Between 1960 and the early 1980s, however, gay characters were still reduced to peripheral status in many plays—or were seen most vividly in musicals like *La Cage aux Folles* (1983), boulevard comedies like *Torch Song Trilogy* (1981), or in broad stereotypes in straight plays. There were exceptions, including Albee's *Everything In the Garden* (1967), LeRoi Jones's *The Toilet* (1964), and the outrageous grotesquerie of Charles Ludlam's Theatre of the Ridiculous, but at the outset of the AIDS epidemic an important change occurred in the theatrical depiction of gays. Homosexual plays became either scathing indictments of American society's failure to adequately respond to the AIDS crisis, as in the plays of Larry Kramer, or dark depictions of the oppression of gays, as in Martin Sherman's *Bent* (1978), which dramatizes the oppression of homosexuals during the Nazi era. However, no gay dramatist seems to directly follow Williams, who, as Delma Eugene Presley writes "made serious efforts to explore the subjects of reconciliation and redemption" (Presley 579) in their work. Before Williams, only Eugene O'Neill faced such questions and, of course, not in the area of sexuality; after Williams, only Kushner, who deals with sexuality centrally.

Despite many similarities between Williams and Kushner, there is at least one obvious difference: Kushner is a dramatist with a strongly political sensibility. Williams is rarely thought of as a political writer, and he himself believed that "only in the case of Brecht that a man's politics, if the man is an artist, are of particular importance in his work" (*Memoirs* 178). In recalling his political awakening, Williams remembered in his *Memoirs* that he came of voting age while working at Continental Shoemakers and "cast my first and last political vote. It was for Norman Thomas: I had already turned Socialist" (*Memoirs* 46). Late in life, his political interests became inflamed by "the atrocity of the American involvement in Vietnam, about Nixon's total lack of honesty and of a moral sense, and of the devotion I had to the cause of Senator McGovern" (*Memoirs* 120), and he continued to long for the emergence of "an enlightened form of socialism" (*Memoirs* 118). Otherwise, Williams's drama is certainly not overtly political, but Kushner argues that "All theater is political. If you don't declare your politics, your politics are probably right-wing. I cannot be a playwright without having some temptation to let audiences know what I think when I read the newspaper in the morning. What I find is that the things that make you the most uncomfortable are the best things to write plays about" (Blanchard 42). The AIDS epidemic had, in essence, pushed gay dramatists toward a more politicized view—even more than had been inspired by the Stonewall era. A politicized gay theatre, for Kushner, is a positive direction. He believes that "America watching the spectacle of itself being able to accept homosexuality is good for America" (Blanchard 42).

Kushner's political awakening began when he was in college. After reading Ernst Fischer's *The Necessity of Art*, he became fascinated with questions of the social responsibility of artists. He grew up in the era reflecting dizzying changes in the way that American society responds to gays, and the influences on his development, as both a human being and an artist, are many and varied. He was inspired, in part, by the writers and artists emerging from the Stonewall generation, by ACT UP and Queer Nation, whose chant, "We're here, we're queer, we're fabulous" pervades Kushner's *Angels* plays. He acknowledges some debt to dramatists like Larry Kramer and Harvey Fierstein, but more directly significant to his development as a dramatist is his deep admiration for Williams: "I've always loved Williams. The first time I read *Streetcar*, I was annihilated. I

read as much Williams as I could get my hands on until the late plays
started getting embarrassingly bad. [...] I'm really influenced by Williams"
(Savran 24). Kushner also admires the plays of John Guare, who "Like
Williams, has figured out a way for Americans to do a kind of stage poetry.
He's discovered a lyrical voice that doesn't sound horrendously twee and
forced and phony" (Savran 24). Kushner aims for lyricism in *Angels*, weaving a tapestry of the crushing human and spiritual issues of the Reagan
era — and beyond — with poignant realism (in the Williams sense) and
epic stature (in both the O'Neillian and Brechtian senses). John Lahr writes
of the connections between Williams and Kushner:

> Not since Williams has a playwright announced his poetic vision with such
> authority on the Broadway stage. Kushner is the heir apparent to Williams'
> romantic theatrical heritage: he, too, has tricks in his pocket and things
> up his sleeve, and he gives the audience "truth in the pleasant disguise of
> illusion." And, also like Williams, Kushner has forged an original, impres-
> sionistic theatrical vocabulary to show us the heart of a new age [Lahr
> 133].

At the very least, if Williams's plays dramatize homosexuality from the
1940s through early 1970s, Kushner's plays clearly provide the next chapter. In technique, particularly in his lyricism, scope, humor, and compassion for his characters, Kushner is clearly indebted to Williams. There are
also distinct differences. For example, all of the major male characters in
Angels are gay — some are "out" and others are "closeted" — but all must
deal with their sexuality as a central part of the action Kushner provides.
In the age of AIDS, sexuality cannot be hidden any longer. Williams's gay
characters are forced by their times to the periphery of mainstream society, while Kushner's have broken through to the center — but not without
great cost. In *Small Craft Warnings*, Williams provides Quentin and Bobby
equal time to reveal their differing perspectives, and Kushner similarly
allows each of his characters ample opportunity to share their private journeys of self-discovery within the complexities, contradictions, and hypocrisies he finds in modern American life.

Drama critics such as John Simon, often accused of homophobia,
disliked the *Angels* plays, particularly finding them pleas "not just for
homosexuality but also and especially for transgression, a life-style of
flouted complaisance and flaunted social unacceptable excess" (Simon
130–131), but despite this the plays generally found acclaim, and perhaps
surprisingly so for an openly gay dramatist in a still homophobic society.
One of the ironies of the success of *Angels* is that the mainstream audience has embraced it, despite the fact that its politics, moral universe, and

views of sexuality are, at least as measured by those elected to public office, are the opposite of what American society claims to believe. It is perhaps in this irony that some of the questions that both Williams and Kushner explore meet. As Kushner wonders, "What is the relationship between sexuality and power? Is sexuality merely an expression of power? Is there even such a thing as 'sexuality'?" (Savran 100).

There is a sense of Greek fatality in *Angels* that can be identified in *The Glass Menagerie, A Streetcar Named Desire,* and *Suddenly Last Summer,* but also an Ibsenite element in its notion that humanity is on the wrong path and that the souls of the past and future will demand retribution. Kushner believes that tragedy, both real and fictional, teaches and changes people. The *Angels* plays are feverish historical dramas about our immediate and current history, but it is the questions Kushner asks that are of greatest significance. What claim can we make to humanity in a nation racially, politically, morally, and sexually divided? Has America chosen an uncompassionate path as part of an inevitable movement toward spiritual decline and death or can this course be changed and renewal be achieved? For Williams, tragically-inspired plays "offer us a view of certain moral values in violent juxtaposition" (*Where I Live* 53), and Kushner provides this conflict in *Angels.* Despite the political predilections of its author, *Angels* attempts to allow both sides their say. Its most lovable character is dying of AIDS, but so is its most detestable; both conservative and liberal characters have admirable moments and reprehensible ones; the strong become weak and the weak become strong. Kushner seems to believe what Williams once said of human experience: "I don't believe in villians or heroes— only right or wrong ways that individuals have taken, not by choice but by necessity or by certain still-uncomprehended influences in themselves, their circumstances, and their antecedents" (*Where I Live* 91–92).

It is in this vein that Kushner's "gay fantasia on national themes" begins. The first *Angels* play, *Millennium Approaches,* opens on a somber scene as an elderly rabbi stands over the coffin of Sarah Ironson, a woman whose difficult life embodies the immigrant experience of her generation. The rabbi berates the congregation for their lack of understanding of the past and the individual journeys of those like the deceased, ending with the ominous warning that "Pretty soon ... all the old will be dead" (*Angels* I: 11). And with them will go the values and certitudes that shaped their lives and our times. Kushner then shifts his gaze to a married couple, Joe and Harper Pitt, and a gay couple, Prior Walter and Louis Ironson, the grandson of the deceased woman. Both relationships are at points of primal crisis when they intersect with the life of McCarthy-era hatchet man and shark lawyer Roy Cohn. Joe is a Mormon lawyer whose conservative politics lead him to Cohn, who would like to place Joe in the Justice Department as his "Roy Boy" in Washington. Joe, however, is caught up in a personal struggle with his long repressed homosexuality. He has lived according to the rules by which he was raised — to be a family man, to be devoutly religious, and to be a conservative Republican. However, he is also miserable. In an agonized plea to Harper, who demands that Joe tell her whether or not he is in fact a homosexual, Joe says what Williams's Brick Pollitt might have said had he a greater level of self-awareness:

> Does it make any difference? That I might be one thing deep within, no matter how wrong or ugly that thing is, so long as I have fought, with everything I have, to kill it. What do you want from me, Harper? More than that? For God's sake, there's nothing left, I'm a shell. There's nothing left to kill. As long as my behavior is what I know it has to be. Decent. Correct. That alone in the eyes of God [*Angels* I: 40].

Joe's life-long conflict with himself is most potently illuminated in a later speech to Harper that reminds of Rev. Shannon's struggle with his vision of a predatory god in Williams's *The Night of the Iguana* (1959), as well as the predatory universe depicted in *Suddenly, Last Summer*:

> I had a book of Bible stories when I was a kid. There was a picture I'd look at twenty times every day: Jacob wrestles with the angel. I don't really remember the story, or why the wrestling — just the picture. Jacob is young and very strong. The angel is ... a beautiful man, with golden hair and wings, of course. I still dream about it. Many nights. I'm.... It's me. In that struggle. Fierce and unfair. The angel is not human, and it holds nothing back, so how could anyone human win, what kind of a fight is that? It's not just. Losing means your soul thrown down in the dust, your heart torn out from God's. But you can't not lose [*Angels* I: 49–50].

When Joe finally acknowledges his homosexuality, he phones his mother, Hannah, in the middle of the night. He painfully reveals his secret to her in a scene that undoubtedly mirrors the experiences of many homosexuals. Kushner himself has said that this scene is taken directly from his own life. After preliminary awkwardness during which Joe admits he has been drinking, he blurts out his confession: "Mom. Momma. I'm a homosexual, Momma. Boy, did that come out awkward. [Pause] Hello? Hello? I'm a homosexual. [Pause] Please, Momma. Say something" (*Angels* I: 75). Hannah is unable to reply directly or even acknowledge what Joe has said, but terminates the call with a burst of sudden anger, shouting "Drinking is a sin! A sin! I raised you better than that" (*Angels* I: 76). Later, Joe encounters Louis, who is in a desperate flight of fear from his long-time lover Prior, who is suffering from the initial stages of AIDS. Racked with guilt at his faithlessness, the politically liberal Louis reflects on the Reagan era, which he sees as a metaphor for his own behavior. He describes himself and Joe as "Children of the new morning, criminal minds. Selfish and greedy and loveless and blind. Reagan's children" (*Angels* I: 74). Louis falls into a brutal, punishing sexual encounter with a stranger in Central Park in a situation that mirrors Quentin's description of the "coarse" experience of homosexuals in Williams's *Small Craft Warnings*. The stranger asks, "You been a bad boy?" Louis can only sardonically reply, "Very bad. Very bad" (*Angels* I: 55).

Meanwhile, Joe's wife Harper, seriously addicted to Valium, and Prior, often delirious as he becomes sicker with AIDS, meet in each other's hallucinations. These scenes are filled with the sort of camp that Williams preferred to avoid. Some critics of *Angels* similarly found the camp to be too stereotypical, but Kushner believes that there is something empowering for gays in drag and a camp sensibility, in the deconstruction of stereotypical images of gays. As a character, Prior combines both wonderment and cynicism, hope and despair in his personality; and is also, at times, outrageously campy. At one point, while in drag, he turns to the mirror on his dressing table and intones "I'm ready for my closeup, Mr. DeMille" (*Angels* I: 30) in his best Norma Desmond imitation. Kushner's use of various forms of humor with all of his characters, but most particularly with Prior, is similar to the ways in which Williams typically broke the unspeakable tension of his most unsettling scenes to show the absurd and grotesque sides of a character's circumstances (*Streetcar*, his masterpiece, offers much humor in Stanley's view of Blanche, and vice versa, for example.) As Williams told Dick Cavett in a television interview: "Much of my pleasure in life comes from the fun, you know, the funny side of people. And if you omit that from them then they don't seem quite real. I don't find people lovable unless they're somewhat funny" ("The Dick Cavett Show"), something Kushner seems to emulate in his depiction of Prior.

Kushner uses a quite different brand of humor with the character of Roy Cohn. Cohn's gleefully bitter corruption is both comic and frightening. One of the most remarkable aspects of *Angels*— and something that is typical of Williams's plays as well — is the way in which sympathetic moments emerge for even the most monstrous and transgressing characters. Roy is a rapacious predator who is first discovered in his command module juggling phone calls and wishing he had eight arms like an octopus. It is Roy's self-loathing that is most unsettling and is most vividly shown in his scathing denial of his own homosexuality:

Like all labels they tell you one thing and one thing only: where does an individual so identified fit in the food chain, in the pecking order? Not ideology, or sexual taste, but something much simpler: clout. Not who I fuck or who fucks me, but who will pick up the phone when I call, who owes me favors. This is what a label refers to. Now to someone who does not understand this, homosexual is what I am because I have sex with men. But really this is wrong. Homosexuals are not men who sleep with other men. Homosexuals are men who in fifteen years of trying cannot get a pissant antidiscrimination bill through City Council. Homosexuals are men who know nobody and who nobody knows. Who have zero clout [*Angels* I: 45].

Roy represents a kind of trickle-down morality in *Angels*—Kushner's notion that if there exists corruption, greed, and bad faith in the ruling class of a society, it will ultimately seep down to each individual within it. As Robert Brustein writes, there are "no angels in America, only angles" (Brustein 30) and *Angels* presents a moral combat set in a corrupted capitalist society represented at various points by the opposing poles of conservative and liberal, gay and straight, transgressor and victim. As in many of Williams's finest plays, *Angels* deftly captures a convergence of past, present, and future. The past, as previously indicated, is symbolized by the death of an elderly Jewish woman. The present is seen in the mantra of greed and self-interest represented by Reagan conservatism, in its embodiment in Cohn, and by a general loss of faith and loyalty, as demonstrated in the behaviors of Joe and Louis. The future is represented by a choice between destruction and change best exemplified at the end of *Millennium Approaches* by the startling appearance of an angel who may be bringing news of either salvation or apocalypse. Fear of the future, moral uncertainty, and a sense of inexplicable loss torment Kushner's characters; in one scene, a nameless, homeless woman predicts "In the new century, I think we will all be insane" (*Angels* I: 105). Kushner raises questions for which there are no easy or simple answers. What lies before us as old values die? How will we find our way without the familiar social, moral, and religious signposts of the immediate past? Can we embrace change before it is too late? Can we make room at the table for everyone? One character ruefully realizes that there is no safety net under these choices, and little guidance in the American experience, for "There are no angels in America, no spiritual past, no racial past, there's only the political" (*Angels* I: 92).

As a dramatist with a decidedly political bent, Kushner is perhaps closer to an Arthur Miller or a Bertolt Brecht than to Williams in this respect. However, both Kushner and Williams reflect on a changing sociopolitical environment within which their characters are caught between two worlds: one that is dying and one that is being born. The centrality of politics in *Angels* can be found most obviously in Roy Cohn, who, for Kushner, is the exemplar of the hypocrisies and failures of conservatism. To Roy, politics is raw power — he revels in his "clout." There is no room for compassion in Roy's view. When Joe confides in Roy his feelings of guilt about his abandonment of Harper, Roy advises that "Life is full of horror; nobody escapes, nobody; save yourself. [...] Learn at least this: What you are capable of. Let nothing stand in your way" (*Angels* I: 58). Roy is haunted by a vision of Ethel Rosenberg, who he had been instrumental in sending to execution for espionage years earlier. This encounter prompts him to proclaim "I have *forced* my way into history. I ain't never gonna die" (*Angels* I: 112). However, Ethel warns "History is about to break wide open. Millennium approaches" (*Angels* I: 112). Kushner's scathing view of Roy as an exemplar of conservatism is balanced by his equally harsh view of traditional liberal politics, which are seen in Louis's self-righteousness and moral impotence. Louis theorizes about politics, but Belize, a gay African American and close friend of Prior, faces the political divide directly when he becomes Roy's nurse. Belize is angry at the horrors of AIDS, which he sees on a daily basis, and the bigotry he encounters on both sides of the political spectrum. He tells Louis that: "I hate this country. It's just big ideas, and stories, and people dying, and people like you. The white cracker who wrote the national anthem knew what he was doing. He set the word 'free' to a note so high nobody can reach it" (*Angels* II: 96). And of Louis, Belize remarks that his liberalism has him "Up in the air, just like that angel, too far off the earth to pick out the details. Louis and his Big Ideas. Big Ideas are all you love" (*Angels* II: 96). Kushner himself is situated on the political left, but it is within Prior's more human and personal politics that Kushner's sympathies lie. Prior grapples with the politics of existence with a profoundly humane and compassionate sensibility. Fear exists in Prior, who recounts a story of one of his ancestors forced to escape in a lifeboat with seventy other passengers when a ship foundered. Whenever the lifeboat sat too low in the water or seemed about to capsize, crew members would hurl the nearest passenger into the sea. Dying of AIDS, Prior says

> I think about that story a lot now. People in a boat, waiting, terrified, while implacable, unsmiling men, irresistibly strong, seize ... maybe the person next to you, maybe you, and with no warning at all, with time only for a quick intake of air you are pitched into freezing, turbulent water and salt and darkness to drown [*Angels* I: 41–42].

At the end of *Millennium Approaches*, an angel appears to a delirious Prior who is frightened, but with moving courage resists his fears: "I can handle pressure, I am a gay man and I am used to pressure, to trouble, I am tough and strong and..." (*Angels* I: 117). At this point, Prior is overwhelmed by an intense orgasm as the angel crashes through the ceiling of his room, announcing that "The Great Work begins" (Kushner, *Angels* I: 119), and the angel at least partially means that working toward a greater compassion for homosexuals is a part of this great work.

In the second *Angels* play, *Perestroika*, the characters continue individual journeys in a darker and even more intellectually complex drama. Kushner says that when he listens to *Perestroika* now he realizes "it has so much about loss—how to deal with it and how not to be deformed by losing" (Raymond 15), a subject Williams and his characters could certainly appreciate. Where *Millennium Approaches* depicts faithlessness and selfishness with compassion while offering a glimpse of the retreating conscience of American society, *Perestroika* finds Kushner's characters tentatively progressing. Despite the overall grimness of much of *Perestroika*, the play finally—and with a moving humanism typical of Kushner's, and Williams's work, brings several of the characters to some measure of forgiveness and a settling of accounts. Most shattering of all may be the scenes in which Belize reluctantly but compassionately nurses the delirious and dying Cohn, despite hateful taunts and threats. At one point, Belize offers Roy advice about getting AZT, an AIDS drug then in its experimental phase, and the mistrusting Roy nastily says, "You're a butterfingers spook faggot nurse. I think ... you have little reason to want to help me," to which Belize wryly replies, "Consider it solidarity. One faggot to another" (*Angels* II: 30). Roy uses his political clout to get the AZT, but it is too late to help him. As he gets sicker, and is transformed, at least in his own mind, into one of the disenfranchised, he vents his fury at his recurring vision of Ethel Rosenberg:

> The worst thing about being sick in America, Ethel, is you are booted out of the parade. Americans have no use for sick. Look at Reagan: He's so healthy he's hardly human, he's a hundred if he's a day, he takes a slug in his chest and two days later he's out west riding ponies in his PJ's. I mean who does that? That's America. It's just no country for the infirm [*Angels* II: 62].

When Roy dies, Belize gets Louis to help him steal Roy's stash of AZT for Prior. In the play's most moving sequence, Louis, appalled to find himself at the bedside of the repugnant Cohn, reluctantly gives in to compassion and joins a ghostly Ethel Rosenberg to chant the "Kaddish" over Cohn's corpse. Similarly, Joe's rigidly Mormon mother, Hannah, cares for the abandoned and increasingly disturbed Harper. While working at her volunteer job at New York's Mormon Welcome Center, Hannah leaves Harper alone with a life-size diorama of a nineteenth century Mormon pioneer family. Harper thinks she sees Joe, her errant spouse, in the image of the "Mormon Father," and pleads for guidance from the "Mormon Mother." When the figure comes wondrously to life and grimly leads Harper toward the next stage of her personal journey, Kushner achieves a transcendent meeting of past and present not at all unlike that in Williams's *Camino Real*, a magical road where the fictions of history and literature converge with reality.

Hannah has lost her son Joe as a result of her rigidity, but visiting Prior in the hospital teaches her tolerance for the "otherness" of homosexuality. She asks Prior if she should come see him again, and Prior, borrowing Williams's most famous—and campiest—line, becomes Blanche Du Bois for a moment. "Please do," he says, "I have always depended on the kindness of strangers." Hannah, unfamiliar with this line, can only reply, "Well that's a stupid thing to do" (*Angels* II: 141). Hannah does return and is no longer a stranger, either to Prior or herself, for she has been visited by Prior's angel and experienced a similarly orgasmic response that has begun her transformation.

The final scene of *Perestroika* is set at the Bethesda fountain in Central Park, with a statue of an angel in its center. It is not at all unlike the one where Williams's repressed Alma Winemuller has her sexual awakening. At the Bethesda fountain a newly created family including Prior, Hannah, Belize, and a repentant Louis meet. A stronger, wiser Hannah asserts Kushner's view of the interconnectedness of all humanity, regardless of race or sexual preference, and the primacy of loyalty and commitment to others. Prior points out the angel of the fountain, his personal favorite in that it is a figure commemorating death but suggesting "a world without dying" (*Angels* II: 147). With Prior's prompting, Louis recounts the story of the angel Bethesda who "descended and just her foot touched earth. And where it did, a fountain shot up from the ground" (*Angels* II: 147). Belize explains that if "anyone who was suffering, in the body or the spirit, walked through the waters of the fountain of Bethesda, they would be healed, washed clean of pain" (*Angels* II: 147). Prior, the prophet, whose AIDS symptoms have stabilized, notes that the healing waters of the fountain are not flowing now, but that he hopes to be around to see the day it flows again. And, in a final statement, this indomitable gay character speaks for those who have come before, from the shadowy figures of Williams's early plays through Kushner's outspoken gay characters:

> This disease will be the end of many of us, but not nearly all, and the dead will be commemorated and will struggle on with the living, and we are

not going away. We won't die secret deaths anymore. The world only spins forward. We will be citizens. The time has come [*Angels* II: 148].

Works Cited

Bell, Arthur. Interview with Tennessee Williams. *Village Voice* 24 February 1972.

Berkvist, Robert. Interview with Tennessee Williams. *New York Times* 21 December 1975.

Blanchard, Bob. "Playwright of Pain and Hope." *Progressive Magazine* October 1994.

Brustein, Robert. "Robert Brustein on Theater: *Angels in America.*" *New Republic* 24 May 1993.

Bryer, Jackson R., editor. *The Playwright's Art. Conversations with Contemporary American Dramatists.* New Brunswick, NJ: Rutgers University Press, 1995.

The Dick Cavett Show. Interview with Tennessee Williams. 1974.

Fisher, James. *The Theater of Tony Kushner: Living Past Hope.* New York: Routledge, 2002.

Frost, David. *The Americans.* New York: Stein and Day, 1970.

Gaines, Jim. "A Talk About Life and Style with Tennessee Williams." *Saturday Review* 29 April 1972.

Jennings, C. Robert. "Interview with Tennessee Williams." *Playboy* XX: April 1973.

Jones, Robert Emmet. "Sexual Roles in the Works of Tennessee Williams." *Tennessee Williams: A Tribute.* Edited by Jac Tharpe. Jackson: University Press of Mississippi, 1977.

Kauffmann, Stanley. "Homosexual Drama and Its Disguises." *New York Times* 23 January 1966: Section 2: 1.

Kazin, Alfred. "The Writer as Sexual Show-Off: Making Press Agents Unnecessary." *New York Magazine* 9 June 1975.

Kerr, Walter. "Talkers, Drinkers and Losers." *New York Times* 16 April 1972.

Kushner, Tony. *Angels in America, Part One: Millennium Approaches.* New York: Theatre Communications Group, Inc., 1992.

_____. *Angels in America, Part Two: Perestroika.* New York: Theatre Communications Group, Inc., 1994.

Lahr, John. "Earth Angels." *New Yorker* 13 December 1993.

The Lively Arts. BBC-TV. Interview with Tennessee Williams. 1976.

Presley, Delma Eugene. "Little Acts of Grace." *Tennessee Williams: A Tribute.* Edited by Jac Tharpe. Jackson: University Press of Mississippi, 1977.

Raymond, Gerard. "An Interview with Tony Kushner." *Theater Week* 20 December 1993.

Rilke, Rainer Maria. "Duino Elegies. The Ninth Elegy." *Selected Works. Vol. II. Poetry.* Translated by J. B. Leishman. Norfolk, CT, and New York: New Directions, 1960.

Savran, David. "Tony Kushner Considers the Longstanding Problems of Virtue and Happiness. An Interview by David Sarvan." *American Theatre* October 1994.

Simon, John. "Angelic Geometry." *New York Magazine* 6 December 1993.

Sklepowich, Edward A. "In Pursuit of the Lyric Quarry: The Image of the Homosexual in Tennessee Williams' Prose Fiction." *Tennessee Williams: A Tribute.* Edited by Jac Tharpe. Jackson: University Press of Mississippi, 1977.

Spoto, Donald. *The Kindness of Strangers: The Life of Tennessee Williams.* Boston, MA, Toronto: Little, Brown and Co., 1985.

Tennessee Williams. Orpheus of the American Stage. A film by Merrill Brockway. *American Masters,* PBS-TV, 1994.

Williams, Tennessee. "The Angels of Fructification." *In the Winter of Cities. Selected Poems of Tennessee Williams.* New York: New Directions, 1956, 1964.

_____. "Let Me Hang It All Out." *New York Times* 4 March 1973.

_____. *Memoirs.* New York: Doubleday, 1975.

_____. *A Streetcar Named Desire.* New York: New Directions, 1980.

_____. *The Theatre of Tennessee Williams. Volume 2.* New York: New Directions, 1971.

_____. *The Theatre of Tennessee Williams. Volume 3.* New York: New Directions, 1971.

_____. *The Theatre of Tennessee Williams. Volume 5.* New York: New Directions, 1976.

_____. *Where I Live: Selected Essays.* Edited by Christine R. Day and Bob Woods. With an Introduction by Christine R. Day. New York: New Directions, 1978.

2

Kushner, Inge and "Little Sheba"

Strange Bedfellows

JEFF JOHNSON

When Prior, speaking to Louis in an early scene from "Millennium Approaches," says, "I warned you, Louis. Names are important. Call an animal 'Little Sheba' and you can't expect it to stick around" (Kushner 26), he is referring of course to William Inge's 1950 play *Come Back, Little Sheba*. But the reference is not a casual inside joke about a sentimental Broadway hit (or to the even more melodramatic movie version of the Inge play, starring Burt Lancaster and Shirley Booth), nor is it merely a literary device to reinforce the perverse sense of campy domesticity shadowing the two men's affair. Instead, by echoing the situation between Doc and Lola, Prior underscores the dyadic tension at the center of his relationship with Louis, that of a seemingly tough realist (Prior) involved with a supposedly romantic, sappy idealist (Louis). But just as in Inge's play, where the roles are reversed, Doc merely pretending to be a clear-eyed rationalist, allowing Lola to masquerade as his dreamy foil, Prior and Louis also play out their role reversals. Prior's cynicism is finally just a front to hide his fear of illness, and Louis's emotionalism nothing but a show of affection worn like pancake make-up to mask his pragmatic core. Just as Doc and Lola must reconcile their disillusionment with their investment in marriage, so too must Prior and Louis come to terms with their emotional disengagement before they can effectively ameliorate their anomie and commit themselves with renewed vigor to life.

The final allusion to *Sheba* in *Perestroika*— not in the facetious exchange between Harper and Prior but when Prior responds to the commands of the angels and confesses during his epiphany, equating God with

Little Sheba, "He isn't coming back" (282)—serves the same function for Kushner as it does for Inge, implying a recognition of abandonment, a coming to terms with the reality of life, when the masks the characters have used to distance themselves from commitment are ripped away. As in Inge's play, when Little Sheba becomes the image expressing Doc and Lola's recognition of the futility of their daydreams and their pining away over the spilt milk of youth, the image of Little Sheba in *Angels* indicates the same truth for Prior and Louis: instead of clinging to idealistic fantasies of uncomplicated love, miracle cures, transcendental hope or divine deliverance, Prior and Louis are left only with each other and the vagaries of love in the face of intolerable suffering and imminent death.

And while Kushner's referencing Sheba certainly acts as an intertextual agent creating a chiasmic connection between two similar relationships, the one in *Angels* demonstrably gay, the other in *Sheba* ostensibly straight, the allusion doubles as a critique of how portrayals of gay relationships have changed since Stanley Kauffmann's seminal and prescient essay "Homosexual Drama and Its Disguises" appeared in the *New York Times* in 1966. Even then, when homosexuality was not acceptable as appropriate dramatic material for mainstream culture, the issue was being debated—true, in a language as codified as any cabalistic dispute, but would anyone even mildly alert to trends in the contemporary theatre scene of the 1960s argue that Inge, Williams and Albee were not writing gay dramas cleverly dressed up as straight theatre? And while Kushner has the luxury of addressing openly the issue of gay love (though, as good art should, his portrayal transcends its gender specificity), his appropriating the theme from *Sheba* also gives the lie to Inge's drama being a straight play, liberating it from its critical and historical tomb where it has lain dormant as a mainly forgotten topical drama about the evils of alcoholism and premarital sex, of lost youth and misspent careers, of simplistic reconciliation based on unconditional love and forgiveness. Kushner's implication, by cross-referencing Inge's play, resurrects *Sheba* as a centerpiece of gay politics and gender subversion. Kushner's use of Little Sheba arguably conjures up the gender politics of the 1950s, the allusion first situates the relationship between Prior and Louis and Doc and Lola as roughly synonymous. Both couples have created insular lives sustained through illusions. They are unable or incapable of accepting the truth of their situations, but in the course of the action they realize that their dreams are an insufficient defense against the complexity of the human predicament.

Doc, a reformed sinner and dry drunk demanding purity in a world he sees as corrupted by venal excesses, suffers a paralytic guilt about his past. His either-or, virgin-or-whore taxonomy mirrors the moral dialectic driving the key conflict in the play. The resolution — the synthesis—can only occur once Doc realizes the truth about people, that they are neither all good nor all bad, merely human. Lola, too, has invested her desire in Marie, only for her Marie represents the sexual vitality and youthful opportunities that Lola was denied when she was a schoolgirl. In the end, however, her resignation is not made in despair. She admits that Little Sheba is not coming back, and the fact that she is "not going to call her anymore" (Inge 69) indicates a reality-check, a chance to see the world as it is so that she might begin to deal with the facts instead of wasting her life mired in fantasy. By the time Doc returns from the hospital, he and Lola both understand that they are left with only one another to salvage what they can of their lives.

Similarly, Prior resists recognizing the hope implied in his doom. He fails at first to embrace his illness, and all that it represents, as an opportunity to understand the beauty of suffering, the intensity it brings to experience. For all its ugliness, his disease sharply focuses his attention on living. Louis, in denial about Prior's condition, surrenders to an escapist's ethic, avoiding the hard work of maintaining love wracked by adversity. Not until he, too, suffers from misplaced allegiance can he recover any authenticity. Once both men achieve a self-awareness that exposes their "bad faith," they can begin an honest relationship, both with themselves and others.

In *Come Back, Little Sheba*, Lola and Doc find themselves at odds with both their social roles and their private expectations. This oppositional positing of conflicting desires is obvious in the contrasting motives of Doc and Lola. Both display public lives that run counter to their natural inclinations. For instance, Doc appears pragmatic, but his cynicism is a product of his unreformed romanticism. Lola seems like a romanticist, but she is actually a hard-nosed realist bent on survival. The implication is clear: their relationship is unnatural. Lola, almost regretfully, admits that as long as Doc stays sober she will "know how you're gonna be when you come home" (Inge 9), as if Doc's domestication has thrown the natural order of things off-balance. In this context, his struggle against alcoholism is a struggle against his savage self, his innate virility, often manifested in animal-like violence, his drunkenness merely defiance in the face of a world willing to crush his spirit for the sake of good behavior.

Lola, sexually frustrated and spiritually disappointed with the predictability of her mundane existence, recognizes this too, and even though he threatens her with physical harm, she understands Doc's climatic drunken rage (the only honest passion in the play). The catharsis after Doc's collapse is clearly sexual, and for a brief moment drains them both of their pent-up energy. By the time Doc has "recovered," Lola has reassumed her proper role in the kitchen and, as if restored to her stereotypically expected role as Doc's wife. Significantly, she offers to cook him breakfast, correcting in the final scene the disjunction that began in the opening sequence when Doc opened the play preparing breakfast for the two women. Doc is bitter that his first sexual episode with Lola led to her pregnancy, bitter because a mid-wife botched the delivery and the baby died in childbirth, and bitter that he lost his inheritance, had to give up medical school and instead became a chiropractor and an alcoholic. So his idealizing Marie — whose name signifying the Madonna takes on existential meaning for him — stems from this desire for expiation. When he sees her drawing, he wants her to "paint lots of pretty pictures" and recalls a painting his mother kept over her mantelpiece that "Made you feel religious just to look at it" (Inge 6). Marie's saying a bath makes her feel "fresh and clean" (7) has a spiritual significance for Doc, denoting his desire for a clear conscience. Inge's directing note describes Doc's reaction to Lola's telling him about Marie kissing Turk as an *"angry denial"* (10), and Doc admits he wants to believe that she is "clean and decent" (11), as if making out with Turk would disqualify her morally from any position of virtue in his ethology.

Doc sets himself up for disappointment by over-investing his faith in Marie, who, even if she were virginal and clean and decent, could never live up to his expectations of innocence. His final disillusionment comes when he hears Turk laughing in Marie's bedroom. Inge's note reads: *"It sounds like the laugh of sated Bacchus"* (44). Then he discovers Turk sneaking out of Marie's bedroom, and his spiritual and physical collapse is complete. He takes the whiskey and goes on a binge. Drunk and blinded by self-pity, he reverses his absolutist morality, calling Lola and Marie "a couple of sluts" and bitterly claiming that Marie will probably have to marry Bruce, "the poor bastard" (56), the same way he was forced to marry Lola. Doc's "slip" (59) and the recognition of his own moral failings prompt him to ask Lola for forgiveness, an ameliorative shift from years of blaming her. The "sad-looking old bird dog" (68) that he has become is still capable of love, and more importantly, being loved.

Doc dotes on Marie's pretense of innocence, describing her as "clean and decent," "clean and fresh," one of the "nice girls" (10–11) who represent for him a simple hunky-dory world in which the sordid grit of existence is deferred, and appearance is the only necessary truth. His struggle is to maintain this chimera of convention, where people assume the roles he assigns them according to what he believes is the proper social codes of normality so that he can locate and define himself within this psycho-theatrical *mise en scène*. To maintain an identity, to project clarity and reason and order, he must, of course, stay sober, but his inclination is to drink, to destroy his carefully constructed ego-identity, to dissolve the established boundaries of personality, to lose himself in the unconscious, wiping out memory of the constantly reconstructed self. In a revealing allusion, Doc is entranced by Schubert, the syphilitic Classicist. Doc envies the composer's ability to arrange and objectify his feelings, but to do so is a trick of the will well beyond Doc's experience; he is best at cheap card tricks, using the same sleight-of-hand by which he hoodwinks himself, half-believing in a world of his own projection.

Lola was "the 'it' girl" (31) who won the Charleston contest at the homecoming dance and had lots of boys calling her for dates. But she recalls how her strict, unforgiving father would punish her for "holding hands" and confesses to Marie that she "never had any fun" (14) until she met Doc, having "saved all her dates" (31) for him. Whereas Doc wants to forget the past, Lola is steeped in it, living vicariously through Marie's exploits with Turk and Bruce and the wistful memories she conjures up in her attempts at intimacy with Doc. He, of course, dismisses her reminiscing, telling her, "you've got to forget those things" (32). His advice is, "If you can't forget the past, you stay in it forever and never get out" (33). But for her, their dating was "the happiest time of our lives" (32). This contrasting approach to events in their past illustrates the fissure in their marriage, Lola relishing the romance of "a nice spring" (32) and Doc regretting all he had to give up because of Lola's pregnancy. But as if to qualify her memories, she repeats the refrain "those years vanished — vanished into thin air" (32), using the same phrase to describe the disappearance of Little Sheba as well as the brief life of the blooms on the lilacs she places on the dinner table she sets for Bruce and Marie.

Her longing to recover her vanished years, however, waxes more pathetic than poetic. Her attempt to flirt with the postman deteriorates into a maudlin complaint laced with painfully personal details about Doc's alcoholism that only embarrasses the postman. Her yearning for romance and a return to that special spring of her youth is embodied in her dog, aptly called Little Sheba, whose name alone is meant to evoke the mysteries of the middle east during the reign of King Solomon, but, like Lola's imagination, the diminutive "little" signifies the reality of her situation. When she pitifully calls for the dog from her porch, she tacitly acknowledges what she and Doc must both confront: the smartest boy in class and the prettiest girl in school were never guaranteed the cozy future they thought they deserved, and there is no going back. In her dream at the end of the play, she seems finally to have accepted the brutal truth, finding Little Sheba — the dreams of her youth — dead and "smeared with mud" (69). If Doc wants to transcend his desire, a victim of excess, Lola wants to embrace desire, to give herself over to it, a victim of denial.

Like Lola, Prior reads his cat's absence as an omen of ill-luck, evidence of which he reveals to Louis: the first signs of Kaposi's sarcoma, "the wine-dark kiss of the angel of death" (Kushner 27). Louis first mentions Little Sheba at his grandmother's funeral, immediately associating the missing cat with death. Prior claims to have done his "best Shirley Booth," calling for Little Sheba to "come back" (27). His calling for the cat to return indicates his desperation, trying to maintain an illusion of optimism, a Panglossian hope in a healthy future. But he senses the truth. After all, he says, "Cats have intuition ... [and] know when something's wrong" (26). Whereas Prior fights to sustain his stoic attitude, Louis panics, fronting denial. But neither can hold his pose. Prior admits that he is afraid that Louis, like Little Sheba, will abandon him when he needs him most, and Louis, recognizing that his panic is felt more for himself than for his lover, confesses to the Rabbi that he is "afraid of the crimes I may commit" (31). The Rabbi reminds him that he is Jewish, not Catholic: "Catholics believe in forgiveness. Jews believe in guilt" (31).

Prior struggles with a very real physical illness, but Louis' dilemma is spiritual, his sickness a lack of character exposing the "neo–Hegelian positivist" (31) beneath his hip, liberal veneer. Ironically, it is Prior who, at first, literally tries to mask his feelings, "applying the face" in one of Harper's hallucinations, claiming, "it was an emotional emergency" (37). He vacillates between stoicism and fear, resignation and anger, his humor failing him as surely as his rapidly deteriorating immune system. But Harper recognizes his innate dignity, claiming in a "blue streak of recognition" to see "a part of you, the most inner part, free of disease," a clear allusion to his calling, his being chosen, like a martyr, to exemplify redemption through suffering. According to Harper, Prior stands on the "[t]hreshhold of revelation" (40).

Louis, on the other hand, retreats into abstractions, couching his emotional response in sophistry, preaching an odd sort of Cartesian dualism that perversely divorces the physical from the conceptual. He struggles not with angels but with denial, commitment and guilt. He flirts with Joe, as if swapping rotten flesh for fresh meat will keep him unsullied and sanctified. Arguing that it is "the shape of a life, its total complexity gathered, arranged and considered, which matters in the end," he dismisses, like an aloof professor with a metaphysical, Hegelian sleight-of-hand, "salvation or damnation" (44)—that is, his own guilty conscience. Prior, with characteristic frankness, debunks his ethos: "it lets you off scot-free" (48). In this context, Louis' plea sounds like a warning: "[D]on't get any sicker" (48).

But of course Prior does. In response, Louis, who remains guiltily healthy, begins to withdraw into diversions and, in the ethical context of the play, further into a moral decline. The night Prior collapses in pain and fever, excreting blood, Louis leaves him in the hospital and trolls the park for a date, looking for someone who will "hurt me, make me bleed" (Kushner 60), hoping his expiation can also be attained through pain. He decides to move out, rationalizing his move in cowardly legalese, talking about "the inevitable consequence of people ... [and] practicalities" (84). Prior accuses him of loving "theoretically," labeling Louis's loss of identity an "editorial 'you'" as opposed to the particular "you ... excluded from that general category" (84–85).

Louis's allegiance, however, remains to himself. His love is categorical, not actionable. His quest for authenticity leads him, at first, further into abstractions. While Prior is undergoing treatment, Louis lectures Prior's former lover Belize on the politics of AIDS, delineating "the limits of tolerance" (Kushner 96), remaining fixed in speculation — or what Belize, who, contrary to Louis, is busy actually dealing with the epidemic on the front lines as a nurse, describes as "playing with your MONOLITH" (99). Belize bottoms lines it for Louis: "it goes bad for you if you violate the hard law of love" (106). This is the truth Louis refuses to recognize, as his evasions lead him finally to the ultimate spiritual compromise: he takes Joe for a lover, a "bisexual Mormon Republican closet case" (222) and, worse, the chief clerk and ghostwriter for a sitting federal judge whose legal opinions reveal a particularly nasty streak of Neanderthal conservatism. Louis's need for forgiveness and expiation has led him to betray his ideals, so his involvement with Joe is ultimately self-destructive, as if by annihilating his own perversion — living categorically — he can recover his authentic, praxeological self. Only at the moment of his most extreme self-abnegation, when he realizes just how much of himself he has sacrificed — having sold out to "an ideological leather bar" (223) — does he recover his integrity. Confronted with the abstract, legalistic opinions of Justice Wilson, Joe defends them with the same insensitivity that Louis used before to explain his cowardice in the face of Prior's disease. Prior then confirms his corruption, receives the painful beating he has long desired, and unfettered by illusions returns to Prior with a genuine sense of his human situation.

Ironically for Prior, as his body declines, his sense of life is enhanced. He has erections — even climaxes with ferocious ejaculations — whenever he suffers a visitation from the angel. His revelations occur through a series of encounters with those who have also experienced disenfranchisement — Harper, Hannah, Belize — and who offer moral guidance as he resists death. Until his illness brought into focus the immediacy of life, Prior lived what Kierkegaard defines as the aesthetic life. Prior confesses: "One wants to move through life with elegance and grace, blossoming infrequently but with exquisite taste" (36), as if style were all, existence reduced to a string of casual, disconnected affairs without a meaningful ethical context. But his illness offers him a pretext for discovering his authenticity, allowing him a chance to make the transition from a deferred, open-ended superficial life to an existential eschatology fraught with significance. The essence of his disease is how the immediate threat to his life intensifies his living. By recognizing that Little Sheba is not coming back, that his illusions of some grand benevolence governing the universe are homespun fantasies, escapist porn, he moves from simply "handling this well" (127) to a richer, intensely subjective understanding of life in action, an ontological immersion into the beautiful filth of carnality.

Prior's struggle with the angel is a struggle against transcendence, a resistance to relinquishing passion, expressing his desire for an earthly life, robust and committed. To negate fear with hope, he must embrace the absurdity of existence and accept the contingency that makes life so precariously precious. The story he tells of the castaways in a leaking lifeboat neatly illustrates his dilemma, as he can now acutely identify with "[p]eople in a boat, waiting, terrified, [...] pitched into freezing, turbulent water and salt and darkness to drown" (48). His ancestors attempt to locate an historical context for his suffering (as if precedence legitimizes calamity) and thereby to prepare him for his calling to prophecy. But Prior rejects the call, announcing (prophetically), "the real world's waking up" (186). His erections become a defense, an assertion of physical aggression in the face of metaphysical dissolution. When the angel reveals the truth — that "The King of the Universe" (195) has left, like Little Sheba, and has abandoned His creation — Prior (with a nod to Sartre) longs not for God but for Louis. His dismissal of the angel's invitation is a reaffirmation of life: "I'm tired to death of being [...] fucked over and now tortured by some mixed-up, reactionary angel" (198). The angel demands "STASIS!" (198), but Prior counters, "I hate heaven" (200). The same logic drives his admonition to Louis when he tries for reconciliation without revelation. Prior tells him, "I can't believe you even have blood in your veins till you show it to me" (239). Prior has, paradoxically, become a prophet, albeit one of those who will muster the courage to "refuse their vision" (255).

Prior ascends to heaven and discovers Little Sheba, dead. But unlike before, he is not bothered. He has learned Hemingway's code (weirdly transforming the drag queen into the lion king): "To face loss. With grace. Is key" (271). He returns the book of prophecy to the angels, content that "God [...] isn't coming back" (282). His optimism in the end is a triumph of this life, this death, free of symbolism and abstractions. In the end, he chooses instinctively: "I want more life" (285).

Besides underscoring the similarities between the two couples in *Angels* and *Sheba*, Kushner's reference also aligns his openly gay play with the more covert homoeroticism in Inge. To suggest that Inge's homosexuality affords him some special sensibility both to limn and erase the expected gender demarcations of his characters is reductive and facile, but to ignore the psychological crisis his sexuality caused in his life seems equally fatuous. Some critics like Albert Wertheim, intent on "reading it gay" (Wertheim 207), force the issue, accusing other critics of imposing agendas that ignore or downplay the homosexuality inherent in Inge's work while promoting their own readings as gospel. Wertheim, in "Dorothy's Friend in Kansas: the Gay Inflections of William Inge," recognizes that "a gay sensibility informs his major plays, is refracted in them, and most importantly permits him special insights, insights derived from his personal experience of gay alterity" (Wertheim 198).

Wertheim's complaint that "critics have been profoundly silent about the homoerotic tones in Inge's work" (Wertheim 198) is empirically accurate but surely not a mystery. One can safely assume that, especially during the fifties, homosexual coding among insiders, including hostile critics, was mutual. Outing of popular and commercially successful playwrights as a McCarthyite tactic could be fatal even for the accuser and may well have threatened the entire industry. Otherwise, beginning with Kauffmann's 1966 article, writers have at least obliquely addressed Inge's "gay inflections," usually as a complementary element to a more comprehensive exegesis, even though the few critics who have written seriously about Inge have shied away from underscoring the "homosexual tones" prevalent in his work.

Wertheim's position is that while claiming his gay reading offers a complete — even absolute — correction of other critical considerations concerning Inge's major plays, his view actually illustrates only a facet of Inge's talent as a playwright. For Wertheim, *Come Back, Little Sheba* focuses on the contrast between Turk, with his "prizewinning phallus" and "the dependable, conventional, sexually colorless" Bruce, peripheral characters who, between them, frame Doc as "a character drawn by a dramatist who brings his knowledge of gay lives, gay neuroses, and alcoholism to bear" (Wertheim 205–206). This subversion enables Inge's audience "to overcome its innate homophobia" (Wertheim 215), but the constrictions of Wertheim's vision also limit Inge's importance, as the gay issues Inge addresses are contained within a larger context that explodes the discourse beyond the narrow application of "gay inflections," exposing a more universal questioning of stereotypes that challenges even Wertheim's reading.

Wertheim argues that Ralph Voss, in his biography *A Life of William*

Inge: The Strains of Triumph, avoids the homosexual "connection except in regard to those works in which an overtly gay man appears" (Wertheim 195). While acknowledging Inge's homosexuality, and citing many reputable sources that testify to the sexual dilemma in his work, Voss does hesitate to draw the obvious conclusion that Inge's understanding of sexually conflicted characters and his uncanny ability to portray dramatically the slippage in practice of fixed gender roles are essentially connected to his own crisis as a closeted homosexual living through a particularly virulently anti-gay decade in American history. Voss documents in detail how Inge was forced to conceal his sexuality, describing him as always "peeking out of the closet" (Voss 256). But the closest Voss comes to asserting that Inge's androgyny is the key to his insight into sexually confused characters is when he writes that Inge, as a gay man in a repressive society, "via analysis understood himself and his upbringing perfectly, and that understanding often informed his art" (Voss 274). Nevertheless, Voss's conclusion that Inge's homosexuality and the psychoanalysis he employed to deal with it "informed" his work reiterates what is evident in the text: Inge carves close to the bone while shaping universal themes out of "small-town dramas" (Voss 275).

The facts of Inge's life, as Voss provides them, clearly imply that no matter how much Inge suffered privately from being "a homosexual during the Eisenhower era" (Voss 274), in his best work he profited artistically from this alienation, gaining significant insight from his own forced sexual duplicity. Voss makes a point of not oversimplifying Inge's epicene insight, but he does document Inge's struggle with a society so puritanically convinced of its moral superiority that it feels compelled to condemn people based on their sexuality. This socially imposed stigma naturally led to Inge's overwhelming sense of guilt, betrayal and anger in a world that would acknowledge him as an artist while condemning him as a homosexual (were he to fess up, publicly).

It is this issue of Inge's aesthetic worth as an artist that concerns Kauffmann in "Homosexual Drama and Its Disguises." In Kauffmann's opinion, Inge's homosexuality, instead of being considered a positive quality that informed his understanding of conflicted characters, is instead a negative trait that explains why many critics (Robert Brustein, for instance) think Inge's depictions of family strife ring patently false. Kauffmann believes that "postwar American drama presents a badly distorted picture of American women, marriage, and society" (Kauffmann 1). He ostensibly argues that society has forced homosexual playwrights to "masquerade," complains that he is "weary of disguised homosexual influence" (Kauffmann 1), and petitions for the honest acceptance of homosexual writers so they might be allowed to render their particular experience into drama. The implication is that homosexual writers are incapable of creating plausible straight characters, as if to write about murder one must be a murderer.

James Fisher underscores this absurdity in a 1995 essay entitled "The Angels of Fructification: Tennessee Williams, Tony Kushner, and Images of Homosexuality on the American Stage." He counters Kauffmann's contention that homosexuals cannot escape their homosexuality and are thus, because of their sexuality, unable artistically to depict any experience outside their supposedly hermetic gay existence. "Kauffmann implies that homosexual writers have no right to write about anything but gay characters—an attitude which would logically imply that men are unable to write about women and vice versa" (Fisher 18).

The key to Kauffmann's complaint is the way he mischaracterizes, through a distorted lens of undiluted bigotry, "the materials of the three writers"—obviously Williams, Inge and Albee—that happen, bizarrely, to include "the viciousness toward women, the lurid violence that seems a sublimation of social hatreds, the transvestite sexual exhibitionism." (Kauffmann 1) Such prejudice might also explain Robert Brustein's facetious description of Inge as "the first spokesman for a matriarchal America" (Brustein 57). It is in fact hard to recognize Inge's work in much of Kauffmann's essay, as what he considers to be most "culturally risky" about "these people" suffering from "this one neurosis" is the camp influence, the "adulation of sheer style," which he considers "an instrument of revenge on the main body of society," sacrificing "social relevance" to promote a "vindictiveness toward the society that constricts and, theatrically, discriminates against them" (Kauffmann 1). When Kauffmann complains that "the marital quarrels are usually homosexual quarrels with one of the pair in costume" (Kauffmann 1), he is undoubtedly referring to Albee's *Who's Afraid of Virginia Woolf?* (1962), but he may as well have been talking about Inge.

As a counterpoint to Kauffmann, Kushner's evocation of *Sheba* inscribes homosexuality with a semiotic that normalizes what has been called the "continuum of gay theatre" (Vorlicky 185), and thereby explodes the very idea of a genotypical "gay drama." Instead of excluding Louis and Prior from the psychological complexity that transcends categorical reductionism, relegating them to the purgatory of two-dimensional presentation where gays are necessarily identified by their sexuality in both the actual theatre and the collective imagination, Kushner integrates them into the arena of human relationships. Their conflicts, both existential and interpersonal, are rendered with the same psychological complexity as Doc and Lola's. Beyond AIDS, bigotry, cultural wars and politics, Kushner's play delves into the mysteries of human nature, locating his characters in the same generic landscape of loss and pain, despair and hope that drives any decent humanistic drama.

By the time *Angels* was staged, instead of allegorical sex, which both hamstrung and *made* Inge, Kushner could employ naturalistic situations without the "prior restraint" limiting Inge in the 1950s. Even so, it was easier for Inge, writing from within the closet, as it were, to be accepted as a mainstream playwright than for Kushner, writing as an openly gay man in the 1990s, to be cast (or maligned) by unsympathetic critics as anything other than an agitprop provocateur (mainly in the "red-state" press, but even James Wolcott dubbed *Angels* a "period piece"). This critical discrepancy may express both cultural and aesthetic prejudice, as Inge's experiments with gendermandering—that is, the subversive manipulation of stereotypes for the purpose of intentionally undermining expected gender roles and destabilizing social norms—never overtly challenged the cultural expectations of his popular audiences, while Kushner's play is transparent: he works as if gender-typing is an irrelevant myth concocted by heartland homophobes determined to protect their moral hegemony (even at the expense of rational discourse). This refusal on the part of Kushner to concede that homosexual couples do not share the same emotional and ethical verities framing Doc and Lola's dramatic dilemma, his insistence on treating his characters as people—not as simple sexual agents—sets *Angels* apart from other plays within the "gay continuum" and assures Kushner a place alongside Inge within the pantheon of classic American playwrights. Yet *Angels* still manages to challenge common bigoted assumptions about homosexuality (resurrected each election cycle as a divisive political wedge issue) exactly because it is unabashedly "gay." It is in fact this duality that gives *Angels* its unique position in the contemporary canon: no matter how many trappings of conventional drama Kushner employs, he still provokes a controversy that Inge never had to confront.

But by grounding his characters in realism not available to Inge, Kushner recovers Inge and realigns *Sheba* outside conventional aesthetic expectations. Kushner recognizes that Inge, in effect, codifies gay love within the linguistic stratagems of a colloquial, heterosexual middle-class lexicography that erases itself even as it subverts the very ordinariness that defines it. He invokes Inge from an essential, structural necessity, and that forms the crux of the allusion to "Little Sheba" as Kushner employs it: to tease out from the ordinariness of life the profound weirdness of individuation. Doc and Louis, Lola and Prior—gay or straight, healthy or ill— with Sheba gone, all they have is each other.

Works Cited

Brustein, Robert. "The Men-taming Women of William Inge." *Harper's* November 1958: 52–57.

Fisher, James. "The Angels of Fructification: Tennessee Williams, Tony Kushner, and Images of Homosexuality on the American Stage." *Mississippi Quarterly*, 49.1 (Winter 1995–96): 13–53.

Inge, William. "Come Back, Little Sheba." *Four Plays by William Inge*. New York: Random House, 1958.

Kauffmann, Stanley. "Homosexual Drama and Its Disguises" *New York Times* 23 January 1966, national edition: section 2:1.

Kushner, Tony. *Angels in America*. New York: Theatre Communications Group, Inc., 1995.

Vorlicky, Robert. *Act Like a Man*. Ann Arbor: University of Michigan Press, 1995.

Voss, Ralph F. *A Life of William Inge: The Strains of Triumph*. Lawrence: University Press of Kansas, 1989.

Wertheim, Albert. "Dorothy's Friends in Kansas: The Gay Inflections of William Inge" *Staging Desire: Queer Readings of American Theater History*. Ann Arbor: University of Michigan Press, 2002, pp. 194–217.

Wolcott, James. "A Descent of Angels." *arts.telegraph* 5 Feb. 2004. 18 November 2004.

3

Blood Relations

Adrienne Kennedy and Tony Kushner

ROBERT VORLICKY

"My plays are meant to be states of mind."—Adrienne
Kennedy, *People Who Led to My Plays*

> *"Even now,*
> *From the mirror-bright halls of heaven,*
> *Across the cold and lifeless infinity of space,*
> *The Messenger comes*
> *Trailing orbs of light,*
> *Fabulous, incipient,*
> *Oh Prophet,*
> *To you..."*
> —Prior, *Angels in America,*
>   *Part One: Millennium Approaches*

Throughout history, artists have provided glimpses into their creative process, insights into the influences on their imaginations, by citing other artists whose accomplishments have had an impact on them. Mid- to late twentieth-century United States dramatists are a particularly vocal, generous group when it comes to acknowledging writers throughout the ages who have inspired their artistry. Edward Albee repeatedly cites, for instance, Chekhov, Beckett, Brecht, Ionesco, Genet, Wilder, and Williams, while Richard Foreman turns to Stein and Brecht, and August Wilson focuses on black playwrights of the 1960s, including Milner, Bullins, Dean, Elder III, Sanchez, and Baraka. David Mamet acknowledges Beckett, Brecht, Pinter, and Williams; Paula Vogel is enamored of, among others, Guare, Fornes, Churchill, Wellman, and Mee; David Henry Hwang cites Chekhov, Brecht, Pinter, Shepard, and Shange; and solo performer Anna Deavere Smith credits Williams, Albee, and Shange.[1]

While mentioned frequently by her peers and theatre scholars as a significant U.S. playwright, experimentalist Adrienne Kennedy (b. 1931) remains one of this country's most under-theorized, unproduced, and unjustifiably unclaimed U.S. playwrights.[2] "With Beckett gone, Adrienne Kennedy is probably the boldest artist now writing for the theater," proclaims Michael Feingold (Sollars xv). Since the production of her first play in 1964, the surrealist *Funnyhouse of a Negro*, Kennedy, an intensely private person, has gone on to write seventeen plays and adaptations that are stuck in a kind of theatre history limbo. Autobiographically shaped content in fragmented, non-realist dramatic form, Kennedy's work does not fit neatly into a recognizable U.S. dramaturgical continuum. Like Gertrude Stein's plays, Kennedy's works defy swift categorization within a discernible, historical trajectory of native playwrights. Instead, as Elinor Fuchs argues, the dramaturgy of Kennedy's early plays, her "mystery or passion plays," is grounded in a European, avant-garde "lineage that can be traced to those brief, often terrifying plays written by the symbolists [Maeterlinck, in particular] just before the turn of the twentieth century and to Strindberg's post–*Inferno* pilgrimage/dream plays" (76–77).[3]

Kennedy, herself, however, is very clear about her indebtedness to a handful of twentieth-century U.S. playwrights. In her critically acclaimed, non-narrative, non-linear autobiography in 1987, *People Who Led to My Plays*, Kennedy repeatedly identifies specific writers and productions, from her childhood to the brink of *Funnyhouse of a Negro* (1936–1961), that sparked her imagination and stimulated her aesthetic, artistic, and cultural self-awareness. Like many playwrights, Kennedy links her passion for the theatre and her eventual career in it from early exposures to theatre and drama through seeing performances and reading scripts. Tennessee Williams and Eugene O'Neill are seminal figures in Kennedy's development. Upon viewing Williams's *The Glass Menagerie* while in high school, for instance, Kennedy writes in her autobiography: "I saw the play and for the first time understood there were other family secrets, family joys and sorrows, just as in my own family" (59). It is this experience of watching an expressionistic play through which, for Kennedy, "the idea of being a writer and seeing [her] own family onstage caught fire in [her] mind" (61). Later, Kennedy would acknowledge the overwhelming impact of O'Neill and, specifically, his *Long Day's Journey into Night*, "the greatest play I have seen on the stage," which, for her, shed "extraordinary light ... on the matrix of his family relationships" (83). After the birth of her first son, Kennedy would note that reading fiction (and ostensibly attending the theatre as well) in conjunction with her own experience of parenting provided a "constant example of how real the unreal is" (82).

Williams, O'Neill, and Arthur Miller (especially Miller's Willy Loman in *Death of a Salesman*) are central in her formative years to fostering Kennedy's inspiration to create theatre. But it is her encounter with Spanish playwright Frederico Garcia Lorca's work in the late 1950s that inspires her actual leap into dramatic writing. Lorca shows her that "imagery is multilayered, that it comes from recovering connections long ago lost and buried" (Kennedy, *People* 98). After having seen *Blood Wedding* (between 1953–1960), Kennedy recalls, "Never again would I be afraid to have my characters talk in a nonrealistic way, and I would abandon the realistic set for a great dream setting. It was a turning point" (108). Kennedy's "turning point" would manifest itself in the creation of her first produced play, the surrealist *Funnyhouse of a Negro*.

Unlike Adrienne Kennedy, Tony Kushner (who is twenty-five years younger than Kennedy) has not written his autobiography. Yet, a reliable source for hearing him speak in his own voice is located in his published conversations. In a series of interviews that Kushner gave in the early 1990s, the author of *Angels in America* readily acknowledged that U.S. playwrights Williams ("Williams is probably all-in-all my favorite playwright and probably all-in-all our greatest playwright") and O'Neill ("I'm very much under the influence, very excited and impressed by the plays and also the life") are significant influences on his writing, as are Brecht and "a lot of British writers" (Churchill, Bond, Brenton, Hare, and Edgar). "In America," Kushner continues, he admires immensely "John Guare, Maria Irene Fornes, [and] David Mamet," along with his contemporaries Mac Wellman, Connie Congdon, Ellen McLaughlin, Holly Hughes, and David Greenspan (Kushner, Myers 235–36). But Kushner saves his greatest praise for his contemporary, and fellow Pulitzer Prize winning playwright, Suzan-Lori Parks. "We may not have anyone who is as absolutely great as Tennessee Williams," Kushner said in a PBS interview in November 1995, "although there are a couple people who I think will be up there. Suzan-Lori Parks will be for sure" (Kushner, Myers 236). And when he was asked earlier that same year to name what playwrights he really "love[s] that aren't being read and done" around the country, Kushner responded, "There's a lot of interesting Adrienne Kennedy that should be reexamined" (Kushner, Jonas 168).

At this point, an intertextuality — a kind of U.S. dramatic lineage — spanning twentieth century U.S. dramatists begins to reveal itself. Both Kennedy and Kushner readily acknowledge the significant impact of Williams and O'Neill on their writings— they find the writings of these earlier playwrights compelling for the depth of their exploration of the familial, for their compassionate humanity, and for their flights of the poetic in life (whether tragic or hopeful) that can be captured in drama. Arguably, one can imagine that Kennedy and Kushner are drawn to the writers' willingness to experiment with and within form: from the realism ignited in such plays as *The Night of the Iguana, A Streetcar Named Desire, Hughie,* and *A Long Day's Journey into Night,* to the expressionism layered in *A Glass Menagerie, Camino Real, The Emperor Jones,* and *The Hairy Ape.* Yet, by her own admission, Kennedy owes her greatest debt to Lorca, whose landscapes of the unconscious, of the dream life, haunt the surrealist settings of Kennedy's radical, early plays of the 1960s, including *Funnyhouse of a Negro, The Owl Answers,* and *A Lesson in Dead Language.* Through surrealism, Kennedy was able to create not only the complexity of character that she desired—least of which is not uncomplicated subjectivity for her women—but also the "multilayered imagery," nonrealistic talk, and dream settings that were stimulated in her imagination by Lorca.

Suzan-Lori Parks, the much admired contemporary of Kushner's, has been unabashedly public about the profound influence that Adrienne Kennedy has had on her own dramaturgy.[4] One can see this in Parks's experimentation with form in her varied usage of surrealism in such plays as *Imperceptible Mutabilities of the Third Kingdom, The Death of the Last Black Man in the Whole Entire World,* and *The America Play.* Both women also liberally rely upon the monologue, a dramatic form Kushner is also keen to employ—from the opening scenes of *Millennium Approaches* and *Perestroika* to the first act of *Homebody/Kabul.*

I would like to suggest that one historical, U.S. dramaturgical lineage of Tony Kushner's originates narratively and structurally with O'Neill and Williams. This line then moves to their avid enthusiast, Adrienne Kennedy, who opens up the earlier writers' experimentation in form by wholly embracing surrealism (vis a vis Lorca's influence) without sacrificing story and character, albeit now in a non-linear, highly theatrical presentation. Taking up the mantle from Kennedy—America's foundational, yet widely unknown woman writer of surrealist drama—are Parks and Kushner who deeply admire Kennedy's work. They are part of a new generation of theatre experimentalists who move effortlessly between realism and non-realism in any given text, as they play with diverse forms as a way to explore character, the boundaries of narrative, and the infinite possibilities of theatricality and performance.

The extent to which Kennedy, the autobiographical avant garde dramatist and Kushner, the socio-political experimentalist, share common artistic ancestry suggests dramaturgical, genealogical linkages between them. This connection is most vividly revealed in the early surrealist works of Kennedy's and Kushner's use of the alternative landscape of surrealism in *Angels in America.* Part of Kushner's dramaturgical roots are located in and inspired by Kennedy's use of surrealism. The roots that connect Kennedy and Kushner are firmly grounded in a culturally specific American consciousness invested in the often fraught relationship between self identity and community, individual free will and democracy. In both writers, albeit to varying degrees and yielding starkly different perspectives, the tension generated by these relationships results in a kind of "rootlessness" that manifests itself in the authors' narratives, dramatic structures, and character developments.

Furthermore, Kennedy and Kushner are intrigued by the creative impulse, often manifest through metatheatrical devices, to play with the conceptualization and staging of history. In addition, both playwrights foreground imagined families on stage and their ancestral relations. Each of these subjects has found its way into the works of Kennedy and Kushner, which, in their hands, suggests a peculiarly "American" theatrical and metaphysical linkage between the playwrights, or what I call, their "blood relations" to one another.

Two striking manifestations of the writers' shared dramaturgical strategies are evident in their liberal approach to action and character. On the one hand, Kennedy and Kushner freely intermingle historical characters with fictional characters in their dramatic worlds.[5] On the other hand, they rely upon "blood relations," usually (deceased) ancestors, within surrealist frames, to complicate or comment upon their protagonists' circumstances in "real time."

Historically specific characters are prevalent in Kennedy's first two plays, the *Funnyhouse of a Negro* and *The Owl Answers*: in the former, Queen Victoria, the Duchess of Hapsburg, Patrice Lumumba, and Jesus share the surrealist, nightmare landscape in the fictional "Negro-Sarah'"s mind; in the latter, Shakespeare, Chaucer, William the Conqueror, and Anne Boleyn readily transform into and co-mingle with such characters as the Bastard, the Owl, Reverend Passmore, the Reverend's wife, the White Bird, and the Negro Man.

There is a radical break from time and history in Kennedy that helps to theatricalize the complexity of her central characters' fractured sense of identity. This dislocation is driven by their lack of racially and sexually determined subjectivity. "I am inbetween," repeats the pasty white Queen Victoria, a sentiment echoed by African Patrice Lumumba, echoed by the embodiment of their interracial progeny Sarah. Sarah's material existence is a compilation of the traces of multiple, marked bodies that have preceded her. She cannot, nor should she have to, escape these markings, but she sees no other way out from her racial and sexual crisis of marginalization than to take her own life. The dramatization and theatricalization in Kennedy of a state of, or an embodiment of "inbetweenness" is not wholly dissimilar, as a trait and device, from the 'inbetweeness' that Prior experiences in

Perestroika as he moves between the worlds of the mortal and immortal, the profane and the sacred ... between the dying and the living. He is neither one or the other — he, alone, is both. He appears to be some kind of a hybrid "relative" of Sarah and Clara.

In Parts One and Two of *Angels in America*, Kushner has the legendary lawyer for the HUAC hearings, Roy Cohn, intermingle with the fictional Joe Pitt during realist scenes in the play. In Part II, when he is dying of AIDS, Cohn slides into the surrealist plane of the unconscious as he hallucinates several conversations with Ethel Rosenberg. In this theatrical dreamscape, temporal history and mortality are suspended so that in a supernatural moment these two characters can fantasize a different historical interaction. Surrealism, which facilitates a break with history, affords Kushner the opportunity to give complete subjectivity to Rosenberg; the accused, the marginalized is not silenced. She is also present to bear witness to the demise of Roy Cohn, her "executioner."

Likewise, fictional characters Prior Walter, who is living with AIDS, and Harper Pitt, a valium addict, dream or hallucinate their ways into each other's unconscious in *Millennium Approaches*. Here, in the surrealist moment, both characters are able to reveal critical truths to one another that would otherwise be denied them in the confines of realist staging. Very simply, Kushner does not construct an implausible coincidence for them to first meet in real time. But this is not to say that they will never meet.

Through metatheatrical techniques and with Benjaminian flair, Kushner creates breaks with reality that serve to radically alter temporal experience. At the Mormon Visitors Center in *Perestroika*, Harper and Prior–who had previously only "met" in the dreamscape — actually meet one another in the flesh. Harper is at the Center under the watchful eye of Mother Pitt, and Prior has come to research angels. In this scene, through an ingenious use of metatheatricality, Kushner populates the diorama of Mormon pioneers with recognizable persons. Harper experiences her husband Joe (who she knows in life) as a character in the Center's diorama of early Mormons' travels to Salt Lake City. Prior sees Louis in the same animated tableau. In this surrealist moment, Kushner creates a space for Harper to be subject of her own noteworthy break with history, with reality. She is able to objectify her husband within the context of speaking plainly, eventually, to the Mormon wife and mother about her sacrifices. This break in stage temporality serves one of Kushner's greater goals: to dramatize the influences and insights that stimulate radical breaks with history that can lead — through knowledge — to individual, and eventually, to collective change.

Kennedy relies upon the interaction of historical and fictional characters to heighten the crisis of origins, self-identity, knowledge, and sanity that her mulatta heroines, Sarah and Clara, undergo. Kennedy's historical figures, from Queen Victoria and Patrice Lumumba to Shakespeare and William the Conqueror embody and activate the racial, sexual, and national identities that are constantly contested as they relate to Sarah and Clara. The fictional protagonists are in an unrelenting state of exile: physically, emotionally, psychologically, and spiritually. Their sense of "rootlessness," of "homelessness" is all pervasive. They are without community. History refuses to acknowledge them, to "place" them, which, in the end, leaves them *outside* the reach of understanding, acceptance, and love. In early Kennedy, historical figures retain stage life, while fictional characters die or remain subjugated.

Quite the opposite happens in Kushner. The historical figure of Roy Cohn is shown living with AIDS on stage, just as is his fictional gay counterpart, Prior Walter. But unlike Prior, Cohn — as in life — succumbs to AIDS. Kushner dramatizes the homophobic, racist's death, but he surrounds the "vanquished queen's" bed with fictional characters who rise, honorably, to the occasion. With personal dignity in tact, Belize and Louis, who says the Kaddish at Cohn's bedside, are joined by the ghost of Ethel Rosenberg. The surrealism of the stage moment brings together past victims (Rosenberg, Jews) and contemporary minorities (gay men, Jews, people of color, women) in the presence of their deceased nemesis. The living fictional characters are invigorated, if not empowered by the death of the historical figure in Kushner's fantasia.

Speaking in 1993, Kushner remarked about the opening scene of Act 3 in *Millennium*, the aptly named "Not-Yet-Conscious." Here, Prior is in his bed having a nightmare, when he is visited by two ancestral ghosts, spectral who he assumes emerge from his possible dementia:

> The first ghostly Prior is a 14th-century squire and the other is a 17th-century gentleman, both from periods of British history when there were terrible outbreaks of plague.... Prior is the only character in the play with a Yankee WASP background; he can trace his lineage back for centuries, something most Americans can't reliably do. African American family trees have to start after ancestors were brought over as slaves. Jews emigrated from a world nearly completely destroyed by European genocide.... As a Jew, my roots disappear into the mists of history, past my great-grandparents and are irrecoverable.... But a certain sense of rootlessness is part of the American character [Kushner, Harris].

The bedside visit from "blood relations" — those who suffered from disease during their own mortal days— signals for Prior the fast approaching first, fully visible visitation from the Angel of America. As the "elegant 17th-century Londoner" confides, "We've been sent to declare her fabulous incipience. They love a well-paved entrance with lots of heralds" (87). Prior engages his ancestors in conversation, talking about their family's genealogy, their own struggles to live with disease, and their mutual fear of the unknown. He gives himself over to the surreal dream state, which, in turn, ushers him into a space filled with personal history and myth. As heralds, Prior's ancestors are the conduits through whom Prior's passage way to "be" with the Angel is sanctioned. Their presence is critical to the ritual, for they name him "Prophet. Seer. Revelator [who bestows] great honor [upon] the family" (88). Within the stage world of non-realism, the ancestral ghosts are empowered to anticipate the shift in Kushner's surrealist narrative, as experienced by Prior, from nightmare to "orgasmic" dream. Furthermore, they signal the Benjaminian 'break with history' that creates, dramaturgically, a space for Prior to think and feel in new ways—a space to come more fully into consciousness. And here it is critical to note that Prior's raised consciousness will eventually led to a resistance to fixity and stasis in favor of fluidity, movement, and change ... a "rootlessness" that Kushner's gay male protagonist enlivens and shares with the spirit of Kennedy's women.

In Kushner's play, the "blood relations" of the ill person are embodied as harmless ghosts who celebrate the fertility and mortality of family lineage. Also, since they, themselves, are among the dead who are specially chosen to speak to Prior, they serve as links between the play's temporal and metaphysical spheres. In this way, the living (Prior), the dead (the ancestors), and the metaphysical (the approaching Angel) are intrinsically connected in Kushner's surrealist, visionary realms, albeit in, preferably, unstable relationships to one another. This instability does not threaten the subjectivity of the gay male protagonist, whether he experiences himself in surreal or realist settings and circumstances.

Throughout *Funnyhouse of a Negro* and *The Owl Answers*, the embodied "blood relations" of Kennedy's heroines, Sarah and Clara, respectively, are agents of terror, confusion, and uncompassionate rejection. They are a far cry from Prior Walter's experience of family in the surreal landscape. In *The Owl Answers*, for instance, the character "She who is Clara Passmore who is the Virgin Mary who is the Bastard who is the Owl" (not unlike the Rabbi who is Hannah who is the World's Oldest Bolshevik who is Henry who is Ethel Rosenberg who is the Angel of Asiatica) is shunned by her father, "The Richest White Man in the Town": "If you are my ancestor," he says to her, "why are you a Negro, Bastard?" (31). This rejection is relatively tame next to those that are expressed throughout the rest of the play, which come from every character with whom Clara comes in contact. Like Sarah, Clara cannot turn to historical or to fictional characters for any sense of ancestral coherence, embrace, or support.

In the surrealist territories of the heroines' minds and experiences—ones in which daughters are overwhelmed by the racial and sexual fixity materialized by their mothers and fathers who insist upon pure, or "untainted" identities—Kennedy captures women who exhaust their capacity to sustain individuation. The ancestral lineages for her interracial protagonists refuse to embrace their newly configured offspring. Rather than celebrating the young women's uniqueness and granting them subjectivity, "blood relations" insist that the women are impure, incoherent, void of historical location, and doomed always to be "less than" others. Their blood betrays their rightful place as individuals within various communities.

While activating these two prominent writing strategies—creating dramatic interaction between historical and fictional characters, coupled with dramatizing in surrealist contexts the dynamics between fictional protagonists and their ancestral relations—Kennedy and Kushner also locate literal and figurative significance in several striking stage images. One of the more imposing images that resonates between the authors is the narrative, semiotic, and symbolic gravity of blood.[6]

For Kennedy and Kushner, the centrality of blood in their work is unmistakable. Blood is either pure, unpolluted, and healthy, or it is tainted, contaminated, and diseased. The tensions in their plays often focus on the kind of blood that circulates in any given body and how that body is coded by one's intimates, one's family, and by the culture at large. The ways in which the writers approach bodies and blood raise issues about their intertextual commentary on race, sexuality, and disease.

Sarah's entrance in *Funnyhouse* is one of the most haunting in modern United States drama, not unlike the opening, memorable image of Hamm's face covered by a bloodied "old stancher" in Beckett's *Endgame*:

> *The light is focused on a single white square wall that is to the Left of the Stage, that is suspended and stands alone, of about five feet in dimension and width. It stands with the narrow part facing the audience. A* Character *steps through. She is a faceless, dark character with a hangman's rope about her neck and red blood on the part that would be her face. She is the* Negro [4].

Early in her subsequent monologue, Sarah mentions that one of "herselves," Queen Victoria, always wants her to talk about "whiteness": "She wants me to tell her of a royal world where everything and everyone is white and there are no unfortunate black ones. For as we of royal blood know, black is evil and has been from the beginning" (5). Juxtaposed to Queen Victoria is another "self" of Sarah's, Patrice Lumumba, liberator of West African Congo, whose black "head appears to be split in two with blood and tissue in eyes" (7). Sarah's various selves cannot reconcile their distinctions in a convincing manner to allow for an integrated coexistence within one's self.

For Sarah and herselves in *Funnyhouse*, blood is intrinsically linked to one's racial identity. It is Sarah's inability to reconcile her interracial identity due to internal (psychological, emotional) conflicts as well as external (cultural, social) racism that forces her to "maintain a stark fortress against recognition of [herself]" (6). Her black blood keeps her "inbetween" (11), a state of being that remains isolated, judged, yet occasionally desired as another's exotic, but expendable Other (implied in her relationship with Raymond):

> They told me my Father was God but my father is black. He is my father. I am tied to a black Negro.... Before I was born at the turn of the century, he haunted my conception, diseased my birth.... He is there with his hand out to me, groveling, saying — Forgiveness, Sarah, is it that you will never forgive me for being black. Forgiveness, Sarah, I know you are a nigger of torment [21].

In *The Owl Answers*, "She who is Clara" cannot gain access to her "Dead Father," who she knows to be her "blood father"; "I am almost white, am I not? ... I am his daughter" (29). But Clara is rejected by her white Dead Father: "You are not my ancestor. You are my bastard ... daughter of somebody that cooked for me" (32). For Kennedy's women, the reality of mixed blood flowing in their veins marks them as "diseased" (21), contaminated, and finally, as rootless undesirables. Clara passionately exclaims to her Dead Father and Black Mother, "You must know how it is to be filled with yearning ... [to] want what I think everyone wants ... Love or something" (36). But it is the blood in her corporeal body, Kennedy suggests, that keeps Clara, the mulatta, from knowing earthly love, a love that embraces and accepts her for who she is, for *all* of "herselves."[6]

Unable to experience love of self and the love of another person in temporal reality (since such love is presumably defined as shared between pure bloods), Clara concludes: "I am only yearning for our kingdom, God"— a God who, when she calls, "the Owl answers" (43). For Kennedy, the Owl embraces the mullata as one of its own; it provides Clara with "life" that rejects the bloody suicide of her "Black Mother who is the Reverend's Wife" and her Biblical, yet prejudicial, salvation. Rather, as Clara, with "butcher knife" in hand, still with her mother's "blood and feathers upon it" readies to murder the "Negro Man" who is trying aggressively to seduce her, the young woman drops the knife "in a gesture of wild weariness" (45). The Negro Man, now "frightened ... backs farther" away from Clara, who falls onto the side of the "burning bed" which is next to the High Altar (made of owl feathers by the Black Mother who is the Reverend's Wife) (45). Next to the bed burning, amidst the altar burning and a "White Bird laugh[ing] from the Dome" (45),[7] Clara "suddenly looks like an owl, and lifts her bowed head, stares into space" and begins to speak (or howl), "Ow ... oww" (45). She is one — and alone — with her "blood" god.

The density of Kennedy's poetic stage imagery is unrivaled in U.S. drama. It is clearly a precursor to the intermingling of diverse story lines, formats, and images that surface in the subsequent writings of playwrights who acknowledge their indebtedness to her, including Suzan-Lori Parks and Tony Kushner. I find Kennedy's literal and figurative reliance upon blood in her surrealist writings essential to capturing her compact narrative aims. For Kushner, and in particular in *Angels in America*, the specific factors of one's blood are no less significant than the crisis of blood facing Kennedy's characters. Prior, not unlike Sarah and Clara, lives with compromised, or less than pure, blood. For this reason, he, too, is castigated by society, turned aside by loved ones, and confronted by his feelings toward mortality and spirituality.

During each of the first three scenes in which Prior and Louis appear alone in *Millennium Approaches*, their dialogue focuses on some aspect of the infected blood in Prior's body. In the first scene he shares with his partner Louis, Prior "*removes his jacket, rolls up his sleeve, shows Louis a dark-purple spot on the underside of his arm near the shoulder*," to which his lover responds,

> That's just a burst blood vessel.
> PRIOR: Not according to the best medical authorities.
> LOUIS: What? (*Pause*) Tell me.
> PRIOR: K.S., baby. Lesion number one. Lookit. The wine-dark kiss of the angel of death.
> LOUIS: (*Very softly, holding Prior's arm*): Oh please...
> PRIOR: I'm a lesionnaire. The Foreign Lesion. The American Lesion. Lesionnaire's disease.
> LOUIS: Stop.
> PRIOR: My troubles are lesion.
> LOUIS: Will you *stop*.
> PRIOR: Don't you think I'm handling this well?
>   I'm going to die [21].

In bed for their next scene together, Louis discusses how the "shape of a life, its total complexity gathered, arranged and considered" is what should "matter in the end." "We who are about to die thank you," responds Prior, for Louis's assessment that is "reassuringly incomprehensible and useless."

LOUIS: You are not about to die.
PRIOR: It's not going well, really ... two new lesions. My leg hurts. There's
   protein in my urine, the doctor says, but who knows what the fuck
   that portends. Anyway, it shouldn't be there, the protein. My butt
   is chapped from diarrhea and yesterday I shat blood.
LOUIS: I hate this. You don't tell me...
PRIOR: You get too upset, I wind up comforting you. It's easier...
LOUIS: Oh thanks.
PRIOR: If it's bad I'll tell you.
LOUIS: Shitting blood sounds bad to me [38–39].

For Louis, who is HIV negative, Prior's "bad" blood sounds unbearable
and unlivable, for himself, and there is no irony when he asks the man living with AIDS if Prior would hate him forever if he "walked out on this"
(40). There is no ambiguity in Prior's reply of "Yes," as he "*kisses Louis on
the forehead*" (40).

Five weeks later, Prior, alone on his bedroom floor with a fiery fever,
is having trouble breathing and standing. Against Prior's pleas to the contrary, a hysterical Louis calls an ambulance, then returns to his boyfriend
who has just "*shit himself.*" "I'm sorry ... I had an accident," Prior says, to
which Louis replies,

   This is blood.
PRIOR: Maybe you shouldn't touch it ... me.... I ... *(He faints)*
LOUIS: *(Quietly)*: Oh help. Oh help. Oh God oh God oh God help me I can't
   I can't I can't [48].

This purging of infected blood — when the internal is manifest externally —
drives a wedge between uninfected Louis and Prior. Kushner's Louis is not
wholly dissimilar from the untainted "selves" who surround, judge, and
desert Kennedy's "diseased" Sarah and Clara. And like Kennedy's protagonists, Prior, when alone earlier, confesses: "I don't think there's any uninfected part of me. My heart is pumping polluted blood" (34).

Yet Kushner departs significantly from his much admired predeces-
sor by obliterating the Aristotelian unities and providing his "polluted"
protagonist with a variety of journeys. Prior moves his compromised body
through several months in real time, and numerous landscapes, from the
experiential to the phenomenal. Kennedy's women stay the course in the
extended dreamscape only to experience, as Sarah concludes,

   These rooms are my rooms.... These are the places myselves exist in. I
   know no places. That is, I cannot believe in places. To believe in places is

to know hope and to know the emotion of hope is to know beauty. It links us across a horizon and connects us to the world. I find there are no places in my funnyhouse.... I try to give myselves a logical relationship but that too is a lie. For relationships was one of my last religions. I clung loyally to the lie of relationships, again and again seeking to establish a connection between my characters [*Funnyhouse* 7].

Unlike his "blood relations," Sarah and Clara, Prior comes to know many *places* during his journey, the most startling (and arguably, illogical) of which is his visitation to Heaven in *Perestroika*. In Heaven, Prior witnesses not only the realm of the Angels, but from a distance he is able to glimpse the Earth of which he chooses to remain a mortal participant. He comes to know Earth as the site for life and movement, of which his infected body only wants more. He comes to know Sarah's illusive "emotion of hope" and therefore to "know beauty" (*Funnyhouse* 7) in spite of, or perhaps because of living with the blood of AIDS. And most astoundingly, he sees and commits to the value of relationships— with Belize, Hannah, and Harper, for instance — that establish human connections with a meaning so profound that, indeed, they become, in Sarah's words, a (secular) "religion" (*Funnyhouse* 7) in and of themselves.

The protagonists in Kennedy's early surrealist plays— women of diseased blood who plummet to the depths of pain, fear, rejection, and loneliness because of their Otherness— live inside Kushner's Prior Walter. Yet, as Harper prophetically and humanely witnesses upon meeting Prior in their shared dreamscape:

> Deep inside you, there's a part of you, the most inner part, entirely free of disease. I can see that.
> PRIOR: Is that.... That isn't true.
> HANNAH: Threshold of revelation [*Millennium* 34].

Whether in death or in life, suicidal Sarah, Clara "who is the Owl," and mortal "prophet" Prior are released to a kind of eternal forgiveness— or an awareness of the mercy and grace in forgiveness— by their authors. Both Kennedy and Kushner value soulfulness and the truth of the soul that can be revealed in life or in death. It is this mysterious and humbling revelation that each playwright brings, uniquely and masterfully, to the United States stage through works of theirs that are blood related.

Notes

1. Albee in Savran *Playwrights* 7, 9; Foreman in Savran *Words* 39; Wilson in Wilson 71; Mamet in Savran *Words* 135–36; Vogel in Savran *Playwright's* 287; Hwang in Savran *Words* 120–21; Smith in Savran *Playwright's* 242, 253.

2. Recent critics focused on improving Kennedy's visibility include the contributors to Bryant-Jackson and Overbeck (among them Elin Diamond, Rosemary Curb, Jeanie Forte, Deborah Geis, Margaret Wilkerson, and Werner Sollars); Robinson 115–49.

3. In "Adrienne Kennedy through the Lens of German Expressionism," William Elwood situates Kennedy's "mutability of forms" within the traditions of German expressionist playwrights (Bryant-Jackson and Overbeck 89).

4. Among her many public remarks about Kennedy, Parks has simply stated, "I'm a fan of hers. I remember a teacher of mine in the English Department at Mount Holyoke. I was walking down the hall one day and she saw me coming and ran in her office and came back out with a book and kind of held it out like I was a train and she had the mailbag and I just took it and kept walking, and I got to the end of the hall and it was *Funnyhouse of a Negro.* So I read it and reread it and reread it and reread it. It also had a hand in shaping what I do. I thought anything is possible. I could do what I wanted to do instead of what I felt I had to do.... I think [the teacher] gave me Adrienne Kennedy to encourage me to do what I thought I had to do instead of what people expected" (Savran *Playwright's* 144–45).

5. A casual glance at Kennedy's unconventionally written autobiography, *People Who Led to My Plays,* suggests the range of individuals—both dead and alive—who captured the writer's imagination. Along with her family members (both immediate and extended) and their acquaintances, Kennedy is moved at a very early age to express her feelings in about souls, witches, magicians, monsters, people in dreams, Frankenstein, and the Devil. Equally, she is obsessed with the world of documented lives: from the Virgin Mary, Jesus, Queen Victoria, Chaucer, Shakespeare, William the Conqueror, Anne Boleyn, and Charlotte Bronte, to Marian Anderson, Eleanor Roosevelt, Helen Keller, Abe Lincoln, Hitler, Clark Gable, and Paul Robeson. All these, and more, captured her attention throughout her elementary school years, 1936–1943. Kennedy's entire life document is shaped, most strikingly, by her personal associations with fictional characters and real people.

6. See Jeanie Forte, "Kennedy's Body Politic: The Mulatta, Menses, and the Medusa" (Bryant-Jackson and Overbeck 157–69).

7. For Kennedy, beds are often sites of enacted misogyny, criminal acts, doomed sex, the creation of displaced children, and murder. In *The Owl Answers,* for example, the bed, which is eventually in flames, is also in front of the High Altar, in the presence of the White Bird. For Kushner, the bed in *Angels* is the site of queer sex and uncontrollable erections—and in front of this bed, the "Angel" descends ("White-Bird"-like) and, eventually, leads Prior to the "high altar" of Heaven.

Works Cited

Bryant-Jackson, Paul, and Lois Overbeck, editors. *Intersecting Boundaries: The Theatre of Adrienne Kennedy.* Minneapolis: University of Minnesota Press, 1992.
Fuchs, Elinor. "Adrienne Kennedy and the First Avant-Garde." *Intersecting Boundaries:*

The Theatre of Adrienne Kennedy. Edited by Paul Bryant-Jackson and Lois Overbeck. Minneapolis: University of Minnesota Press, 1992: 76–84.

Kennedy, Adrienne. *Funnyhouse of a Negro*. 1962. *Adrienne Kennedy in One Act*. Minneapolis: University of Minnesota Press, 1988.

_____. *The Owl Answers*. 1963. *Adrienne Kennedy in One Act*. Minneapolis: University of Minnesota Press, 1988.

_____. *People Who Led to My Plays*. New York: Knopf, 1987.

Kushner, Tony. *Angels in America, Part One: Millennium Approaches*. New York: Theatre Communications Group, Inc., 1992.

_____. *Angels in America, Part Two: Perestroika*. New York: Theatre Communications Group, Inc., 1994.

_____. Interview with Kim Myers. *Tony Kushner in Conversation*. Ed. Robert Vorlicky. Ann Arbor, MI: University of Michigan Press, 1998: 231–44.

_____. Interview with Susan Jonas. *Tony Kushner in Conversation*. Edited by Robert Vorlicky. Ann Arbor: University of Michigan Press, 1998: 157–69.

_____. Interview with William Harris. "The Secrets of *Angels*." *New York Times* 27 March 1994: H5.

Robinson, Marc. *The Other American Drama*. Baltimore, MD: Johns Hopkins University Press, 1997.

Savran, David. *In Their Own Words: Contemporary American Playwrights*. New York: Theatre Communications Group, Inc., 1988.

_____. *The Playwright's Voice: American Dramatists on Memory, Writing and the Politics of Culture*. New York: Theatre Communications Group, Inc., 1999.

Sollars, Werner. "Introduction." *The Adrienne Kennedy Reader*. By Adrienne Kennedy. Minneapolis: University of Minnesota Press, 2001.

Wilson, August. "The Ground on Which I Stand." *American Theatre* September 1996: 14–16, 71–74.

4

Then and Now

W.H. Auden, Christopher Isherwood, Tony Kushner, and Fascist Creep

DAVID GARRETT IZZO

A necessary Preface as a matter of timing: Arthur Miller died during the writing of this essay. After Brecht, perhaps no other modern dramatist was as socially and politically pointed and poignant as Miller. He said, "Attention must be paid." These words also fit the plays of W.H. Auden, Christopher Isherwood, and Tony Kushner. Of Miller, Bob Herbert, in his Op-Ed in the *New York Times* of 14 February 2005 wrote:

> The individual, in Mr. Miller's view, had an abiding moral responsibility for his or her own behavior, and for the behavior of society as a whole [online].

The late 1920s and the 1930s, and the 1980s to the present (February, 2005), share certain socio-economic-political patterns that one can identify for their similarities. Both eras have the symptoms of fascist creep. The earlier period went from just creep to a terrible reality. Today, there is creep but one hopes the terrible reality will never occur. Throughout history it has been the artists and intellectuals that first recognized the antecedents of totalitarianism, which made them targets to be removed before they could spread the alarm. Then and now will be examined here through comparisons of the two eras and three dramatists: W.H. Auden and Christopher Isherwood then, and Tony Kushner now.

Tony Kushner: ... art can help change people, who then decide to change their own lives, change their neighborhood, their community, their society, the world. I don't think art alone changes people, but consciousness, the life of the mind, is a critical force for change and art helps the shaping of consciousness ... watching theater teaches people a way of looking

56

at the world with a doubleness of vision that's immensely useful — transformative, even.... Art has a power, but it's an indirect power. Art suggests. When people are ready to receive such suggestion, it can and does translate into action.... Truth is never finally entirely graspable, but neither is it entirely unknowable; glimpses of it come to the courageous, the curious, the diligent, the kind-hearted, the generous [Higgins, online].

In January of 2005 there is a great need for the diligent, kind-hearted and generous, as one can see from the following excerpts:

The Bush-Cheney Administration's assault on civil liberties is starkly authoritarian and must be resisted with every bit of strength the broad left can muster. The question here is whether we are experiencing a lurch to the right by the governing elites or actually witnessing the rise of an American fascism [Sheasby, online].

The American Fascist Movement would like to welcome all — from newcomers to veterans — to its online store! Be sure to take advantage of our constant sales and stock up! Order now, and help fund the only movement of American Fascism! [American Fascist Movement, online].

Tony Kushner as co-editor has published an essay collection (*Remembering Cable Street: Fascism and Anti-Fascism in British Society*) on the nature of British fascism from 1931 to 2000, which of course begins with Oswald Mosley and the British Union of Fascists. No, not the American dramatist — rather a British scholar with the same name, which, while it may seem merely coincidence, is rather an ironic truth-telling as both Kushners are concerned with the nature of fascism, not just as history, but as a contemporary undertone of an insidious drone that is getting louder on a daily basis. The *other* Kushner, the one who writes plays, as early as 1996 wrote a parable about Nazi Germany, *A Bright Room Called Day*, that was meant more as a cautionary warning than just a reflection of a past no longer relevant. Kushner is always relevant. He is a very politically and socially activist writer. His plays are self-evidently intended to teach as well as entertain in the Brechtian manner. A Kushner theme is "fascist creep." As a gay dramatist in the present age of neo-homophobia, Kushner, as a minority, understands the role of the dissident outsider whose victimization is not just a tangential example of isolated small brush strokes but speaks to potentially greater threats of more broadly applied blanket strokes. In the early 1930s W.H. (Wystan Hugh) Auden and his best friend, Christopher Isherwood, were also gay, but they were closeted as the era required by threat of criminal charge. Dramatists, they also

wrote plays as parables of fascist threats. Both had been in Berlin before
and after Hitler's ascension and saw the creeping fascism slowly take over
a browbeaten populace. Their vision of fascist creep was not just about
Germany; they saw it at home in England with Mosley and his cohorts.
Then and now: Déjà vu all over again. The similarities are apparent
between then and now about how these three gay dramatists and intellectuals depict fascist creep. And the U.S. is not alone. Britain is no less
immune to neo-fascism and a yearning for a neo–Great Oswald:

> What next? How soon will there be a murmur rising higher for a man like
> Mosley, his dynamic approach to life at last forgiven? But men like Mosley
> are rare. Will one emerge, as the great voice still echoes down the years,
> calling "Britain awake"? [Friends of Oswald Mosley, online].

One need only do a quick Google search to see that the crazies are alive
and well on both sides of the Atlantic. This is noted so that in a discussion of Kushner's present and Auden and Isherwood's past, the sense of
their concern with fascist creep was not, and is not, overstated. And if one
should think that the above references are cherry picking of extreme but
isolated asininely fatuous examples, read on:

> *New York Times*   January 26, 2005
>
> **EDITORIAL OBSERVER**
>
> **The Difference Between Politically Incorrect and Historically Wrong**
>
> **By ADAM COHEN**
> [In] "The Politically Incorrect Guide to American History...," Thomas
> Woods ... fulminates against the Civil Rights Act of 1964, best known for
> forcing restaurants and bus stations in the Jim Crow South to integrate,
> and against Brown v. Board of Education [online].

Poor Orwell. Could even he have imagined that his formula for rewriting
history in *Animal Farm* and *1984* would come to pass in the United States
of today? Come to think of it, Orwell *did* imagine it; that's why he wrote
his cautionary and didactic novels. Auden, Isherwood, and Kushner also
have didactic intentions even while teaching these lessons through theatrical parables. Both the old fascism of the 1930s and the neo-fascism of today
can be seen to fit the following definition of fascism by Roger Griffin:

> Central to this idea type is the concentration on the fascist's obsession
> with the nation's current decadence and imminent rebirth (palingenesis)
> in a nebulously conceived post-liberal order. It is arguably this myth of

the regenerated national community thriving within a new type of state which forms the elusive "fascist minimum." In other words, it is the common denominator not only between the many different ideologies of national renewal which converged in fascism, but the programmes of the revolutionary nationalist movements most often associated with generic fascism (e.g. the Spanish Falange, the Romanian Iron Guard, the Finnish IKL), despite significant surface divergences conditioned by the unique historical situation and cultural climate of each nation-state concerned. This ideal type of generic fascism can be formulated as follows: Fascism is a genus of political ideology whose mythic core in its various permutations is a palingenetic form of populist ultra-nationalism [online].

Griffin's notion of a "fascist minimum" developing into a "populist ultra-nationalism" fits recent political events in the America of the past 24 years and Europe between the wars. In the 1930s, organized labor was an enemy, particularly communists (whom the Nazis blamed for setting fire to the Reichstag, thus inflaming the people against the CP, even though it was likely the fascists who did the actual burning). In the 1980s, organized labor also became the enemy, with Reagan setting the tone by firing the air striking traffic controllers. Today, there is much anti-union sentiment, even though the very same people who feel this way enjoy whatever benefits and labor laws preventing abuse of workers that organized labor fought to get for them. This is biting the hand that feeds. Intellectuals and artists are also the enemy both then and now. Janet Jackson's bare boob gives an excuse for the righteous right to raise hell over the neo-decadence, which must be repressed while the birth of a new moral order strikes back at the New York and Hollywood liberal elite. One recalls Bush spitting out the words "Hollywood types" at his pep rallies while his adoring fans booed the very people that make the movies and music they pay for. This, while Bush's niece is a model in New York and his cousin Billy Bush carouses on *Access Hollywood*. Howard Stern has been banished to satellite radio for doing exactly the same thing he's been doing for years—why—new moral climate, new enemies. Mel Gibson was forgiven for being a "Hollywood type" because he made *The Passion of the Christ*, which turned into a neo–second resurrection as if the circus was coming to town. (This author is not anti-spirituality. Indeed, a major component of his work as a literary theorist is based on the premise that a spiritual force, aka God, *does* exist.) So-called Decadence, as in the tribute to Mosley above, is one excuse fascists rally around to bolster their real wish: Control. One can learn this from the 1930s.

The Berlin that first Auden, then Isherwood visited from 1929 to 1933 began with the "decadent" avant-garde art and sexual excess of the late Weimar Republic that was later targeted by the Nazis as the devil that must be destroyed. All of this, too, was blamed on the communists, intellectuals, artists, and homosexuals who, along with Jews, were that era's bogeymen. Invoking these "decadent" people was a recruiting tool for fascism. One knows the historical drill: the more things change, the more things remain the same. An example of "the same" is an editorial in the 4 January 2005 *New York Times.*

Leave No Sales Pitch Behind

President Bush's No Child Left Behind Act is slowly dawning on ... high school students ... military recruiters can blitz [with] pitches.... This is ... possible under ... part of the law that requires schools to provide the names, addresses (campus addresses, too) and phone numbers of students or risk losing federal aid [online].

In the 1930s, Hitler also appealed to the lower middle class and poor, many of whom were unemployed and needed others to commiserate with and scapegoats to blame. Hitler provided both. Indeed, in 1930, Isherwood wrote an essay about "The Youth Movement in Germany." The recruiting by the U.S. military sounds much like the Patriot Act's provision of forcing librarians to tattle on their constituents' reading habits. A reader who borrows *Animal Farm* might be considered a subversive because Orwell's "fairy tale" is a handbook on how to turn an egalitarian enterprise into a totalitarian state. Conversely, this reader might not be persecuted but praised and recruited for the CIA. Is this a stretch? Perhaps not any more than approving in the new U.S. attorney general a person who advocates methods of torture that stop just short of organ failure or death. Is it too much of a stretch that such a person might make the leap to using these same techniques on American citizens he or the state doesn't like?

As for Reagan, it was he who inspired Tony Kushner's activist drama career. In an essay/interview, Fernando Quintero writes about what motivated Kushner to write his play *A Bright Room Called Day:*

[It] was written ... in response to his "overwhelming sense of despair" following the re-election of former President Reagan. The play depicts a group of artists and political activists struggling to preserve themselves in Berlin during the rise of fascism in the 1930s ... parallels are drawn between Reagan and Hitler [Quintero, online].

Quoted in the *New York Blade,* Kushner said, "I wanted to write about the times. I wanted to write about being gay and I was horrified by Reagan for his lunatic posture in foreign affairs and his repulsive response to AIDS" (Robinson, online).

Kushner said that he considered *Bright Room* as more than just a "coy metaphor, and saying 'watch out, it could happen here' [fascism], the point of *Bright Room* is that the Holocaust is only useful as a standard of evil if you're actually willing to apply it, and if you don't apply it, if it's set up as a unique metaphysical event that has no peer [that is, thinking it couldn't happen again], then those people really died for nothing" (McLeod, 143).

Often the past can tell us about the present as well, as in this *New York Times* film review of 5 January 2005:

> MOVIE REVIEW | HITLER'S HIT PARADE: It's the Nazi Era, but It Looks So Familiar
>
> By A.O. Scott
>
> ... as the film's title makes clear, these ditties and scenes come not from Hollywood but from Nazi Germany, and they are arranged to emphasize the dark irony that such wholesome blandness and suave sophistication could be part of the self-image of radical evil [online].

The subtitle for this review, ""It's the Nazi era, but it looks so familiar," is a message that Kushner has understood for the since Reagan's re-election that moved him first to despair, then to the act of artistic creation in the manner that Nietzsche called *ressentiment*— that is, a rush of creative emotion resulting from pent-up moral outrage. Kushner, like all artists, counts on audience identification with issues that are raised by the art of anguish: "I am happiest when people who are politically engaged in the world say, 'Your play meant a lot to me; it helped me think about something, or made me feel like I wasn't the only person who felt this way'" (Bernstein, online).

Auden said this in a similar manner many years earlier: "The reaction one hopes for from a poem is that the reader will say, 'Of course I've always known that, but I've never realized it before'" ("Interview with W.H. Auden," 139).

Auden said that an artist couldn't tell people what to do; he could only tell them parables from which one could make self-discoveries. Ideally, this is what art does; it points one towards an epiphany without doing so polemically. The effect is more genuine than the hammer approach of crude didacticism. Art *does* teach, but pointing toward revelation is much more effective than demanding it.

Auden and Isherwood's reaction to fascism was not based on any singular moment like Kushner's impression of Reagan's re-election. Their awareness was developed over time and even before Mussolini, Hitler, and Mosley began operating. For Auden and Isherwood, the concept of a fascist mentality began at their prep schools. A recurring theme of the Auden generation was its hatred for their prep schools — at least by the artists and intellectuals, the "aesthetes," as opposed to the "hearties." The aesthetes recalled that their schools were more about preparing the upper class to preserve and protect the British Empire from the working class than about education. Empire-protection was the "end" and had as its means in the prep schools an "honor system" that put the aesthetes against the hearties, with the latter the willing majority in enforcing the honor code. The "hearties" played games both physically and mentally against the "aesthetes" and lower grades. The hearties were expected and encouraged by their schools to demand obedient conformity and were given the power to use or abuse corporal punishment in order to get it. Conformity meant strict adherence to the school's rules of conduct. Students were encouraged on their "honor" to tell on each other when rules were violated. Auden, writing in 1934, remembers this honor system as egregiously dishonorable:

> I believe no more potent engine for turning [students] into neurotic innocents, for perpetuating those very faults of character which it was intended to cure, was ever devised.... The best reason I have for opposing fascism is that at school I lived in a fascist state ["The Liberal Fascist," 325].

As homosexuals Auden and Isherwood were doubly fearful. The trial of Oscar Wilde was not such a distant memory in the 1920s. Isherwood would later say of this school-induced fear, "Paranoia is a kind of heightened awareness which makes one see how extraordinary ordinary life is — or can seem, if one wishes" (*Diaries*, 756). (Kushner, in *Bright Room*'s New York Shakespeare Festival version had three "interruptions," with the third subtitled, "Berlin 1930: The Politics of Paranoia.") Any minority, herein homosexuality specifically, is aware of its outsider status and the paranoia this entails.

While writers of the mid-to-late 1930s responded to actual fascism in Europe, the Auden generation's writings of the early 1930s were initially responses to the homegrown fascism of the public schools. In 1938 when Isherwood published the autobiographical *Lions and Shadows*, he subtitled it "an education in the twenties." The fear and paranoia detailed in this book were derived from his public school but were also readily understandable to a readership feeling its own fear and paranoia about the fascism across the water. Isherwood's message to readers was that they would be able to relate the contemporary fascism of the 1930s to the de facto fascism of the public schools in the 1920s.

A central event of 1933 was the publication of *The Brown Book of Nazi Terror*. Without byline, the book was a chronological list of crimes during and after the Nazis' rise to power. German communist Willi Munsterberg was tacitly credited with putting it together. Since the Nazis had avowed their intention to destroy communism, the communists countered with this effort that was translated into twenty-three languages and sold 600,000 copies throughout Europe and America. Even up to the day before *The Brown Book* became widespread news, the British still pretended that Hitler was just another buffoon like Mussolini and both were someone else's local problem. Yes, one had heard things, but one imagined these were rag press exaggerations promulgated by the Communist Party. However, the book's introduction by the esteemed Lord Marley attested to the veracity of the facts, and the facts defied — if not credence — decency.

Samuel Hynes writes in *The Auden Generation*: "If *The Brown Book* was a true history of existence in what had been a civilized European country, then it compelled any ordinary reader to alter and extend his sense of reality, of what was possible to men in the twentieth century. If it was true — and no one questioned the essential accuracy of the reporting — then reality meant something other, and worse, than men had thought and human beings were capable of greater evil than liberalism had allowed for. *The Brown Book* did not create this change — the Nazis did that — but it helped force a recognition of the change upon western consciousness" (130).

There is also recognition by artists and their audiences feeling fear and paranoia about the 1980s and early 2000s. Kushner shares his recognition in his writings of the 1980s and 1990s, including the obviously antifascist *Bright Room Called Day*, and the almost as obvious *Angels in America*. And are there still aesthetes and hearties? What is George Bush, if not a pseudo-frat-party-flyboy who avoided the Vietnam War and was an undeserving Yale legacy product and former party animal who feels entitled to his existence, as do his coterie of privileged characters that would like to undo the New Deal. This is not a meritocracy in charge, but a "Poshocracy" (Isherwood's word for the 1920s "old men in high places," aka *The Others*) of money and noblesse oblige.

One difference between then and now is that Kushner does not have to hide his sexual orientation under threat of jail. This does not mean that gays and lesbians are yet fully free from bigotry, animosity, and discrimination — unless they are celebrities. Why is it that Melissa Etheridge, Ellen DeGeneres, Nathan Lane etc. appear regularly in living rooms across the United States on television, even in red states, but would be much less welcome in person by certain segments of the American population? Or is it that certain segments of the population that previously didn't give much of a damn have been inflamed by Republican gay bashing? Maybe they still don't give a damn but can't admit to it in any kind of public

accounting such as on the job, at religious services of whatever denomi-
nation, and just about any other nexus of group interaction where there
is always that pressure to conform and be one of "us."

For Auden and Isherwood British gay bashing was hardly unknown in
the 1920s and 1930s. In Isherwood's 1960 novel, *Down There on a Visit*, the
section titled "Ambrose" details the memory of the gay Ambrose (based on
the very real Francis Turville-Petre) being harassed and thrashed at Cambridge in the late 1920s. In his 1976 autobiography of the years 1929–1939,
Christopher and His Kind, Isherwood is very clear that what motivated Auden
first, Christopher second, to visit Berlin was because of what they found
there — "boys" — in a non-judgmental, non-paranoid environment (before
Hitler) without the accompanying fear that always existed in Britain.

Certainly, Auden and Isherwood's first play, *The Dog Beneath the Skin*,
replicates much of the Berlin club nightlife (the Cozy Corner was later
made famous in *Cabaret*) in the Ninevah Hotel scene. Owen Brady writes
that because the scene is "done in a crude and rowdy cabaret style [it] suggests all that is venal, gross, and inhumane about capitalist materialism....
Because they are grotesques, the Announcer and Madam Bubbi [from Isherwood's Berlin boyfriend "Bubi," about whom Auden wrote his poem,
"The Loved One] serve to mock the romantic illusions they endorse. Love
becomes mere appetite and sexual pleasure an edible commodity; the
Ninevah girls perform crudely and are selected by the hotel audience for
consumption. [Is this not today's Reality TV?] ... the association of the
Berlin Cabaret with English self-aggrandizement ... threaten the theater
audience's nationalistic illusion of sanity, civility, and order..." (161). Overall, Brady argues that a great deal of campy and outrageous stage business
was meant to be a free-for-all backdrop to the campy and outrageous
script. (Isherwood would define High and low camp in his 1954 novel, *The
World in the Evening*.) Auden and Isherwood had clear intentions in criticizing British society but conceded that a theater audience would need to
be entertained as well as enlightened to make sure there *was* an audience.
Kushner would agree — entertainment can have a message, but entertainment is the first requirement, and the message is best taught as parable.

For Auden, the sincere writer writes to please himself while convey-
ing a universal message that can also please an audience: "Poetry is not
concerned with telling people what to do, but with extending our knowledge of good and evil, perhaps making the necessity of action more urgent
and its nature more clear, but only leading us to the point where it is possible for us to make a rational and moral choice" (Introduction, "The
Poet's Tongue," 327).

As regards "rational and moral choice" in *The Dog Beneath the Skin*,

Edward Mendelson notes, "The pattern introduced beneath the wonder-ings of the hero amounts to a parabolic lesson in history. This takes the form of a progress from innocence to experience, of two opposed kinds: the revolutionary awakened in the hero and the reactionary hysteria that emerges in the village" (*Early Auden*, 101). Auden and Isherwood had made their own progress from innocence to experience as witnesses to the Nazi terror in Berlin. The play's hero, Alan Norman, is selected by his village to search for a missing heir, Sir Francis Crewe, whose return might bring some stability back to the town. Alan is sent off with pomp and circum-stance across the border and to unknown frontiers where he has burlesque adventures. Norman sets out with the village's favorite "dog" as a com-panion. Alan returns home with the heir, Francis, who in fact had dis-guised himself as the "dog" years before, and had been in the village all along. Alan and Francis find that their village has become a fascist enclave with the concomitant fear and paranoia this entails.

It is during Alan and the dog's quest beyond the village that they encounter the grotesque absurdities that represent contemporary Britain's blindness towards reality. Owen Brady states, "Alan and the dog continue their quest for the lost Sir Francis in Ostnia's red light district, a landscape where souls have sought powerful deflections and intoxicating substances, sexual pleasures and drugs, to escape the harsh reality of the industrial urban capitalism. The chorus grounds the middle class audience in a hard reality, taking them imaginatively from "a square of Georgian houses" to a place where "chimneys fume gently above us like rifles recently fired" (218). Another escape for Europeans was into the jingoistic nationalism of rabid fascism under a Hitler, Mussolini, or Mosley. (There was a recent British film, *Liam*, which astutely depicts the early 1930s seduction of the disenfranchised into the British Union of Fascists.)

To depict the faux revelry veiling morbid despair, the Auden's play *The Dance of Death* (1934), and the Auden-Isherwood plays *The Dog Beneath the Skin* (1935), *The Ascent of F6* (1936), and *On the Frontier* (1938), employed variations of the *danse macabre* motif as a signature of Auden and the Group Theatre. At the request of Rupert Doone, the artistic leader of the Group Theatre who had worked with Jean Cocteau in the 1920s, Auden wrote a multiform performance piece called *The Dance of Death*, performed in 1933. This was the initial time a *danse macabre* was featured. Auden and Doone's intended symbolism signified an overall metaphor of the stale, bourgeois British chasing foolish diversions to ward off the clear reality that their way of life was mortally wounded. Auden and Isherwood had written copiously of this deadly decline in their previous art and, for Auden, essays. British and European upper class decadence, a decadence that tried to ignore the reasons that World War I happened — and might happen again — was not abating but worsening. In the 1920s Aldous Huxley's bitterly cynical satiric novels and T.S. Eliot's nihilistic *The Waste Land* were the early harbingers of a slow decay that now speeded up in the 1930s with the havoc wrought by the Depression.

In his era Kushner has recognized American decadence since the Reagan 1980s. *A Bright Room Called Day* and *Angels in America* also fight against decadent indifference, as a moral failing that won't see the forest for the trees. Kushner was greatly influenced by socialist Walter Benjamin's metaphor of the "Angel of History" that Benjamin described upon seeing the Paul Klee painting "Angelus Novus," itself a *danse macabre.*

> *Benjamin*: ... [There is] an angel looking as though he is about to move away from something he is fixedly contemplating. His eyes are staring, his mouth open, his wings are spread. This is how one pictures the angel of history. His face is turned toward the past. Where we perceive a chain of events, he sees one single catastrophe which keeps piling wreckage and hurls it in front of his feet. The angel would like to stay, awaken the dead, and make whole what has been smashed. But a storm is blowing from Paradise; it has got caught in his wings with such violence that the angel can no longer close them. This storm irresistibly propels him into the future to which his back is turned, while the pile of debris before him grows skyward. This storm is what we call progress [257–58].

Benjamin clearly intimates that often chaos precedes learning. Before Benjamin, Soren Kierkegaard, the nineteenth century existential Christian polemicist, said, and Auden, a great admirer of Kierkegaard, repeated, "Life is learned backwards, but must be lived forwards" (25). Benjamin echoes Kierkegaard's axiom. Kushner read Walter Benjamin's *Understanding Brecht* and "Theses on the Philosophy of History." In a *Bright Room Called Day*, a character says, "History repeats itself, first as tragedy, then as farce." (This message also features in Thornton Wilder's *The Skin of Our Teeth*; see Fisher in *Thornton Wilder: New Essays.*)

> Kushner ... shares Benjamin's belief that history (social, political, and personal) teaches profound lessons and he understands that the concepts of apocalypse and the afterlife are fraught with the same struggles, confusions, and pain encountered in real life. Kushner is inspired by Benjamin's assertion that, as [Kushner] describes it, one is "constantly looking back at the rubble of history. The most dangerous thing is to become set upon some notion of the future that isn't rooted in the bleakest, most terrifying idea of what's piled behind you" [Fisher, 7].

Preparing for a better future is predicated on not repeating the mistakes of the past but learning from them. Throughout history this has been much easier said than done.

Fisher continues:

> *The Angels* plays, feverish historical dramas about America's immediate and contemporary history, examine many themes, but are held together by Benjamin's conception of the ruins of history as the price of progress. *Angels* depicts, with varying degrees of anger, humor, and empathy, a poignant and epic tapestry of the substantial societal and spiritual issues facing humankind — and Americans in particular — at the dawn of the new millennium. Presenting a moral combat represented at various points — and on various fronts — by the opposing poles of conservative and liberal, gay and straight, victimizer and victim, *Angels* also deftly captures a convergence of *past* (dying old values and certainties symbolized by the death of the elderly Jewish woman who journeyed from the Old World to America and by the Diorama of a Mormon pioneer family), *present* (selfishness, faithlessness, and isolation, as typified by the era itself, archconservative politician Roy Cohn, and by a perceived decline of compassion in American society at the end of the twentieth century), and *future* (represented as a choice between further deterioration or an acceptance of the necessity of change, as exemplified at the end of *Millennium Approaches* by the startling appearance of an angel who may bring news of salvation or of apocalypse [55].

And metaphorically the audience must also choose salvation or apocalypse.

While Kushner sees the past as the hard lessons upon which progress will be made, Auden and Isherwood also saw lessons to be learned from the past, but even more so they resented the past as their personal albatross. This resentment developed into their theme of an ancestral curse and family ghosts. "The tyranny of the dead," wrote Auden: "One cannot react against them" (*Journal*, quoted in Mendelson, *Early Auden*, 25). The Auden generation seemed haunted by the past. Auden and Isherwood rebelled against the Others, or, in line with the title of Isherwood's first novel, *All the Conspirators*, the "old men" who they felt had caused the events leading to World War I and its aftermath that damaged the psyches of the Auden generation. Auden used the terms "ancestral curse" and "ghosts" in his poems with the cryptic intent of signifying his contempt for the cant and rant defenders of the British Empire: teachers at the old school, preachers, politicians, and the "Poshocracy," the British upper middle and upper classes. Included as Others were the widowed mothers of World War I, such as Isherwood's, and the guilt they subjected their bound sons to.

Despite different eras, Auden, Isherwood, and Kushner depict societal

decay with very comparable approaches. Audiences then and now consider similar questions that are posed in their work. The answers may not
be didactically provided in the plays, but by their absence — as depicted
by the decay and lack of compassion towards others in both eras— audiences will intuitively see and feel that there are holes needing to be filled
with some kind of new wisdom — whatever that may be.

In the particular universes and zeitgeists of Auden, Isherwood, and
Kushner, this wisdom would have some general underlying basis as a form
of socialism, which at the very least would be the dictum *Do unto others
as you would have them do unto you.* Auden, Isherwood & Kushner all
stopped short of communism (a much bigger paradigm of choice in the
1930s that is almost irrelevant now). Auden, much more of an ideologue
than Isherwood at this time, read and wrote about Marxism, but a more
benign, socialistic Marx. Kushner has been greatly influenced by social-
ists Walter Benjamin and Raymond Williams.

One must be reminded here that while *Ideas* were deliberately given the
light of day by all three dramatists, the trio still believed that ideas would
fall flat and be underappreciated if there was no entertainment value in presenting the ideas. Auden said a poet (or dramatist) must be a mixture of spy
and gossip with a lot of good news to report in the most entertaining way
possible. Auden's 1937 essay "In Defense of Gossip" combined his view of
the inclusiveness of poetic subject matter with a view concerning the force
behind the creation of poetry. Auden writes: 'Gossip is the art form of the
man and woman in the street, and the proper subject for gossip, as for all
art, is the behaviour of mankind" ("In Defense of Gossip," 1371).

This essay suggests that the source of both art and gossip is an ordinary
curiosity about life around us— a curiosity shared by all — and that art mirrors this curiosity. Hence, this is a defense of poetry as well as a defense of
gossip, and ideally it should convince the man in the street that reading poetry
is a "popular" and not just a highbrow source of enjoyment and satisfaction,
just as one enjoys the tabloid gossip pages and TV gossip shows. In real life,
a "gossip" session, besides being about people telling what they themselves
and others are doing, is also a vehicle to talk about one's self in comparison
to those "others." When the artist "gossips," he does best when he arouses
both interest and sympathy through the gossip's entertainment value.

Kushner agrees: "The theater always has to function as popular entertainment. Or at least the theater that I do, because I don't have the talent
for doing anything else. It has to have the jokes and it has to have the
feathers and the mirrors and the smoke" (*Tony Kushner in Conversation*,
63). Kushner also believes that art should have news value that audiences
can relate to: "It is immensely difficult, if not impossible, to write a play

intended to enter into public discourse that is free of any reference to current events, to news. It's hard to understand why anyone would want to" ("Notes About Political Theater," 29). While Kushner points to Brecht as an inspiration for political theater, the political messages in Kushner's plays come from Walter Benjamin and Raymond Williams. In Williams' 1985 essay, "Walking Backwards into the Future," its title imitative of Kierkegaard's axiom, Williams writes:

> The idea of *a society* was to distinguish one form of social relationships from another, and to show that these forms varied historically and could change. Thus, in thinking about the longstanding problems of virtue and happiness, people who began from the idea of a society did not immediately refer the problems to a general human nature or to inevitable conditions of existence; they looked first at the precise forms of the society in which they were living and at how these might, where necessary, be changed. The first uses of *socialist*, as a way of thinking, were in deliberate contrast to the meanings of *individualist*: both as a challenge to that other way of thinking, in which all human behaviour was reduced to matters of individual character and more sharply as a challenge to its version of human intentions. Was life an arena in which individuals should strive to improve their own conditions, or was it a network of human relationships in which people found everything of value in and through each other...? The power of private capital to shape or influence these decisions is replaced by active local and social decision, in what is always in practice the real disposition of our lives [and that there is] an immense and widespread longing for this kind of practical share in shaping our own lives.... The public interest is not singular but is a complex and interactive network of *different* real interests. A Sharing plan begins from an acknowledgement of *diversity*, and encourages the true social processes of open discussion, negotiations and agreement [283–86].

Concerning sharing, Auden wrote many essays in the 1930s that preview Williams' ideas, including: "The Group Movement and the Middle Class" (1934), "The Good Life" (1935), "Psychology and Art Today" (1935), and "Psychology and Criticism" (1936). (See Appendix.) A main theme for Auden was that mass depersonalization must be broken back down into smaller personal groups working together for the good of the whole and against the 1930s' Poshocracy. For example, in 1934 "The Group Movement...," Auden wrote, "Today the light which has been shed by Freud and Marx on the motivation of thought makes it criminal to be uncritical, and no movement, secular or religious, which is afraid to examine dispassionately and to acknowledge openly what self-interest would make it want to believe, is worthy of anything but contempt" (89–90).

Could have been said yesterday.

A post–1960s Poshocracy solidified with Reagan in the 1980s. Reagan was the anti–Williams (and anti–Auden and Isherwood, who likely would not have tolerated Reagan any more than Kushner did). Fisher wrote:

> *Angels*, like most of Kushner's work [and the Auden-Isherwood plays], argues for a reordering of American society along the lines suggested by Williams socialist theories. Laced throughout *Angels* is the call for a re-evaluation of old certitudes, whether they be political, social, religious (or moral), or personal. A reformed society built on progressive, compassionately humanistic doctrine that draws its strength from the hard lessons of the past is central to both Williams' theories and *Angels*. For the characters in the play, proceeding into the unknown future seems too frightening, too painful, and too confusing. Walking backward into the future, as William suggests, is a possible route—finding in the values of the past both the triumphant and the catastrophic. When Prior Walter invites the audience to imagine more life at the end of *Perestroika*, he does so with his eyes firmly fixed on what is behind him as well as what might be in front. It is a guarded optimism, won through terrible personal ordeals and a belief in the power of humanity to survive its own failings [58].

If one chooses to see life as lessons learned after overcoming obstacles, one will learn from both bad and good, or, as Thornton Wilder wrote in 1930, "I praise all living, the light and the dark" (*The Woman of Andros*, 115).

The educative approach that Auden, Isherwood and Kushner employ is a kind of magic realism that uses fantastic (and sometimes seemingly absurd) elements to highlight the bitter realities that might (and would) have seemed too realistically harsh to portray straight up without the levity of fantasy. "*The Dog Beneath the Skin* ... has a two-part agenda. First, it is an all-out theatrical assault on British commercial theater, especially middle-class romantic comedy. Second, it wants to expose the dangers of the comfortable British bourgeois assumptions. The radical mixing of theatrical forms ... hoped to open the eyes of bourgeois British audience to the danger of its own personal and social self-delusions and in so doing create the possibility of a more humane society" (Brady, 152). Kushner also challenges assumptions with fantasy and credits Brecht for the ways he

> [M]arried the illusion/reality paradigm at the heart of all Western theater since the Italian Renaissance and Shakespeare to its counterpart in Marx.... Theater, like dialectical materialist analysis, examines the magic of perception and the political, ideological employment to which the magic is put ["Notes About Political Theater," 27].

Auden said that white magic is art; black magic is propaganda. The difference is that art teaches as parable, but an audience must discern the lesson of its own accord as a self-revelation; propaganda is didactic and false, influencing by lying. Propaganda was a concern of Kierkegaard, who influenced Auden's views on the public's propensity for believing propaganda. Kierkegaard believed the anonymous Public was the bastard child of the Industrial Revolution, universal education, and mass media. This Public can be influenced by the media but cannot be held accountable for any resulting behaviors that these media appeals might provoke. The Public comprises individuals who can be manipulated in general but need not be responsible for anything in particular because they are not identifiable as specific human beings. Media can influence an anonymous Public to take sides on an issue; yet, these unidentifiable individuals can remove themselves from subsequent results by fading into their anonymity as a so-called silent majority. In effect, by reading and hearing the news in private, one can be moved to love or hate another person or group without the personal scrutiny or judgment that might involve the conscience. Anonymity can be irresponsible. The anonymous Public becomes the proverbial "They" that authority figures can invoke to praise conformists and chastise nonconformists. This concept of a Kierkegaardian Public is crucial in understanding the rise of propaganda in the 1930s. How did this Public and its anonymity come about? In the agrarian and small-town culture before the Industrial Revolution, anonymity was less prevalent, and thus the concept of an impersonal Public is not as applicable. The anonymous Public emerged from the depersonalized, industrialized city-state where mass production necessitated regimentation among workers. This regimentation required a universal basic education that allowed workers to function in their roles as cogs in the mechanized city. These workers would then consume the goods they read about in advertising and perpetuate their own existences in a slavish cycle. Universally, if minimally educated, this easily influenced Public consumes media and not necessarily with great discernment. As Auden said in *Letter to Lord Byron* (1937), "Our age is highly educated / There is no lie our children cannot read" (83). It was one thing for the mass producers to influence the Public to become mass consumers through advertising, but it became something quite nefarious when tyrants used the media to influence the Public to be mass followers through propaganda.

> *Kierkegaard*: The public is a concept which could not have occurred in antiquity because the people en masse, *in corpare*, took part in any situation which arose and were responsible for the actions of the individual, and, moreover, the individual was personally present and had to submit

at once to applause or disapproval.... Only when the sense of association in society is no longer strong enough to give life to concrete realities is the press able to create that abstraction 'the public,' consisting of unreal individuals who can never be united in an actual situation or organization — and yet are held together as a whole.... A public is everything and nothing, the most dangerous of all powers and the most insignificant" [41–43].

Propaganda became a tool for dictators to fool the public in the 1920s and 1930s. In the post–World War II era, the media took even greater control of images and "big lies" to be seen and told over and over: *There are Weapons of Mass Destruction about to be set off in Central Park; marriage is between a man and a woman only. Social Security is going to be broke (in 60 years).* These are distractions that play on fear, and fear leads to head-fogging anxiety. After World War II there were forty years of Cold War anxiety followed by the temporary reprieve at the end of the Cold War in 1979 when Americans had no common cause or enemy to give them a basis for solidarity. If there is no cause for solidarity, then there is no outer focus that joins people but an inversion to a focus on Me! Me! Me! Me! The media is only too happy to help adoring egos adore themselves with mirror reflections of what one would imagine one wants to be like with shows such as *Entertainment Tonight* and *Access Hollywood* providing the mirror of celebrity for egos to vicariously imitate. (This perception of the end of the Cold War is a theme of Don DeLillo's Reagan-induced novel *Underworld*.)

So when Kushner talks about illusion and reality, this is not just about theater but about the duality of each individual's self-perception that is juxtaposed with that individual's perception of celebrities, and then further juxtaposed with some kind of external reality of how he and others he considers in his "club" see the *Other*.

Auden said that human relations begin with one's looking out at others in an oppositional, often adversarial way: "I am I; you are not I." He also said, as Kushner does above, that art undoes this separation by taking the particular case and showing how it is universally understood, meaning that we are actually more alike than we are different, though many people will not accept that the *Other* is not really an alien.

Anxiety about the *Other* creates fear and suspicion. Auden's, Isherwood's and Kushner's plays are about the anxiety and suspicion in their different eras, which are not so different since human nature replicates itself each generation with only the nomenclature, nuances, and scenery changing.

This generation's folly has a context that readers can put Kushner's plays into. A review of the context for Auden and Isherwood is helpful and can point out the similarities of their 1930s with the U.S. of the past 25 years.

The Auden Generation

Many of the British writers between the wars (1919–1939) indicted the failed liberalism that they felt led to World War I. They also believed that the punitive Treaty of Versailles that ended the first war would lead to a second. The 1920s emphasized the residual shock of the war with a cynical nihilism as represented by T.S. Eliot's *The Waste Land* in 1922 and the novels of Aldous Huxley. Huxley summed up the 1920s by portraying the seemingly purposeless frivolity of the middle and upper classes that actually masked pervasive despair. Eliot and Huxley were adults during the war and fully understood the events that caused it, the horror of the war itself, and the debilitating consequences that followed it. The immediately following writers of the 1930s, though only some ten to fifteen years younger and exemplified by W.H. Auden, Christopher Isherwood, and Stephen Spender, were distanced from the causes of the war but became the inheritors of the war's effects. Rather than being cynical nihilists as were the 1920s writers, they became cynical idealists who rejected their predecessors and wished to create a socialist world inspired by the public experiment of the Soviet Union and the private experiments discovered through Freud and psychoanalysis.

In the 1930s they contributed to a redefining of the male hero (and anti-hero) by moving him toward his more contemporary configuration that Kushner and his contemporaries know very well — the sensitive man. Auden's generation witnessed a precipitous end to pre-war traditions. This new world was confronted by an unknown future that might be a socialist utopia, a fascist tragedy, or both. From that era's uncertain perspective to this era's uncertain perspective, the anti-hero's changing face has been a progress of different masks. Auden's generation saw a precipitous end to a traditional European liberalism that was instead heading toward fascist chaos. And Kushner's generation sees a precipitous end to 1960s liberalism that is heading toward a neo-fascism.

The anti-hero's evolutionary process began after World War I when writers such as Huxley blamed the war's causes on the "old men" in high places, aka the Poshocracy. Today the new Poshocracy are the beneficiaries of Bush's tax cuts. The 1930s writers also recognized the paranoia of the middle and upper classes who feared that the Bolsheviks would take over Britain and redistribute their bourgeois wealth. Today, these are the people who enjoy the tax cuts and want to preserve them without sharing. In the 1920s the bitter war heroes such as the martyred poet Wilfred Owen, and the disengaged cynics depicted by Huxley and Eliot, became magnets for the youthful intelligentsia who would become fervently engaged activists in the next decade. Today, Kushner is a magnet for the youthful intelligentsia who will become fervently engaged activists in the next decade. In the late 1920s, Auden and Isherwood began their consideration of the anti-hero as the person who makes the heroic trek that actually only proves he is weak until he finds the inner peace that is truly strong. In the 1930s the Auden generation developed the "mythified" dichotomy of the Truly Strong and Truly Weak Man. This dichotomy is standard operating procedure for Kushner and his present fellow artists.

Although the Strong Man and Weak Man can be distinct individual personas, more often the Strong Man and Weak Man represent conflicting aspects within the same person. Auden's generation developed this mythos by emphasizing the conflicts of divided minds that anticipated the future of literary characterization ushered in by Auden's *Age of Anxiety* after World War II.

The dichotomy of the Truly Weak and Truly Strong Man was depicted tacitly in Auden and Isherwood's art from 1928 forward. In 1938, however, Isherwood's autobiographical *Lions and Shadows* explicitly traces the Truly Strong and Truly Weak theme. The book's subtitle is "an education in the Twenties," and this was shared by many in the Auden-Isherwood generation, one which endured the guilt of *not* having been in the war. Consequently, they were unable to prove themselves as had the noble dead war heroes, including Isherwood's father. These martyred fathers, husbands, brothers, uncles, sons, cousins, and friends were eulogized endlessly and were a constant source to Isherwood and his peers of a latent, or not-so latent, guilt by comparison. This contrast engendered psychological insecurity that was magnified by widowed, possessive mothers who were intent on dominating their sons.

There was an Us against Them mentality. To Isherwood, "Them," or the Others, meant the Poshocracy who had caused the war in order to protect and preserve the British traditions and class divisions that had given them disproportionate advantages—as is now being done by the beneficiaries of Bush's tax cuts. Auden and Isherwood categorized this antagonism as one requiring "Tests" that would prove they were just as capable as the noble dead had been. For example, Isherwood purchased an unneeded motorcycle in order to emulate T.E. Lawrence. The goal of these Tests was to make the journey over a metaphorical Northwest Passage within the mind and over the border/frontier of the old world and to a new world of promise. Initially, for Auden and Isherwood, this new world meant Berlin in 1929 before Hitler took power. Similar pseudo-heroic posturing of the 1920s was soon to be trivialized by the harsher realities of the next decade: Hitler and Mussolini, propaganda emerging to its full power, Stalinism, and the travesty of the Spanish Civil War. For the Auden generation this world of the 1930s was one of pervasive paranoia with shadowy deals and betrayals thought to be *de rigueur*. By *Lions and Shadows* in 1938, Isherwood was quite clear that the unconscious, symptomatic acts he described concerning school life in the 1920s now had a more consciously recognizable context in the 1930s. The "Test" was now understood to have been a symptom caused by the much more profound thematic dichotomy of the Truly Weak or Truly Strong Man.

The Truly Weak Man (exemplified by T.E. Lawrence) suffered from a compulsion to prove himself by seeking, confronting, and passing tests of rebellious derring-do. It did not matter whether the tests were actual or imagined. (Is not the Roy Cohn of *Angels* the exemplar of the Truly Weak Man who compensates by being an evil prince of paranoia?) Conversely, the Truly Strong Man is pure in heart. In *Lions and Shadows* Isherwood defines the Truly Strong Man in the terms "spoken of by the homicidal paranoiac whose statement is quoted by [the German psychologist] Bleuler: 'the signs of the truly strong are repose and good-will ... the strong individuals are those who without any fuss do their duty. These have neither the time nor the occasion to throw themselves into a pose and try to be something great.'" Isherwood adds, "In other words, the Test exists only for the Truly Weak Man: no matter whether he passes it or whether he fails, he cannot alter his essential nature" (19). The Truly Weak Man can pass individual tests, but he can never truly be satisfied because the underlying subconscious needs that are motivating the tests are not really being assuaged.

The Truly Weak Man must try to decipher the psychological compulsions that push him to prove himself so that he can aspire to overcome them and become Truly Strong instead. In the interim his bifurcated self struggles to reconcile these conflicting urges, resulting in a duality of a private face and a public face. There is a confusion of his public and private spheres, inner and outer personas, real and fantasy worlds. Consequently, no real distinction exists, only an ambiguous blurring of inner and outer, public and private, Truly Weak and Truly Strong.

As regards the dissemination of the Truly Weak and Truly Strong mythos, Isherwood, who was three years older than Auden and five years older than Spender, befriended them in the late 1920s and his influence became apparent as they incorporated his themes into their own work. Isherwood's themes of the Truly Weak and Truly Strong Man, us against them, and the divided mind became the staging area for those who gave homage to Auden as the *de facto* leader of his generation. Britain's Angry Young Men of the 1930s emulated Isherwood by emulating Auden.

As the decade progressed, the satiric tone that was highlighted in the writings of the early 1930s gave way to more alarmist poetry, essays and other prose that were warnings concerning the advance of fascism. The principal theme portrayed within these warnings was the conflict of the Truly Weak Man and the Truly Strong Man who battle with public and private personas. Auden summarized this duality succinctly in 1932 with his dedication of *The Orators* to Stephen Spender:

> Private faces in public places
> Are wiser and nicer
> Than public faces in private places.

If one feels comfortable enough to wear his private face in public, showing his true self without resorting to masks and posturing, then one is pure-in-heart and Truly Strong. Easier said than done, and the Auden generation knew this was a path to seek, rather than a destination assured. The hero's worthiness comes from the search, and the sincere search is the goal in itself.

After the collective trauma of the war to end all wars, and the equally collective despair about the world that had allowed it to happen, many among the not so rich blamed the upper classes for the war and grew more intolerant of acquiescing to the old class divisions. The working class demanded better conditions and struggled against violent opposition to organize themselves. The psychic damage of the war affected more than just the working class, and was responded to by the Freudian revolution which asserted that the world inside the mind was as much or more important than the world outside it, and that if one could better understand and change his or her mind, one might better understand and change the world. And if all the answers were not in the mind, there was a possible solution in the pseudo–Marxist/communist revolution of the USSR. The rise of the great experiment of the Soviet Union in the 1920s was first seen as the secular New Jerusalem by the workers/socialists of the world and their compatriots among artists and intellectuals. During the 1930s, however, their hopes were betrayed, as Stalin's totalitarian version of the USSR proved to be no better than the rabid fascism of Hitler, Mussolini, and Franco that would lead to World War II.

During this tumultuous era the Auden generation felt compelled to respond to these events, to become socially responsible and actively *engagé* in trying to address them. It was "in" for the artist/man of letters to have and express points of view about the news of the world. Auden and his peers certainly had opinions and did not hesitate to share them through their art and essays. Today, there are far fewer artists who are willing to go against the power structure. Bruce Springsteen resisted taking public sides for 30 years until the 2004 election when he feared for his children's future. Fortunately, Kushner has taken sides all along, as did his antecedents, Auden and Isherwood, also artists, also gay. As members of a minority, the three have always understood their outsider status, resulting in great sympathy for underdogs of all kinds. Today, it seems that approximately half the U.S. population — the blue half — are underdogs. Kushner is a spokesperson for the underdogs.

In this volume, in the editor's book on Kushner, and in many other venues, Kushner and his plays have received generous media and critical coverage, and *Angels* was seen on HBO and is now on DVD. One already knows or can find sources to learn a good deal about Kushner and his activist plays. Conversely, while Auden and Isherwood have received their due as poet and novelist, their plays have been branded period agit-prop and are hardly read and never performed. Nonetheless, since their period closely resembles this period, their plays could now be read and seen as if written in the last year. Moreover, as if similar eras produce similar approaches to drama, in the plays of Auden-Isherwood and Kushner there are the elements of "magic realism" and, indeed, a coalescing of a yearned-for inner mystical undifferentiated unity as a counter to the outer hurricane of external reality and the separating alienation of conflicting egos. In the 1930s both Auden and Isherwood were grasping at different strands of possible solutions to the world's problems; yet, in their plays, they seemed to move toward mysticism — or the transformation of the inner self—for a solution to how one faces outer tumult. In the 1940s Auden became a Christian existentialist and Isherwood the foremost spokesperson for the Eastern philosophy of Vedanta, which is the antecedent to all forms of mysticism under an umbrella called the Perennial Philosophy. In this context one can examine the plays of Auden and Isherwood, after which will come a look at Kushner's own mystical and political inclinations.

The Plays of Auden and Isherwood: The Dog Beneath the Skin *(1935), and* The Ascent of F6 *(1936)*

In 1933 Auden had written the play *The Dance of Death* for Rupert Doone and the Group Theatre, and this newly emerging company wanted more from Auden, the icon of the avant-garde. He discussed a draft with Isherwood, who made substantive suggestions. Auden decided that Isherwood should get credit and co-write the play with him. There was some resistance from Doone as well as from T.S. Eliot at Auden's publisher, Faber

& Faber. Auden would not yield. The result was *The Dog Beneath the Skin*. *Dogskin*, as they called it, is a satirical farce with serious undertones. The quest saga was the parable form that Isherwood and Auden implemented for the three plays that they wrote in collaboration. The questors, whether satirical as in *Dogskin* or serious as in *The Ascent of F6* and *On the Frontier*, ventured into the public chaos on a metaphorical search for inner peace in the private sphere. The plays were explicitly political, tacitly metaphysical. The villains are Truly Weak; the heroes are Truly Strong. In fact, they are also one and the same, and represent the mystical dialectic known as the Reconciliation of Opposites—two poles come in conflict in a never-ending effort to find a metaphysical balance in the world.

    Dogskin was a parable of current events using humor to satirize the serious issues "beneath the skin" of the farce. (The authors got their title from the line "the skull beneath the skin" from Eliot's "Whispers of Immortality.") *Dogskin* owes much to Gilbert and Sullivan, Thornton Wilder, and Brecht's plays *Threepenny Opera* and *The Rise and Fall of the City of Mahagonny*. *Dogskin* became a parable with absurd content barely masking rebellious intentions.

    Throughout the play a Chorus comments on the action in the didactic mode. In the play's prologue, the chorus invokes the idyllic and pastoral British past and compares it to the Depression present.

    The town's vicar, another ancient Other, as in Isherwood's *The Memorial* and Auden's *The Orators*, exhorts the village to select a questor who will preserve the past by bringing back the "missing" heir, Sir Francis Crewe. Alan is sent off as the hero-savior with jingoistic fervor. His search includes the usual Isherwood-Auden staples of spies and secret agents. The play has left-leaning implications that capitalists are bad while socialists and communists are good. A visit to a red-light district includes a stop at the Cozy Corner, the name taken from the boy bar Isherwood and Auden had frequented in Berlin. In addition to the red-light foray, Norman and the "dog," named Francis after the subject of their search, meet, among others, two journalists, a king, a crooked financier, a surgeon and his students in a medical school, and the inmates of a lunatic asylum who are led by "The Voice of the Leader." This leader spouts rabid fascist nonsense. After the asylum, they go to Paradise Park. Norman asks a poet he meets in the park if he knows the missing heir. The poet, pointing to his head, answers: "Here. Everything's here. You're here. He's here. This park's here. This tree's here. If I shut my eyes they all disappear" (95; all quotations here are from the 1935 edition.). The poet reminds the audience of the ephemeral nature of the search and the illusory status of the human condition, which the poet attempts to reflect in the "here" of his imagination. After Norman and the dog take a nap in the park, the Chorus states: "Dear sleep, the secretary of that strange club / Where all are members upon one condition, / That they forget their own importance..." (112). Whether in dreams or in life, only when the ego is suspended are people truly equal.

The satire belies the serious undertone of the Isherwood-Auden schema. There is little difference between the various groups encountered. The lunatics are no more paranoid than "normal" people are. Negative behaviors are a result of living in a capitalist world that produces inevitably deleterious conditions. These conditions are perpetuated by a devotion to the past that ignores current crises such as the Depression and fascism. As postulated by the park poet, reality is in the eye of the beholder. Nothing exists outside each mind's uniquely self-designed perception. The cultural compulsives or the collective subjectivity of societal attitudes and pervasive propaganda distorts this individual perception. These attitudes are the obstacles Alan encounters on his quest (Test) over the Northwest Passage. Norman learns that solutions are not to be found externally. Answers must be found within.

In a long monologue the "dog" confesses to what the audience already knows, that he is Francis. He explains that he took on his dog disguise to "sever all ties with the past." Masked, he observed the foibles of human nature as a spy amidst the subjects of his study: from this view he learned that all were playing at "charades" of self-deception and wearing their public masks in both public and in private. (People acted and spoke in front of a "dog" as they never would have in front of people.) He learned that people form masks because they are overwrought with neuroses and psychoses that make them easy prey to outside influences. Echoing the Paradise Park poet, Francis says, "Too many ideas in their heads! To them I'm an idea, you're an idea, everything's an idea" (146). These archetypal ideas, once pure, are now tainted by societal influences that have "subjectivized" them so that they have come to supersede the reality of immediate experience.

Alan and Francis (as himself) return to their village for the last scene. The Chorus precedes the final scene by saying: "Do not speak of a change of heart, meaning five hundred a year and a room of one's own, / As if that were all that is necessary. In these islands alone, there are some forty-seven million hearts" (155). Bourgeois comfort and complacency are not enough to bridge the gaps created by separate egos that should otherwise strive for an ego-less undifferentiated unity. Each of the forty-seven million hearts is another island within the islands; each wears a mask as a shield to conceal vulnerability, but while these shields try to prevent pain, they also deny love from access. The Chorus continues with a reiteration of the Isherwood-Auden schema:

Man divided always and restless always: afraid and unable to forgive: /
Unable to forgive his parents. / An isolated bundle of nerve and desire,
suffering alone, / Seeing others only in reference to himself: as a long-lost
mother or his ideal self at sixteen. / Dreaming of continuous sexual enjoyment or perpetual applause. Some turn to ... solutions of sickness or crime:
some to the ... sport of the moment. / Some to good works, to a mechan-
ical ritual of giving. / Some have adopted [a] system of beliefs or a political programme, others have escaped to ascetic mountains. / Or taken
refuge ... among the boys on the bar stools, on the small uncritical islands.
/ Men will profess devotion to anything; to God, to humanity, to Truth,
to Beauty: but their first thought on meeting is 'Beware!' / They put their
trust in Reason or feelings of the Blood but will not trust a stranger with
half-a-crown [156].

(The "feelings of the Blood" refers to the obsolete "life-worship" of D.H.
Lawrence, once an Auden favorite but now considered by Auden as a false
hope.) After this litany of the Truly Weak, the Chorus suggests that the
only hope for each individual is a transformation from within. Norman
and Francis return to the village only to find that it has succumbed to fascist influences. The vicar makes a long speech of patriotic cant and rant,
warning of what will happen if the enemy succeeds: What the vicar imagines sounds as if Isherwood and Auden had read Aldous Huxley's 1932
novel, *Brave New World*: "No family love. Sons would inform against their
fathers, cheerfully send them to the execution cellars. No romance. Even
the peasant must beget that standard child under laboratory conditions.
Motherhood would be by license. Truth and Beauty would be proscribed
as dangerously obstructive. No books, no art, no music" (167). A villager,
who lost both her sons in a previous war, responds that this cant will only
get more children killed.

Francis, having revealed himself, tells them: "I've had a dog's-eye view
of you for the last ten years.... I was horrified and fascinated by you all"
(172). He continues with a scathing evaluation that amounts to Isherwood
speaking for himself. (Isherwood wrote the prose passages.) "I thought such
obscene, cruel, hypocritical, mean, vulgar creatures have never existed
before.... As a dog, I learnt with what a mixture of fear, bullying, and con-
descending kindness you treat those whom you consider your inferiors,
but on whom you are dependent for your pleasures" (172–74). The play ends
with Francis declaring he will join the Anti-Others of the world to spread
the truth about the Others of the Poshocracy. He departs with his first
recruits, including Alan, and the Chorus concludes with a paraphrase of
the communist dictum "To each his need: from each his power" (180).

The Dog Beneath the Skin turns the Isherwood-Auden schema into a blend of parable and didacticism. The themes that dominated their individual works coalesce in collaboration: Francis as "dog" and then Francis as rebel broadly manifest the duality of private and public, inner and outer, Truly Weak and Truly Strong. Norman's quest is a Test beyond the borders and over the Northwest Passage. Nothing is learned from this quest except the realization that external quests and Tests are for the Truly Weak. Realization is circular, not linear. One must return to one's inner self. Before the quest, Francis had been in the village all along, just as the answers to society's problems are hidden in each individual all along if one turns inward to seek them. *Dogskin*, even though staged by the Group Theater as a burlesque aiming for political laughs, is a metaphysical exercise signifying Isherwood and Auden's call for a change of heart. The sensitive man who wishes to become Truly Strong seeks this change. With *Dogskin* as a warm-up, Isherwood and Auden's next play would explore the same themes more seriously, with the metaphysical intentions front and center.

In *The Ascent of F6* the hero/anti-hero Michael Ransom represents what Isherwood and Auden had learned in their lives and through their work over the previous ten years. Ransom would be the symbolic star of his decade and the anti-hero role model for the future, including Kushner's future.

Michael Ransom's very name carries with it the implication of a man held hostage. Ransom is a captive of the past who becomes a victim of it when that past inflicts its inexorable will on him through the Others. In *Dogskin* the burlesque still had one foot in the pseudo-fascism of the British public school with the other foot stepping towards the new school of real-world fascism. *The Ascent of F6* has both feet firmly rooted in current events, and the Old School is no longer a source of satire in light of these events. Isherwood and Auden's concern about current events demanded tangible responses in the more public forum of the theater. In his 1934 essay on T.E. Lawrence, Auden explicitly stated the dichotomy of the Truly Weak and the Truly Strong Man. Until then this dichotomy had only been expressed through tacit parables. *In The Ascent of F6* the Truly Weak and the Truly Strong Man are defined explicitly and T.E. Lawrence is the role model for both.

The listing of the play's characters "in order of their appearance" begins with "Michael Forsyth Ransom" followed by "Sir James Ransom (his twin brother)." The twinship is a metaphor. They are actually two halves of the same person. The play begins with Michael Ransom's existential monologue that is inspired by Ransom having just read in Dante that men "were not formed to live like brutes, but to follow virtue and knowledge"

(11). Ransom, a weary cynic, says of Dante, "a crook speaking to crooks." Then after calling Dante an aristocratic Other, Ransom asks, "Who was Dante to speak of virtue and knowledge?" (12) (Auden will also quote from Dante's Canto XXVI of the *Inferno* where Ulysses listens to false advice and leads his men to doom, a foreshadowing for Ransom in the play.) Ransom questions if, to Dante, "virtue and knowledge" really meant a quest for power. Ransom secretly despises the world of his own upper class: "the generals and industrial captains: justifying every baseness [of their] schoolboy lives" (12). Ransom has retreated into the solitude (and Tests) of mountain climbing.

Ransom speaks bitterly that it would be better to be dead or ignorant than be caught in the "web of guilt that prisons every upright person ... oh happy the foetus that miscarries and the frozen idiot that cannot cry 'mama!'" (14). Ransom may be an aesthete who was tormented by hearties. He may also be an aesthete who disguised himself as a hearty and suffers the guilt of having conformed instead of being his true self. Ransom is a cynic; he is Francis Crewe without the satire. From the hero's disappointment with life, the anti-hero is born.

The scene shifts to a typical middle-class British couple at home and describes their middle-class routine as one of stultifying, spirit-killing ennui. They are listening to the wireless. Mr. A: "I'm sick of the news. All you can hear is politics." Mrs. A: "They will ask for our children and kill them; sympathise deeply and ask for some more." Mr. A: "There is nothing to make us proud of our race.... Nothing to take us out of ourselves. Out of the oppression of this city.... Give us something to live for. We have waited too long" (17–18). This middle-class couple will appear frequently as a contrast to the behind-the-scenes manipulations of the Others. Mr. and Mrs. A represent the anonymous public who know only the propaganda they are fed by a manipulated media.

The next scene emphasizes the contrast of Mr. and Mrs. A with the Others by shifting to, as per the stage directions, "Sir James Ransom's room at the Colonial office. On the wall ... hangs a large boldly-printed map showing British Sudoland and Ostnian Sudoland. The frontier between the two colonies is formed by a chain of mountains: one peak, prominently marked F6, is ringed with a red circle" (19). Sir James, the evil twin, speaks as a stereotypical Other about the Sudoland problem. This British colony, with socialist Ostnia's influence, has been yanking at its colonial chains. The Others denounce socialism and Lord Stagmantle proudly boasts: "We were out to smash the Labour Government ... and, by God, we did" (21). The "by God" is a hint of a church-sanctioned imperialist hypocrisy. James forms a plan to inflame public opinion into wanting to keep Sudoland for the British: An expedition will scale the previously insurmountable mountain, F6. Propaganda will arouse British pride and the public will wish to defend their prize, F6, and this means retaining control of British Sudoland at all costs. F6 is also known as the "Haunted Mountain," and Lady Isabel recalls that it is reputedly protected by a "guardian demon" (23). The General retorts that this is a "fairy-tale." James, however, always the politician, responds: "A fairy-tale is significant according to the number of people who believe in it..." (26). He is suggesting that propaganda can manufacture nefarious "fairy-tales" to suit a hungry public starved for self-serving news. James tells the Others that he will recruit his brother, the famous climber, to lead the expedition. Next the audience watches Mr. and Mrs. A listen to the first wave of propaganda on the wireless: "The haunted mountain [is] inhabited only by monks [who] practise a mysterious cult ... and there are wonderful tales of their mystical and psychic powers" (29). Isherwood and Auden foreshadow the metaphysical messages to come later in the play.

In Scene III we return to Michael Ransom and meet his climbing fellows: the Doctor, Lamp, Shawcross, and Gunn. Ransom is the magnetic leader; Shawcross and Gunn are his devoted followers. Gunn is a jokester, conniver and compulsive Test-seeker. Shawcross is a fawning worshipper. (The name of Shawcross has meaning in that Shaw was the second name that T.E. Lawrence feigned when he reenlisted in the R.A.F. anonymously as a "common" soldier, after having been the fabled Lawrence of Arabia; later he took the name of Ross to further reduce himself to anonymity.) Gunn is a court-jester worshipper, appealing through humor. Shawcross is judgmental of Gunn and a snitch when Gunn is caught in some petty connivance. Shawcross and Gunn are still living as honor system schoolboys in the British public school mentality; they are the younger boys trying to please the older leader of the senior class— Ransom. Shawcross and Gunn are Truly Weak. Ransom understands this undercurrent and is suitably patient with each. Still, recalling his opening monologue, he himself has his own undercurrent of stark cynicism towards his fellow men.

The Others, led by James (a precursor to Kushner's Roy Cohn in *Angels*), visit Michael and his gang to persuade Michael to surmount F6. James tries flattery on Michael: "In all humility I say it— my brother is a great man" (39). Michael sees through this, recalling their childhood when James would whine and wheedle for what he wanted. He tells James to cut the subterfuge and get to the point. James starts off: "In the name of His Majesty's Government, I have come to make you an important proposition —," but Michael does not want to hear it and interrupts: "Which I unconditionally refuse" (40). The invocation of king and country is enough to repel him. "I know your propositions, James: they are exceedingly convincing. They contain certain reservations. They are concerned with prestige, tactics, money, and the privately pre-arranged meanings of familiar words. I will have nothing to do with any of them. Keep to your world. I will keep to mine" (40). The Others and the opposing Anti-Other are clearly in conflict, with the Others manipulating their world through a secret code of "familiar words." James tempts Michael the mountain-climber by telling him that the goal is F6. Michael questions: "What does your world have to do with F6? Since boyhood, in dreams ... F6 is my fate.... But not now, not like this" (40). Lady Isabel tries to manipulate him by shamelessly impugning his manhood: "I see it in your eyes, you are afraid." She confronts Michael with a Test. He does not succumb to the bait. "I am afraid of a great many things.... But of nothing which you in your worst nightmares could ever imagine" (41). This alludes to his angst in the opening monologue. Ransom realizes that he has inner demons spurred by some hidden guilt. He also realizes that in his efforts to be Truly Strong and refuse this Test, he knows that he is, like anyone else, also Truly Weak because otherwise he would feel no temptation. Speaking of temptation, the Others pull out their ace. There is a knock on the door. James says: "Here is somebody who may be able to persuade you."

> RANSOM [with a cry of dismay]: Mother!
> MOTHER [advancing to Ransom]: Michael, I am so proud—
> RANSOM [recoiling]: You too! No, it isn't impossible! Your shadow adds to
> theirs, a trick of the light [42].

His mother — an archetypal Auden generation mother — knows no bounds for laying on guilt and shame. Michael tells her that when he and his brother were boys she neglected him in favor of James, of whom he was jealous; hence his guilt and retreat into solitude. She invokes the memory of their father saying that James was like him: "He cannot live an hour without applause.... But you, you were to be truly strong who must be kept from all that could infect or weaken; it was for you I steeled my love deliberately and hid it. Do you think it was easy to shut you out? But I won. You were to be unlike your father and brother, you were to have the power to stand alone.... There was a mother who crucified herself to save her favorite son from weakness" (45). On this pathetic note Michael gives in.
    His mother, in her twisted effort to make Michael Truly Strong, succeeded superficially, but left him with a core of vulnerability as seen in the bitterness of his opening meditation on Dante in Act One. The past lurks always in the psyche to disturb the present. The great irony is that his

mother, who claims she withheld her love to make him strong so he could "stand alone," won't let him. Mrs. Ransom gives back the love she withheld, but since this is only a ploy to make him Truly Weak and accept this Test, she contradicts herself. After having succeeded in their entrapment, the Others leave, and Ransom has a dream (or nightmare) that punctuates his own particular mother-son conundrum. Michael hears his mother tell him she will be with him always, right to the top of the mountain. Her son's tormented voice is heard far off, frightened: "It's the demon, mother!" (53). The line is deliberately ambiguous as it could refer to the mountain-as-demon or the mother-as-demon.

Act Two begins "in a monastery on the Great Glacier." Shawcross tells Michael that Gunn "steals." Michael laughs, calling Gunn an essentially harmless "magpie." Ransom also notes to Shawcross that he hasn't changed much since he was a heart captain at school, meaning that he epitomizes the Old School's faults. Shawcross fawns some more while still slipping in his derision of Gunn, whom he refers to as being fearful of F6. Michael tells him it is the fear that pushes Gunn: "Being frightened is his chief pleasure in life" (60). Shawcross knows that only two climbers can actually reach the summit of F6 and begins his campaign to be chosen. He jealously calls Gunn a "neurotic." Shawcross and Gunn are Truly Weak, only differing in approach. Shawcross needs approval from his hero Ransom to validate himself. He endures Tests for Ransom's sake. Gunn needs Tests for his own sake.

Gunn wonders if the monks communicate by "telepathy" in some secret code known only to them (62). The monks unnerve Gunn because his instinct tells him that they understand that his compulsion to live dangerously is a weakness. The monks have a magic crystal in which one can glimpse one's future if not necessarily realize what that future means. The reflections are also omens of death.

Alone, the monastery's abbot and Ransom philosophize. This dialogue signifies Isherwood and Auden's shift away from the distracting public chaos and into private spheres where the only true salvation can be found. Ransom reveals to the Abbot that when it had been his turn to look into the crystal he saw the "ragged denizens" crying out for help and he wonders if their cry was for him to save them. The Abbot tells him "Only God is great" (68), implying that if fate chooses him to be a savior, so be it, but he cannot put this burden on himself if he is doing so as a compensation for some secret guilt. The Abbot warns Michael not to let his Western sensibility discount the idea of a demon on the mountain, telling him that the peasants, unencumbered with the veneer of civilization, "see it more clearly than you or I. For it is a picture of truth. The Demon is real.

Only his ministry and his visitation are unique for every nature. To the complicated and sensitive like yourself ... his disguises are more subtle.... I understand your temptation. You wish to conquer the Demon and then to save mankind." The Abbot continues:

> Nothing is revealed [in the crystal] but what we have hidden from ourselves.... Your temptation ... is written in your face. You could ask the world to follow you and it would serve you with blind obedience; for most men long to be delivered from the terror of thinking and feeling for themselves.... And you would do them much good. Because men desire evil, they must be governed by those who understand the corruption of their hearts ... but woe to the governors, for by the very operation of their duty, however excellent, they themselves are destroyed. For you can only rule men by appealing to their fear and lust; government requires the exercise of the human will: and the human will is from the Demon [70–72].

And the Demon (the ego) is a metaphor for the neuroses and psychoses that result from the conflict of trying to shake off the shackles of the past. Ransom asks the Abbot what choice he has but to climb the mountain. The Abbot answers: "There is an alternative, Mr. Ransom; and I offer it to you.... The complete abnegation of the will" (72). Ransom asks what this means, but they are interrupted before the Abbot can explain.

In the mystic's purview the "abnegation of the will" is the eradication of the willful ego's lower-case self in favor of Vedanta's transcendent upper-case Self. But can any ruler abnegate his will? Isherwood and Auden understood that the process of ruling corrupts even the well-meaning man. Hero-worship entails that a hero fill the needs of the Truly Weak. The amorphous public will objectify the hero and give him an image that no man can possibly live up to. The hero feels compelled to try and match their image of him. A Truly Strong Man, if asked to be a leader, would wish to maintain his private face in public places, but he would find that this private face may not be the face his public expects or wants. The Truly Weak Man who becomes a leader does not have this problem; his mask is always in place to fit the vision others have of him and indeed need of him.

After he and the Abbot are interrupted, Ransom wonders: "Is it too late for me.... There was a choice once ... I made it wrong, and if I choose again now, I must choose for myself alone, not for these others" (74). He implores some greater power to help him: "Save us from the destructive element of our will, for all we do is evil" (74). The term "destructive element" came from the title of Stephen Spender's 1935 book of literary criticism.

Spender asserted that the technique in the middle to late novels of Henry James was a prelude to literary modernism. Spender said that James used interior monologues to tacitly express beliefs in absentia through stating unbelief, or that by having the characters reject certain ideas, readers inferred new ideas antithetically. Further, Spender analyzed James, Yeats, Eliot, and D.H. Lawrence as exemplars of "unbelief" from which the astute reader should derive new beliefs. Spender declared that there must be a "tearing-down" of the old before there can be a "building-up" of the new. In *F6* Isherwood and Auden convey their understanding of this process, having spent ten years tearing down the influences of the past. The building-up of new beliefs must have some underlying metaphysical basis so one can act in the world as a Truly Strong Man, uninfluenced and unimpeded by the needs of the individual ego. To know this is to know also that the public will resist the ideals behind such a theory. Further, what is the belief that will supplant the unbelief, socialism? Communism? Mysticism? These are only words if the private face cannot find its balance in the public chaos. In 1937 Isherwood and Auden were not yet certain of the answers, but they knew enough to pose the questions.

As Ransom and the others climb, a skull is found and, like Hamlet, Ransom speaks to it. Hamlet is Ransom's literary role model; both are internally conflicted concerning their mothers and driven by forces they cannot control or fully understand. As with Hamlet, Ransom's angst will supply ample blood sacrifices. In *F6* the first to die is Edward Lamp, in an avalanche. Ransom says of Lamp: "the first victim to my pride" (86). Back in England Lamp is lionized by the media as the newest martyr for the cult of the dead.

Ransom decides that Gunn, not Shawcross, will go with him to the summit. Ransom tells the doctor that Shawcross can't deal with the Test because he is a nervous wreck and the climb is too emotionally connected with his self-esteem. This makes him a risk. (It took one to know one.) Ransom informs Shawcross, who does not take the decision well. Shawcross, unable to bear what he considers to be his failure, jumps to his death. Shawcross saw in his hero Ransom what his lack of self-esteem prevented him from seeing in himself. No actual hero can live up to such a follower's ego-derived vicarious need.

In the next scene Gunn dies of exhaustion as he and Michael are just short of reaching the summit. Ransom thinks that this is Gunn's good luck for he has achieved the release of death that "extricates you now from the most cunning trap of all," which is life (102).

Ransom goes on, nears the summit, and collapses. At the summit he sees a veiled unidentifiable figure. The Chorus is in the background wearing the monks' cowled robes. They recite: "When shall the deliverer come to destroy this dragon?" (106). After a fanfare of trumpets, James Ransom

appears as the Dragon. He spews propaganda. Michael rises and steps into
the circle of light around the Dragon. James signals and life-size chessmen
appear. Their ensuing debate is a matter of gamesmanship. All of the play's
characters encircle the twin brothers. The middle-class couple grumbles
about their dull lives. The General tells them that they have it easy compared to the brave climbers. Maybe so, but one's egocentric everyday life
goes on. Mr. and Mrs. A can only suffer for themselves; they cannot feel
what the climbers felt or what another feels. For Mr. and Mrs. A, as for
any individual, one's own existence is paramount. Another's suffering may
be apprehended intellectually, but it is an abstraction viscerally, even to
one who is well meaning and tries to empathize. One's intellect cannot live
in another's body. (Later Auden would use this theme in the poem "Musée
des Beaux Arts.") Of course, the rich Others find it easy to chastise others not so rich. Lord Stagmantle shallowly asserts that money isn't everything: "I know there are far too many people who have too little. It's a
damned shame, but there it is" (110).

Mrs. A asks, "Why were we born?" She does so in despairing ennui,
not as a philosophical inquiry. James misinterprets her meaning and sar-
castically mimics Michael's scholarly bent by responding with ad hoc non-
sense about the "immensity of the universe" (110) in which the life of the
individual has no importance but to pass the torch, die, and be forgotten.
Michael protests that this is a twisted paraphrase of how he truly feels. His
thoughts were distorted just as a controlled media manipulates propaganda. James taunts him, repeating what Michael said to him in Act One:
"Keep to your world. I will keep to mine" (111). The chess game com-
mences. Michael wins. James falls dead and is eulogized by the Others, who
continue their patriotic cant and accuse Michael of murder.

The Abbot appears in a judge's wig and robe. Michael cries out that
he is innocent and that the Demon gave the sign for his brother's death.
The Abbot calls as witnesses the victims of Michael Ransom's pride. Shawcross appears and implicates the former subject of his hero-worship. Gunn
and Lamp follow and are also of no help to their friend. The Abbot asks
Michael if he wishes to appeal to the all-seeing crystal. The Abbot looks
into it and tells Ransom that the Demon was not the temptation. Ransom
realizes his pride was the temptation. He is found guilty to a chorus of:
"'Die for England!' All lights are extinguished below; only the [veiled] Figure and Ransom remain illuminated. Ransom turns to the Figure, whose
draperies fall away, revealing Mrs. Ransom as a young mother" (117).

Then darkness hides the stage. The sun rises; the stage is empty, except
for the body of Ransom at the summit. He has been dead or near death all
along. The preceding scene was an illusion, or perhaps the dream vision

of one dying. After his death, Ransom is praised by the Others as, indeed, having died for England. James says: "He had many sides to his character and I doubt if anyone knew the whole man. I as his brother certainly did not. He had an almost feminine sensibility which, if it had not been allied to great qualities of soul and will-power and a first class intelligence, might easily have become neurotic...." James, indeed, did not know him. What he said of his brother is true, but a misinterpretation reversing the real meaning. If his brother was "neurotic," it was not due to a "feminine sensibility" (or sensitivity). This sensibility had more likely ameliorated his mental illness instead of worsening it; that is, at least until he had given in to the temptation of his masculine side, which led him to charge up F6. Had his feminine sensibility been stronger, he might not have let his manly pride push him to accept the mission that killed him and his friends. His past, in the symbolic form of his young mother, overcame the common sense of his sensitive, feminine side.

Ransom failed because he gave in to the public chaos instead of listening to his private sphere. His inner Self had an intuition for mysticism as revealed in his conversation with the Abbot. The Abbot had told him that the secret to his salvation would be in the "abnegation of the will," but Ransom could not resist his ego and he succumbed to the temptations of worldliness that his mother represented. Isherwood and Auden created a character that was the defining figure for their generation. Michael Ransom was an aspiring Truly Strong Man who was overwhelmed by Truly Weak temptation. He was a realistic anti-heroic hero; his divided, angst-filled being had a conscience. Ransom cared — too much! Had he cared less and not been so vulnerable, he might have ignored the appeals of the Others and acted more in self-preservation. Ransom was the sensitive man who had an intuition that it is in the world of the spirit where answers might be found. His intuition, however, became clouded by his ego.

For Isherwood and Auden, Michael Ransom's quest represented their quest. Ransom was their last hope for the 1930s. Metaphorically, his failure would signify the futility that would overcome their iconoclastic generation when it was unable to prevent World War II. This generation, with all its activism, had not been able to save the world. When the decade ended, all that was left for them to do was to try and save themselves by somehow turning inward. Just as Kushner took Benjamin's idea of the past as that which one must understand to deal with the present and future, Auden and Isherwood saw the past this way as well, but in the 1930s the past was still more of an enemy to be disavowed and rejected, and less of a teacher. Later in their careers, they would see history more as Benjamin and Kushner see it.

Then was then. Kushner is now.

Tony Kushner: Activist Jewish Mystic

> *Tony Kushner is drunk on ideas, on language, on the possibility of changing the world. His talent and his heart are incendiary, combustible, explosive, heartbreakingly vital and on-target.* — Larry Kramer

> *Kushner has been a revitalizing force in American drama.... His influence on the development of American theater may ultimately equal that of O'Neill or Williams. His drama daringly mixes fantasy and reality — as tragedy and comedy — to blend together elements of the past, present, and future of the world of his play, the lives of his characters, and the society in which he lives.... An understanding of Kushner's political beliefs is essential ... as his socialist politics are never far from the surface. Although most critics and audiences think of Kushner almost solely as a "gay dramatist," it is truly the case that he is a "political dramatist" who happens to be gay.* — James Fisher

> *Every living creature has a heart, and every heart a thread.*
> *And He of Holy Wisdom draws all the threads together.*
> *From the fiery threads is woven time, and thus new days are made;*
> *Unto the heart is given, unto the spring is given.*
> *As the spring pours waters through the days, the heart of the world looks on.*
> *And so the World continues, until the world is gone.* — Tony Kushner, from his adaptation of S. Ansky's *A Dybbuk*

Angels in America, Kushner's anti–Reagan and anti–Bush AIDS and gay-sympathetic play, is not subtle at all about the playwright's didactic intentions. Kushner gives critics the very beneficial service of providing numerous sources in which he explains himself. Kushner's own words reveal him as an articulate, erudite, and passionate spokesperson.

> *Kushner:* Since it's true that everything is political (though not exclusively so) it becomes meaningless to talk about political and nonpolitical theater, and more useful to speak of a theater that presents the world as it is, an interwoven web of the public and the private [quoted in Fisher, 1].

Kushner's "web of the public and private" is like the Auden and Isherwood duality of "public/private" as a *modus operandi* for life and literature. If characters (and people) were exactly what they seemed, life would be saner, safer, and also a numbing bore. Kushner is not boring; he knows that oppositions, duality, and ambiguity fuel the universe, and they provide the emotional and intellectual fire in his plays. And while he challenges audiences intellectually, as did Auden and Isherwood, Kushner knows that people wish to be entertained as well as enlightened. Kushner was born in New York City in 1956, and he grew up as a Jew in Louisiana. He has admitted to being very closeted. In 1974 he returned to New York City to attend Columbia. Things changed quickly and sharply as he fell in love with the New York theater scene and embraced his gayness. Milestones for him were Richard Schechner's production of Brecht's *Mother Courage and Her Children* which, Kushner thinks, "is the greatest play ever written," (1) and Richard Foreman's version of *The Threepenny Opera*. Brecht became Kushner's model for political theater in terms of technique and social activism. "I believed that theater, really good theater, had the potential for radical intervention, for effectual analysis. The things that were exciting me about Marx, specifically dialectics, I discovered in Brecht, in a wonderful witty and provocative form. I became very, very excited about doing theater as a result of reading Brecht" (quoted in Fisher, 6). Ultimately, Brecht would lead Kushner to Walter Benjamin and to Raymond Williams, and these three, along with Jewish mysticism (Kabbalah), would inform Kushner's views on political theater, his interpretation of historical forces, a definition of socialism, and the need for personal and then collective transcendence.

After reading Brecht, Kushner read Walter Benjamin's *Understanding Brecht* and "Theses on the Philosophy of History." For Kushner, the history that repeats itself in both *A Bright Room Called Day* and *Angels in America* was the 1980s of Reagan, neo-conservatism, AIDS phobia, and homophobia. Today little has changed. Both plays use past history/tragedy to illustrate/teach in the present. *Bright Room*'s metaphor is Nazi Germany, and *Angels* uses Roy Cohn (who embodied the oxymoron of being a "gay homophobe") among others. Throughout Kushner's work Brecht provides the "how," Benjamin, the rationale, Raymond Williams, a future solution, and mysticism, to form his concept of social activism.

The realm of socialism, Williams posits [in "Walking Backwards into the Future," 1985], is more than merely a place for "stranded utopians and sectarians." Williams' concept of a socialist society significantly shapes Kushner's conception of America under Reagan, who was the anti–Williams. For Kushner, Reagan began an abandonment of the notion of a society concerned with the "longstanding problems of virtue and happiness." A reformed society built on a progressive, compassionately humanist doctrine that draws its strength from the hard lessons of the past is central to both Williams' (and Benjamin's) theories and *Angels* (quoted in Fisher, 57).

In *Angels* Roy Cohn symbolizes the sum total of the Reagan era. Another character in *Angels* points to Cohn, who is dying of AIDS, and says, "I'll show you America. Terminal, crazy, and mean." Fisher wrote: "Cohn represents a kind of trickle-down morality in *Angels*—Kushner's notion that if corruption, greed, and bad faith exist in powerful members of a society, it will ultimately seep down into each individual.... *Angels* presents a battle of political angles—conservative and liberal ideologies in moral combat against each other as the historical failures and hypocrisies within each are challenged" (62).

While Kushner leans on Brecht, Benjamin, and Williams for an underlying philosophy behind his plays, it is Tennessee Williams "spirit" and his homosexuality that became Kushner's inspiration for the tone of his plays. This is interesting because Isherwood was an early mentor to Williams just as he had been to early Auden when he provided more of the realistic counterbalance to Auden's poems and plays. Isherwood was definitely and unequivocally gay before Auden as well. Shortly after leaving Oxford, Auden was briefly engaged to a nurse and not a male one. Williams arrived in Hollywood in 1953 with a letter of introduction from Isherwood's good friend, New York dance impresario Lincoln Kirstein, and they began a strong friendship. Isherwood stayed with Williams and his companion Frank Merlo in Key West, Florida, during the filming of *The Rose Tattoo*. Isherwood also introduced Marguerite Lamkin to Williams. Originally from Louisiana, she aided Williams in perfecting southern dialect and dialogue for the film version of his play *Cat on a Hot Tin Roof*. Perhaps Isherwood influenced Williams' spirit, who then influenced Kushner. Fisher finds "significant parallels ... between *Angels* and the plays of Williams: both feature classically inspired epic passions, both depict dark and poetic images of the beautiful and the horrifying aspects of existence, both create a stage language at once both naturalistic and poetic, both ponder the distance between illusion and reality, both explore the nature of spirituality from a grounding in classical and modern thought, and both deal centrally and compassionately with complex issues of sexuality from a gay sensibility" (67).

There are many more influences on Kushner: Marx, Trotsky, Christianity, Judaism, and Eastern versions of spirituality, German Classicism, poets Rilke and Stanley Kunitz, recent contemporary theater—Richard Foreman, Harvey Fierstein, Charles Ludlam, Larry Kramer, Terence McNally, Paula Vogel, and Britons including Caryl Churchill and David Hare. Kushner's intellectual curiosity is wide and diverse and he brings this breadth to his art and essays just as Auden did in his art and essays. Both were/are voracious readers in all disciplines, and both students of life, assimilating, processing, amalgamating, synthesizing, and then effusing the outcomes of their prodigious mulling into words.

Regarding mysticism/spirituality in *Angels in America*: "Angels have long been symbols of spiritual significance. Residing in a realm somewhere between the Deity and His Creations, angels watch over humanity as unspeakably beautiful harbingers of hope and death. Kushner turned to Walter Benjamin's image of the Angel of History as the guiding metaphor" (Fisher, 54).

The very nature of a play with angels as a metaphor signifies mystical interest. Kushner's adaptation of S. Ansky's *A Dybbuk* (1914), confirms this. A "dybbuk" is a Jewish soul that is restless, brooding, and homeless (a Michael Ransom), and this soul attempts to enter the body of another person to try for a resolution. The male character Chonen, a student of the Kabbalah, is promised to Leah by his father, but Leah's father wants a more lucrative match. He breaks the vow and she marries another. Chonen starves himself to death, a spiritually bereft death, his soul wanders, and it inhabits Leah. This type of possession is also featured in the Japanese Noh plays, and Yeats took the idea from the Noh and reprised it his Celtic legend plays. "Kushner and Ansky share an insider-outsider attitude about Judaism — admiring its mystical beauty, its moral imperatives and questions, and its otherworldliness, while also finding themselves at a distance from its rigidities..." (Fisher 145). Throughout history, the initial forms of religions derived from mystical antecedents that were not rigid. The mystical branches also keep their distance from dogma and religious orthodoxy. The dybbuk, Chonen, is exorcised from Leah. Nonetheless, when Leah dies, she and Chonen are reunited.

"The importance of the play's subtitle, *Between Two Worlds*, is, in part, that the play works on dual levels: [The character Solomon says,] 'Death resides in life, male in female, the spiritual in the female, religious doubt in devotion, evil in goodness, social well-being in private acts, Hasidism in modernity, the holy in the profane.' This is a near–Upanishadic accounting of the Reconciliation of Opposites" (Fisher 150). By the character saying "in" for each pair, rather "to" or "versus" or "against," Kushner has enunciated the purest essence of how the opposites are working in tandem by design to fuel the fission of evolving consciousness. Kushner is an activist and speaks his mind concerning socio-political-economic-gay issues; he knows that each individual must change from within before he can truly act in the world.

Ansky's version and Kushner's end with this same verse:

> Why did the soul,
> Oh tell me this,
> Tumble from Heaven
> To the Great Abyss?
> The most profound descents contain
> Ascensions to the heights again... [9, 106–7].

The cycle of evolving consciousness— depths and heights, the reconciliation of opposites— is the course of progress. Events, even when calamities and obstacles, are lessons to be learned by humanity — if humanity chooses to do so.

Fisher published his first criticism on Kushner in 1999, which compared Kushner to Thornton Wilder in an essay titled "Troubling the Waters: Visions of Apocalypse in Wilder's *The Skin of Our Teeth* and Kushner's *Angels in America.*" (The chapter on *Angels* in Fisher's Kushner study is also called "Troubling the Waters.") That earlier essay hinted at Fisher's future book on Kushner and the book's subtitle, *Tony Kushner: Living Past Hope:*

> In *Angels*, Kushner's apocalyptic harbinger is an angel and, in the final scene of *Perestroika*, the play's survivors meet at Central Park's Bethesda Fountain — which features a statue of the biblical angel who "troubled the waters," the subject of one of Wilder's early "three-minute" plays, "The Angel That Troubled the Waters," 1928. Kushner uses this imagery at the end of *Perestroika* and throughout both plays he "troubles the waters" of American life in a way that permits revelation to his characters, just as Wilder's invalids hope for a cure to their ills and a new beginning. In "The Angel That Troubled the Waters," the angel asks the Healer, "Without your wound where would your power be?" [149]. The characters of both *Skin* and *Angels* grow strong from their suffering, just as the cripples in "The Angel That Troubled the Waters" are healed [395].

Indeed, without his wound how could the healer truly understand the suffering of others? Hence, compassion and healing are partners. (In Mendelson's book, *Early Auden*, he devotes chapters to Auden's youthful wish to be a healer and redeemer.) Just like Auden and Isherwood, Wilder and Kushner are two dramatists who do not mind overtly displaying personal and sociopolitical agendas in their work. (Wilder's 1931 short play, "Pullman Car Hiawatha," was an inspiration for *Dogskin*.) Wilder's intentions may have been subtler, but he was no less emphatic. Kushner's anti–Reagan, AIDS- and gay-sympathetic play has clear intentions. Kushner has written or adapted many more plays than just *Angels in America*, and in Fisher they are all explored as a continuous/contiguous narrative of Kushner's singular dramatic identity.

Fisher's main theme for Kushner in his study *The Theater of Tony Kushner: Living Past Hope* carries over from that first Wilder/Kushner essay: Kushner's plays, however often they may depict pain and suffering, are ultimately all about the political possibilities for hope and healing. Fisher sets all of Kushner's plays in this framework:

A Bright Room Called Day: "Kushner severely tests his faith in hope in ... a dark, despairing work illuminating issues of political engagement (past and present), survival, and fear in an era of great social evil ... the rise of Hitler" (21).

Hydriotaphia, or the Death of Dr. Browne (An Epic Farce About Death And Primitive Capital Accumulation: "Death dominates.... Throughout [Kushner's] imaginative rumination on the life of Sir Thomas Browne ... Kushner imagines the period in which capitalism was born" (38).

Slavs! Thinking About the Longstanding Problems of Virtue and Unhappiness: "The emphasis is on political debate and governmental failure as seen through the sad consequences of a country — the crumbling Soviet Union of the late 1980s" (93).

Other chapters analyze Kushner's one-act plays and his adaptations, which, by their choice, also signify Kushner's sociopolitical concerns: *The Illusion*, from Corneille's *L'illusion Comique*; *Stella*, from Goethe; *St. Cecilia, or The Power of Music*, from a story by Heinrich von Kleist; *A Dybbuk*; Brecht's *Good Person of Setzuan*; and *Widows* (as in those of Chile's "The Disappeared"), written with Ariel Dorfman from Dorfman's novel.

Fisher's book draws its subtitle from part of a speech spoken by Prior Walter (after Walter Benjamin) in *Perestroika*, the second of the *Angels* plays:

> "We live past hope." This line, more than any other in Kushner's oeuvre, captures the intent of his drama: a belief that despite centuries of historical and personal tragedy, we must progressively face inevitabilities of a future we cannot know while, at the same time, learning from an often tragic and destructive past we know only too well. Belief in progress, in compassion, in the transformative power of love, in true community, is the religion Kushner offers for the new Millennium [Fisher 13].

Auden and Isherwood also lived past hope and against fascism with a "belief in progress, in compassion, in the transformative power of love, in true community," in the 1930s and then found hope in the progressive 1960s. Life goes in cycles. Hopefully this present era of fascist creep will wear thin just as the conservative 1950s wore thin, leading to the progressivism of the next decade.

Works Cited

Anonymous. americanfascistmovement.com/afmstore. 5 February 2005.
Auden, W.H. "The Group Movement and the Middle Classes." *Oxford and the Groups*. London: Blackwell, 1934: 89–103.
_____. "In Defense of Gossip." *The Listener* 18 (1937): 1371–1372.
_____. Introduction to *The Poet's Tongue* (1934). *The English Auden*. New York: Random House, 1976: 327–330.

_____. "Letter to Lord Byron." *Collected Poems*. New York: Random House, 1976.

_____. "The Liberal Fascist." (1934) *The English Auden*. New York: Random House, 1976: 321–327.

_____. *The Orators*. London: Faber & Faber, 1932.

Auden, W.H. and Christopher Isherwood. *The Ascent of F6*. New York: Random House, 1937.

_____. *The Dog Beneath the Skin*. London: Faber & Faber, 1935.

_____. "The Dog Beneath the Skin." *Plays and Other Dramatic Writings*. Princeton, NJ: Princeton University Press, 1988: 189–293.

Benjamin, Walter. *Illuminations, Essays, and Reflections*. Translated by Harry Zohn. New York: Schocken Books, 1968.

Bernstein, Andrea, "Tony Kushner." Mother Jones.com. 23 February 2005.

Brady, Owen. " Chorus and Character in Auden and Isherwood's *The Dog Beneath the Skin*: A Poetic Shaggy Dog Story for a Revolutionary Theater." *W.H. Auden: A Legacy*. West Cornwall, CT: Locust Hill Press, 2002: 151–172.

Brask, Per. Ed. *Essays on Kushner's Angels*. Winnipeg, Manitoba: Blizzard Publishing, 1995.

Cohen, Adam. "The Difference Between Politically Incorrect and Historically Wrong." www.nytimes.com/2005/01/26/opinion/26wed4.html?ex=1264482000&en=c2a6ca3e 4e1d17c3&ei=5090&partner=rssuserland. Editorial. *New York Times*. 4 January 2005.

Fisher, James. *Tony Kushner: Living Past Hope*. New York: Routledge, 2002.

_____. "Troubling the Waters: Visions of Apocalypse in Wilder's *The Skin of Our Teeth* and Kushner's *Angels in America*." *Thornton Wilder: New Essays*. West Cornwall, CT: Locust Hill Press, 1999, 391–407.

Friends of Oswald Mosley. www.oswaldmosley.com, 2/3/05.

Griffin, Roger. "British Fascism: The Ugly Duckling." *The Failure of British Fascism*. London: Macmillan, 1996: 141–165. Online, ah.brookes.ac.uk/history/staff/griffin/publications.html, 23 February 2005.

Herbert, Bob. "The Public Thinker." Op-Ed, *New York Times* 14 February 2005.

Hynes, Samuel. *The Auden Generation*. Princeton, NJ: Princeton University Press, 1976.

Isherwood, Christopher. *Diaries, 1939–1960*. New York: HarperCollins, 1996.

_____. *Lions and Shadows*. London: Hogarth Press, 1938.

Kierkegaard, Soren. *The Living Thoughts of Kierkegaard*. Bloomington, IN: Midland Books, 1962.

Kushner, Tony. *A Bright Room Called Day*. New York: Theatre Communications Group, Inc., 1994.

_____. *Death & Taxes: Hydriotaphia & Other Plays*. New York: Theatre Communications Group, Inc., 2000.

_____. "Notes About Political Theater." *Kenyon Review* XIX, nos. 3/4, (summer/fall 1997): 19–34.

_____. *Plays by Tony Kushner*. New York: Broadway Play Publishing, 1992.

_____. *Slavs!* New York: Broadway Play Publishing, 1996.

_____. *Thinking About the Longstanding Problems of Virtue and Happiness*. New York: Theatre Communications Group, Inc., 1995.

_____. *Tony Kushner in Conversation*. Ann Arbor: University of Michigan Press, 1998.

Kushner, T. and N. Valman. *Remembering Cable Street: Fascism and Anti-Fascism in British Society*. London: Vallentine Mitchell, 1999.

McLeod, Bruce. "The Oddest Phenomena in Modern History." *Iowa Journal of Cultural Studies* 14, no. 1 (spring 1995): 143–153.

Mendelson, Edward. *Early Auden*. New York: Farrar Straus & Giroux, 1981.

Quintero, "Political Struggles in a Bright Room." *Berkeylean* 1 November 1995. Online, www.berkeley.edu/news/ berkeleyan/1995/1101/struggles.html, 23 February 2005.
Robinson, Gerard. "Activism through Art." *New York Blade* 2 July 2004: 10.
Scott, A.O. "Hitler's Hit Parade: It's the Nazi Era, But It Looks So Familiar." *New York Times* 5 January 2005: E5.
Sheasby, Walter. "Fascism and the American Polity." January 13, 2004.
Spender, Stephen. *The Destructive Element.* London: Jonathan Cape, 1935.
"Ten Questions for Tony Kushner." www.nytimes.com/2004/06/04/readersopinions /kushner-questions.html?ex=1140670800&en=2f24e178a3aa0c99&ei=5070.
Wilder, Thornton. *The Woman of Andros.* New York: Albert & Charles Boni, 1930.
Williams, Raymond. "Walking Backwards into the Future." *Resources of Hope: Culture, Democracy, Socialism.* London and New York: Verso, 1989.

5

Stonewall, "Constant Historical Progress," and *Angels in America*

The Neo-Hegelian Positivist Sense

DAVID KRASNER

> Since a man is to be judged according to the direction he has given him-self, he is in this act free, let the external features of the act be what they may. As no one can successfully assail a man's inner conviction, and no force can reach it, the moral will is inaccessible. A man's worth is estimated by his inner act. Hence the moral standpoint implies the realization of freedom [Hegel 1996: 105].

Early in Tony Kushner's *Angels in America*, Part I, Prior Walter informs his lover of four years, Louis Ironson, that he has AIDS. The scene takes place at the close of funeral services for Louis's grandmother. Louis and Prior leave the service to sit together on a park bench. Prior remarks: "Bad timing, funeral and all, but I figured as long as we're on the subject of death" (I: 22). Louis takes the news badly; he is uncomfortable with blood and suffering. In the next scene, Louis seeks guidance from the same Rabbi who delivered his grandmother's eulogy.

LOUIS: Rabbi, what does the Holy Writ say about someone who abandons someone he loves at a time of great need?
RABBI: Why would a person do such a thing?
LOUIS: Because he has to. Maybe because this person's sense of the world, that it will change for the better with struggle, maybe a person who has this neo–Hegelian positivist sense of constant historical progress towards happiness or perfection or something, who feels very powerful because he feels connected to these forces, moving

uphill all the time ... maybe that person can't, um, incorporate sickness into this sense of how things are supposed to go. Maybe vomit ... and sores and disease ... really frighten him, maybe ... he isn't so good with death.

RABBI: The Holy Scriptures have nothing to say about such a person.

LOUIS: Rabbi, I'm afraid of the crimes I may commit [I: 25].

In 1996 I directed *Angels in America*, Part I. During one rehearsal the actor playing Louis asked: "What does Louis mean when he says, 'neo–Hegelian positivist sense of constant historical progress towards happiness or perfection or something.'" I replied at the time with boilerplate psychological realism: "Louis is groping for excuses." While I believe this is true, I have since come to believe that more compelling reasons underlie Louis's remarks.

Critical analyses of Louis's comments have run the gamut from outright dismissal to dialectical comparisons. Alisa Solomon, for instance, says that Louis "prattles about being a guy with a 'neo–Hegelian positivist sense'" (Solomon 127). Mike Nichols's HBO production of the play appears to follow Solomon's appraisal, expunging the line and the paragraph. While cutting simplifies, it also effectively minimizes Louis's complexity, reducing the betrayal to an unspecified act of selfishness. Martin Harries and Art Borreca compare Louis and Prior, with Louis's secular liberalism diminished next to Prior's characterization as seer. Louis's symptomatic humanism, Harries writes, "denies the existence of 'angels in America'" (Harries 192). Borreca more or less concurs, saying that Louis "rationalizes his treatment of Prior," as well as establishes himself as the "dialectical opposite to Prior as prophet." Borreca adds that Louis is "a liberal rationalist who subscribes to the myth of a progressive, enlightened America but whose interpretation of these ideals is as misplaced as his abandonment of Prior is cowardly" (Borreca 249). Louis represents liberal Enlightenment (he is, after all, working his way through *Democracy in America*) and he indeed "rationalizes" his betrayal, a rationalism owing much to Hegel's quintessential ideas of freedom.

This essay will examine Louis's phrase "neo–Hegelian positivist sense" in order to illuminate his larger purpose in the play. This will be done in light of the fact that Louis's outlook actually changes by the end of *Angels in America*, Part II. At the beginning of Part I Louis defends his betrayal by appealing to two related themes, one directly and one indirectly inferred: first, Hegel's concept of freedom, and second, the gay revolution known as Stonewall. Hegel's ideas of freedom and the 1969 political events of Stonewall where gays and lesbians resisted oppression in New York's Greenwich Village, form Louis's justification. Although neither Louis nor anyone else in the play mention Stonewall, I submit that the movement's impact resonates. For Louis, the gay liberation movement that emerged from Stonewall represented a newfound freedom, what might be deemed in Louis's terms as the historically positivist-progressive struggle towards utopia. Louis frequently evokes the term "freedom" throughout Parts I and II of *Angels in America*; however "freedom," as Louis comes to realize, is "heartless" (I: 72). His conflict is not merely owing to his neurosis (though he admits to being neurotic throughout the play), but rather, as this essay will attempt to demonstrate, his struggle emerges as the play's representation of the Hegelian mind/spirit (*Geist*) in conflict with the flesh. Louis's trajectory through Parts I and II charts his progress from Hegelian freedom, with its emphasis on abstraction, to his understanding of the body, flesh, and the responsibility freedom entails.

Where Hegel and Kushner's Louis converge is in their belief that reason and freedom are, in Louis's words, a "constant historical progress." History according to Hegel is the process by which reason proceeds towards universal claims of freedom. In *The Philosophy of History*, Hegel says: "The only Thought which Philosophy brings with it to the contemplation of History, is the simple conception of *Reason*; that Reason is the Sovereign of the World; that the history of the world, therefore, presents us with a rational process" (Hegel 1956: 9). For Hegel, reason is a process, not a result, evolving through various stages before attaining universal freedom. Freedom for Hegel (and Louis) is, according to Stephen Eric Bonner, "the rational unfolding of history" (Bonner 22), and this unfolding aims towards the highest attainment of the rational spirit, what Hegel calls *Geist* (translated as spirit or mind).

Hegel begins Chapter 6 of his *Phenomenology of Spirit* by saying that "Reason is spirit (*Die Vernunft ist Geist*)," wherein spirit is the "the object of consciousness— the pure category — raised to the concept of reason" (Hegel 2001: 1). He emphasizes that the "*living ethical* world (*lebendige sittliche Welt*) is the spirit in its *truth*" (Hegel 2001: 4), and that "spirit is present as *absolute freedom* (*absolute Freiheit*)," yielding a "self-consciousness grasping itself" (Hegel 2001: 104). The "highest actuality," he maintains, "is the freedom and singularity of the actual self-consciousness itself" (Hegel 2001: 107). "*In itself*," he contends, "freedom is precisely this *abstract self-consciousness* (*abstrakte selbstbewußtsein*) that exterminates within itself all distinction and any persistent of distinction. As such an abstract self-consciousness, it is its own object; the *terror* of death is the intuition of this, its negative essence" (Hegel 2001: 109). Hegel's dichotomy between abstract self-consciousness and death is for Louis emblematic of his striving towards absolute freedom and spiritual enlightenment unsullied by disease and deteriorating flesh. The objective is reason, which leads to freedom; nothing can come between Louis and his quest for the absolute spirit, which for him translates into reason (rationality) and freedom. The Hegelian notion of *Geist* as freedom, Charles Taylor reminds us, must emerge as "quintessentially reason." Reason "is most fully realized when one follows in thought and action the line of rational, that is, conceptual, necessity." This rational necessity, or rational subjectivity, opens the way towards "the freedom of *Geist*" (Taylor 29). Rational subjectivity, once it is recognized as such, encourages the individual's autonomous freedom; reason guides the individual in his or her choices. As Taylor points out, *Geist* must "flow of necessity from the Idea, from Spirit or Reason itself. Hence Spirit must ultimately rebel against anything merely given" (Taylor 76). This is Louis's goal; rebellion against that which is given (obstacles such as Prior's illness) and progress towards spiritual contemplation — pure, abstract thought — devoid of responsibility to the material, i.e., flesh and blood. Louis thus experiences what Walter Benjamin terms "this storm ... we call progress" (Benjamin 258), a progress that rejects the past (which, for Benjamin, is often blood-soaked ruins), and marches ahead unencumbered by past consequences and responsibilities. Louis, despite his guilty feelings, turns his back on his four years spent with Prior; for all his rhetoric about freedom and ethics, his lack of ethical accountability opens the way for his impoverished morality.

Hegel and Louis are also united in constructing a view of moral duty. Hegel modifies Kant's categorical imperative, which claims that one must *"act only in accordance with that maxim through which you can at the same time will that it become a universal law"* (Kant 31 [4:421]). In his effort to seek radical autonomy, Kant (influenced by Rousseau) sought to jettison nature's directives and emphasize volition. Kant is not altogether clear how we enact this postulate; as Stephen Körner observes, Kant's original formulation of the categorical imperative "is hardly a case of logical deduction" (147). Suffice to say, Kant employs every effort to make rational actions coincide with a universal (moral) law. Hegel's critique of Kant's categorical imperative maintains that it imposes a negative freedom — what one ought not to do. According to Hegel, "once this principle [categorical imperative] is accepted, the rational can announce itself only as limiting this freedom. Hence it is not an inherent rationality, but only a mere external and formal universal" (Hegel 1996: 35). Hegel seeks to expand the notion of freedom, incorporating the negative and the positive. In his book, *Queer Social Philosophy: Critical Readings from Kant to Adorno*, Randall Halle asserts that Hegel charted the process "through which the state comes to contain both negative determination and positive determination, freedom from *as well as* freedom to" (Halle 74), the "state" being the ultimate will of the people. Freedom for Hegel is not simply the actions one must restrain from, but also actions one must take; and freedom is not imposed from the outside, but part of consciousness and will. Louis initiates his drive towards freedom, which entails abstracting or extracting freedom from any association with the body — in short, blood, as well as human bonding — and thus rationalizes his abandonment of his lover during the time of his greatest need. This is supported in the opening of Act Two. The scene takes place at night, around Christmas of 1985; Prior is, according to the stage directions, "*alone of the floor of his bedroom; he is much worse*" (I: 47). Prior cries out to Louis, who is evidently no longer sleeping in the same bedroom as Prior. Louis tries to convince Prior to call an ambulance and go to the emergency room, but Prior is too afraid. He pleads with Louis to avoid calling for help. As Louis tries to help Prior back to his bed, Prior, the stage directions say, "*shits himself.*"

> PRIOR: I'm sorry, I'm sorry.
> LOUIS: What did...? What?
> PRIOR: I had an accident.
> (*Louis goes to him.*)
> LOUIS: This is blood.
> PRIOR: Maybe you shouldn't touch it ... me ... I... (*He faints*).
> LOUIS: (*Quietly.*) Oh help. Oh help. Oh God oh God oh God help me I can't I can't I can't [I: 48].

Louis is unable to incorporate into his Hegelian ideals blood, feces, and the deterioration of his lover's flesh. Louis first evokes "God," but when that fails he simply states the obvious: "I can't." What he "can't" do is deal with "blood," because blood, flesh, and mortality are antithetical to his idealization of abstract (self-conscious) freedom.

Louis searches for self-knowledge throughout the play. His efforts are solipsistic, but genuine. His moral imperative is total "freedom" and what it requires. Obstacles to this process might "enslave" him. In this Louis finds Hegel a kindred spirit. According to Hegel, freedom is a thought carried through to its logical conclusion; the slave, incapable of freedom, is therefore incapable of pure thought. Hegel says: "Thus the self-consciousness, which purifies its object, content or end, and exalts it to universality, is thought carrying itself through into will. It is at this point that it becomes clear that the will is true and free only as thinking intelligence. The slave knows not his essence, and not to know himself is not to think himself" (Hegel 1996: 29–30). Hegel is concerned with the way freedom depends on

volition and ethics (since enslavement deters the slave's capacity for volition, the slave is ipso facto a non-thinking person; however, the slave for
Hegel is capable of evolving). Freedom, according to Hegel, is a "fundamental phase of will," and "Will without freedom" is "an empty word."
Volition, moreover, "is a special way of thinking; it is thought translating
itself into reality; it is the impulse of thought to give itself reality" (Hegel
1996: 11). Ethics identify the need for creating a particular connection
between means and ends, and the means and the ends for Hegel must be
speculative as well as inclusive of all thought, ideas, and opinions. Hegel
asserts that all contributors to consciousness are true or partially true
because each contribution is a part of a teleological progression of consciousness that results in an all-encompassing conclusion. Everything leads
to an absolute standpoint; thus, the march forward towards this absolute
must incorporate all rational forms including those deemed contradictory.
The endpoint arises through stages; no opinion or idea is entirely wrong —
all are absorbed in the process.

The notion of absorbing all thoughts is essential in describing Louis's
most compelling needs; throughout the play he is ambivalent about any
single truth or any single commitment, but nonetheless retains a voracious appetite for ideas. But Louis's ideas at the beginning of the play are
speculative and abstract; they are contemplative but rarely adhere to people or objects. In discussing law, for example, he says to Prior that law
"should be the question and shape of a life, its total complexity gathered,
arranged and considered, which matters in the end, not some stamp of
salvation or damnation which disperses all complexity in some unsatisfying little decision — the balancing of the scales" (I: 38–9). Louis's Hegelian
point is that a small act (small in his terms) fails to incorporate the total,
absolute spirit of consciousness. Reason, according to Hegel, provides
knowledge of reality by apprehending things in their concrete interrelat-
edness with other things; it grasps things in their totality and interconnectedness. Reason aims towards wholeness rather than parsing things
from other things. For Hegel, as it is for the law courts, the only truth is
the whole truth, even if the truth is abstracted in the mind. According to
Allen W. Wood, for Hegel a "free volitional agent, capable of abstracting
completely from its desires and situations," creates an "external sphere"
in which "the person's right of arbitrary freedom must be recognized by
others" (Wood 217). This point summarizes Louis's rationalization; Louis
is a free agent, who in his efforts to understand himself and others, must
form an "external sphere" capable of "abstracting completely from desires
and situations." Prior responds bluntly by acknowledging Louis's abstract
logic and appeal to abstract freedom: "I like this," he says, "very zen; it's

... reassuringly incomprehensible and useless. We who are about to die thank you" (I: 39). Louis justifies leaving the mortally ill Prior with Hegelian rationale: do not judge a single act but consider the totality of the person's actions. Prior is aware of Louis's intentions, and counters by bringing the discussion to the level of the body, a body that is dying at that.

Louis's reasoning is based on Hegel's abstract freedom detached from the flesh. Hegel divides freedom and volition along three lines. First, he identifies free will as a "caprice," a stage of desire — "mere impulse" — consisting of the individual "doing what one likes" (1996: 24, 25). Second, he considers "reflective will," a stage more advanced than caprice but not yet ascending to objective freedom. In "reflective will," the agent reflects on moral actions and considers their consequences, but still the agent is encased in subjectivity: "the subjective side is still different from the objective," he says (Hegel 1996: 25). The third and highest attainment of freedom is "rational will." (1996: 30) The third stage involves self-awareness, but also involves a process of overcoming (*Aufhebung*) desires, appetites, and reflection, thereby raising freedom "into the universal," which "constitutes the activity of thought" (Hegel 1996: 29). Reality is to be considered, but only as a process. Thought rather than concrete reality is the ultimate goal, which can obtain "freedom." In his book *Hegel's Idea of Freedom*, Alan Patten claims that this third stage of rational will "involves a more *complete* abstraction from one's actual desires, inclinations, and so on," yielding "a grounding in reason that *goes all the way down*: it is opposed to any process of determining one's ends that stops at contingently given desires and inclinations" (Patten 51). This describes Louis as well: he will stop at nothing in his effort, as Patten says, to go "all the way down" to absolute thought and abstract (detached) freedom, unsullied by illness, disease, and the flesh. Though Louis does not abnegate desires, he is seeking nullification of commitment. He will be undeterred by what he calls the "stamp of salvation or damnation which disperses all complexity in some unsatisfying little decision"; rather, he incorporates all in the Hegelian absolute spirit, "the balancing of the scales," as he says, even if this process towards universal spirit means betrayal.

Louis abandons Prior in a quest for Hegelian absolute freedom of pure thought, but his "success" in triumphing over association with the disintegration of his lover's body in pursuit of a purely mental utopia comes at great personal cost. He extols in his liberated sensibilities, pluralistic openness, and radical-left politics that reveal his Hegelian absolute freedom, but he chooses to ignore the material reality and tragic consequences of AIDS. As a result, he has lost touch with the material side of his humanity. He is obsessed with the concept of freedom unrelated to the body, the flesh, and the material; but it is recognizing the flesh, body, and ultimately material pain that Kushner identifies as essential to our humanness. This is the lesson Louis must learn through the course of two plays, and which instigates the character's evolution. Oscar Eustis, one of Kushner's dramaturges and close associate throughout the development of the play, asserts: "What became clear [in the course of Kushner's creating *Angels in America*] is that the difficulty in these people changing *was* the subject of the play" (quoted in Lahr 48). Louis goes through the difficult struggle to change. He must, in the end, come to the conclusion that the concept of freedom and openness in the abstract realm without materiality is a vapid signifier and ideologically bankrupt.

Struggle informs the play. On the one hand, Stonewall is an important phenomenon for Louis because it represents a positive liberating struggle. According to Kushner himself,

> The Stonewall Riots happened in New York in 1969, the night that Judy Garland died, when all these drag queens refused to be arrested and taken out of a bar — the beginning of the gay movement in the States and I guess elsewhere. The moment said we're not apologizing for the sex, and we're not going to stop having it, we are involved in a very legitimate experiment, we're not going to be embarrassed or ashamed, or deprived of something we're working on, that our historical mission is to investigate — that was the first moment of real political sophistication in gay liberation since Stonewall [quoted in Vorlicky 22].

Although not explicitly noted in the play, I maintain that the Stonewall uprising Kushner refers to generates Louis's attempt to seek a positive worldview, embrace freedom, and maintain an ethical stance. The radicalism that took root via Stonewall becomes Louis's inspiration to advance it several steps further towards utopic freedom. The positive direction, in this case, might refer to Louis's "Hegelianism"; however, what Louis cannot embrace is the physical setback symbolized by his lover's AIDS. For Kushner, James Fisher observes, the AIDS epidemic had "pushed gay dramatists toward a more politicized view ... even more than had been inspired by the activists of the Stonewall era." This "politicized gay theater" was Kushner's way of ensuring "a positive direction" (Fisher 69). Louis thinks he has taken a "positivist" direction, but he misconstrues the revolution's fundamental political goals. The realization of his mistake is the process he must undertake throughout the course of two plays.

Kushner does not reject Hegel out of hand. He understands and endorses Hegel's goals of historical change as well as Hegel's demand for a capacious consciousness, one that embraces all thoughts and ideas. Freedom for Hegel necessitated an ongoing struggle to the process that is history. Since events and forces change, individuals ought to be made aware that what was freely chosen yesterday may not be available today (or tomorrow). Consequences of group actions, such as Stonewall, transform conditions and establish new conditions. The world spirit takes on changing forms, demanding a concomitant evolution of one's ethical stance. Louis's idealistic struggle as part of a Hegelian "world spirit" is a mixture of subjective absolutes as well as an incorporation of other subjectivities within their place in history. Hegel, however, departs from Kushner when he describes idealism in relation to finite thought rather than in the body; in *Science of Logic* he says that idealism "consists in nothing else than in recognizing that the finite has no veritable being. Every philosophy is essentially an idealism or at least has idealism for its principle" (Hegel 1969: 154–55).

For Kushner, like Hegel, freedom is subject to constraints imposed by institutions arising from consciousness in its progress towards the speculative "absolute spirit." But for Kushner, contra Hegel, speculative spirit that nullifies the flesh is unacceptable. Speculative thought, which is the basis of Hegelian metaphysics, involves freedom in specific concrete conditions, but it always seeks to transcend the material. For Hegel, real progress takes place in the mind and not necessarily in the material world (though he hopes it will ultimately manifest itself in concrete reality). As Louis progresses through the play, he comes to realize that freedom and the absolute spirit devoid of flesh is insubstantial. In an extended rant to his friend Belize during the opening of Part I, Act III, Louis contemplates "freedom." Here Louis takes a less positive approach to freedom, and in so doing initiates further the modification of his attitude. Louis:

> I mean it's the really hard thing about being Left in this country, the American Left can't help but trip over all these petrified little fetishes: freedom, that's the worst; you know *Jeane Kirkpatrick* for God's sake will go on and on about freedom and so what does it that mean the word freedom, when she talks about it, or human rights; you have Bush talking about human rights, and so what are these people talking about, they might as well be talking about the mating habits of Venusians, these people don't begin to know what, ontologically, freedom is or human rights, like they see these bourgeois property-based Rights-of-Man-type rights but that's not enfranchisement, not democracy, not what's implicit, what's potential within the idea, not the idea with blood in it [I: 89–90].

Louis is beginning to realize that spirit without blood is an abstraction without substance. His nemesis in the play, Roy Cohn (based on the real-life lawyer and anti–Communist), is the antithesis to Louis: he understands flesh and appetites without moral inhibitions. Although Cohn represents unbridled avarice and hedonism, he also understands (which Louis does not) that flesh is Realpolitik with grass-root consequences. Politics for Cohn exists not in the abstract, but in digestion, blood, and raw meat. For example, in his efforts to persuade Joe, Roy's acolyte, to serve as his point-man in Washington, Cohn asks Joe if he would be his "well-placed friend in the Justice Department." Joe replies that this appointment, manipulated by Roy and his sycophants, might be "unethical." Roy asks Martin, who has joined them for dinner in order to help persuade Joe, to take a walk. Alone with Joe, Roy calls attention to Joe's inability to consider the body:

> Roy: Un-ethical. Are you trying to embarrass me in front of my friend [Martin]?
> Joe: Well it is unethical, I can't...
> Roy: Boy, you really are something. What the fuck do you think this is, Sunday school?
> Joe: No, but Roy this is...
> Roy: This is ... this is gastric juices churning, this is enzymes and acids, this is intestinal is what it is, bowel movement and blood-red meat — this stinks, this is *politics*, Joe, the game of being alive. And you think you're.... What? Above that? Above alive is what? Dead! In the clouds! You're on earth, goddamnit! Plant a foot, stay a while [I: 68].

Both Joe and Louis actually believe they are above corruption as well as the body; they fail to understand the flesh and its relationship to politics. This is likely the basis of their mutual attraction. In the next scene Joe joins Louis on a park bench during lunchtime outside their place of work, where Joe devours several hotdogs. Joe, a Republican, and Louis, a Democrat, are mutually attracted despite (or perhaps because of) their opposite views. Joe admires Louis's "freedom," but he is also petrified, largely because of his fear of coming out. Louis is nonplussed.

> Joe: Yes, I mean it must be scary, you...
> Louis: (*shrugs*) Land of the free. Home of the brave. Call me irresponsible.
> Joe: It's kind of terrifying.
> Louis: Yeah, well, freedom is. Heartless, too.
> Joe: Oh you're not heartless.
> Louis: You don't know. Finish your weenie [I: 72].

Louis is coming to terms with the notion of "freedom" as something un–Hegelian. By *Angels in America*, Part II, his struggle to change is coming to fruition.

During Part II, subtitled *Perestroika*, Louis and Joe move in together. However, Louis discovers that Joe was Roy Cohn's assistant. Repulsed by the thought that he is having sex with someone who had sex with Roy Cohn (though in fact Joe never had sex with Roy, but was merely wooed by Roy for political purposes) Louis challenges Joe, echoing Joseph Welch's famous accusations made at the Army-McCarthy hearings: "Have you no decency, sir? At long last? Have you no sense of decency?" (II: 106). Their argument escalates into a brawl, with Joe getting the better of Louis. At the end of the scene, Louis is on the floor with a bloody nose, while Joe stands over him saying:

> JOE: *I hurt you!* I'm sorry, Louis, I never hit anyone before, I...
> LOUIS: Yeah yeah get lost. Before I really lose my temper and hurt you back. I just want to lie here and bleed for a while. Do me good [II: 111].

Louis's final line — "Do me good" — should not be construed as mere guilt-feelings for abandoning his lover Prior. Bleeding is part of having flesh. Louis is not necessarily being "punished" for transgressions, but rather he is experiencing what Elaine Scarry calls the ineffability of the body in pain that "resists verbal objectification" (Scarry 12). Louis is going through, albeit on a smaller scale than Prior, physical pain and suffering that allows him to understand Prior's agony. But he is also learning the limits of discourse and with that the limits of Hegelian rationalism.

In Act 5, Scene 3, of Part II, Roy Cohn is dead, but his stolen AZT bottles are still useful for others too poor to obtain them. Belize, a nurse, contacts Louis in order that he might abscond with the remaining bottles of AZT (Louis can sneak them out without notice because he, unlike Belize, is not on the hospital staff and therefore unlikely to be checked by security for stealing drugs). Since Louis is Jewish, Belize also asks him to recite the Kaddish, the prayer for the dead, for Cohn. He implores Louis to forgive Cohn, despite Cohn's politics. Louis resists, first for political reasons, then confessing: "I know probably less of the Kaddish than you do, Belize, I'm an intensely secular Jew, I didn't even Bar Mitzvah" (II: 122). Yet Louis recites the Kaddish perfectly. Finishing, Belize says, "Thank you Louis, you did fine." Louis replies, "Fine? What are you talking about, fine? That was fucking miraculous" (II: 123).

For Kushner, the Kaddish recitation is his character's "constant historical progress," one that involves the Hegelian spirit without negating the flesh. It is Louis's epiphany; he can now make amends with Prior and, at the close of Part II, befriend him once more. In the final scene of Part II, Louis, Prior, Belize, and Hannah (Joe Pitt's mother, who has come to

New York to assist her son but ends up assisting Prior instead), sit beneath the statue of the Bethesda angel in Central Park. They discuss current events, specifically the end of the Cold War and the collapse of the Soviet Union. Louis approves of Perestroika and the advent of socialist democracy initiated by Gorbachev, calling the Russian leader the "greatest political thinker since Lenin" (II: 143). Prior turns away from the three and addresses the audience. Prior:

> On a day like today. A sunny winter's day, warm and cold at once. The sky's a little hazy, so the sunlight has a physical presence, a character. In autumn, those trees across the lake are yellow, and the sun strikes those most brilliantly. Against the blue of the sky, that sad fall blue, those trees are more light than vegetation. They are Yankee trees, New England transplants. They're barren now. It's January 1990. I've been living with AIDS for five years. That's six whole months longer that I lived with Louis [II: 144].

Prior's speech evokes images of living things (trees), the "physical presence" of the sun, and locale (New England). He also describes time in relationship to the body ("living with Louis, living with AIDS"), and the body in relationship to the earth. Prior incorporates the flesh in his language and thought, never letting one supersede the other. It is fitting, then, that Louis, still discussing politics, speaks the following:

> LOUIS: Whatever comes, what you have to admire in Gorbachev, in the Russians is that they're making a leap into the unknown. You can't wait around for theory. The sprawl of life, the weird...
> HANNAH: Interconnectedness...
> LOUIS: Yes.
> BELIZE: Maybe the sheer size of the terrain.
> LOUIS: It's all too much to encompass by a single theory now.
> BELIZE: The world is faster than the mind [II: 144].

It is appropriate for Louis to abandon the certainty of a single theory, Hegelian or otherwise. The environment spins in and through rational notions of truth or absolutes. Hegel's notion of historical evolution bears out fruitfully, but the absoluteness of Hegel's abstract theory and the certainty of progress are proven suspect. Louis has learned, as the other characters know all along, that Enlightenment, liberal reason alone fails to encompass freedom in any real sense. The world cannot assert its volition for freedom and progress through "positivism," but rather must accept the importance of human relationships and the ever-changing nature of the body. Harold Bloom has called Kushner a "theological writer," which is true to the extent that *Angels in America* is, in Kushner's words, a "struggle and pursuit between the human and the divine" (both quoted in Lahr 42). It should be added, however, that the play also represents a Hegelian struggle that seeks to reconcile the flesh and the ideal. Louis, as well as the other characters in the play, journey to find their way to unification of mind and body, flesh and spirit. In this way, Kushner asserts his commitment to a compassionate world.

Works Cited

Benjamin, Walter. "Thesis on the Philosophy of History." *Illuminations.* Edited by Hannah Arendt, translated by Harry Zohn. New York: Schocken Books, 1968.
Borreca, Art. "'Dramaturging' the Dialectic: Brecht, Benjamin, and Declan Donnellan's Production of *Angels in America*" *Approaching the Millennium: Essays on* Angels in America. Edited by Deborah R. Geis and Steven F. Kruger. Ann Arbor: University of Michigan Press, 1997: 245–260.
Bronner, Stephen Eric. *Of Critical Theory and Its Theorists.* New York: Routledge, 2002.
Fisher, James. *The Theater of Tony Kushner: Living Past Hope.* New York: Routledge, 2002.
Geis, Deborah R., and Steven F. Kruger, eds. *Approaching the Millennium: Essays on* Angels in America. Ann Arbor: University of Michigan Press, 1997.
Halle, Randall. (2004). *Queer Social Philosophy: Critical Readings from Kant to Adorno.* Urbana: University of Illinois Press.
Harries, Martin. "Flying the Angel of History." *Approaching the Millennium: Essays on* Angels in America. Edited by Deborah R. Geis and Steven F. Kruger. Ann Arbor: University of Michigan Press, 1997: 185–197.
Hegel, G. W. F. *Philosophy of History.* Translated by J. Sibree. New York: Dover, 1956.
_____. *Science of Logic.* Translated by A. V. Miller. Atlantic Highlands, NJ: Humanities Press, 1969.
_____. *Philosophy of Right.* Translated by S. W. Dyde. Amherst, NY: Prometheus, 1996.
_____. *Spirit: Chapter Six of Hegel's Phenomenology of Spirit.* Translated by Hegel Translations Group. Indianapolis: Hackett Publishing Company, 2001. The German original from: http://gutenberg.spiegel.de/hegel/phaenom/pha6b302.htm.
Kant, Immanuel. *Groundwork of the Metaphysics of Morals.* Translated by Mary Gregor. Cambridge: Cambridge University Press, 2002.
Körner, Stephen. *Kant.* New Haven, CT: Yale University Press, 1955.
Kushner, Tony. *Angels in America, Part I: Millennium Approaches.* New York: Theatre Communications Group, Inc., 1992.
_____. *Angels in America, Part II: Perestroika.* New York: Theatre Communications Group, Inc., 1993.
Lahr, John. "After Angels: Tony Kushner's Promethean Itch." *New Yorker*, 3 January 2005: 42–52.
Patten, Alan. *Hegel's Idea of Freedom.* Oxford: Oxford University Press, 1999.
Scarry, Elaine. *The Body in Pain.* New York: Oxford University Press, 1985.
Solomon, Alisa. "Wrestling with *Angels*: A Jewish Fantasia" *Approaching the Millennium: Essays on* Angels in America. Edited by Deborah R. Geis and Steven F. Kruger. Ann Arbor: University of Michigan Press, 1997: 118–33.

Taylor, Charles. *Hegel and Modern Society*. Cambridge: Cambridge University Press, 1979.

Vorlicky, Robert, ed. *Tony Kushner in Conversation*. Ann Arbor: University of Michigan Press, 1998.

Woods, Allen W. "Hegel's Ethics." *The Cambridge Companion to Hegel*. Edited by Frederick C. Beiser. Cambridge: Cambridge University Press, 1993: 211–233.

6

Queer Politics to Fabulous
Politics in *Angels in America*
Pinklisting and Forgiving Roy Cohn
ATSUSHI FUJITA

Tony Kushner's widely acclaimed *Angels in America,* was broadcast as
an HBO-TV mini-series (premiering on December 7 and 14, 2003) over ten
years after its Broadway production. Various media promoted and reviewed
this program every day at the end of 2003 confirming that *Angels* is a great
work and that Kushner is one of the most important playwrights in the
United States today. (For example, Nancy Franklin says, "*Angels in America*
is the most important play of the last decade" [Franklin 125].) Moreover,
taking into consideration that the politics of gay people — and gay marriage
in particular — has been and continues to be a controversial issue.

This paper will discuss this play in terms of queer theory and politics. In various writings by queer theorists, there seem to be two issues at
stake: how queer can remain unessentialized; how queer theory can be
politically effective. Kushner adds a new meaning to queer politics in *Angels
in America*. In interviews and writings, Kushner presents the concept of
the "fabulous," which includes deconstructive analyses of historical contexts and incorporates practical politics after the AIDS epidemic.

It is an outstanding element of *Angels,* compared to other plays, to
suggest "fabulous" politics. Therese Jones analyzes AIDS plays by separating them into two generations. Characteristics of the first generation AIDS
plays are their traditional forms, sentimental and assimilationist tones,
and depictions of a revised notion of family values in the time of AIDS.
(Among the important works are Larry Kramer's *The Normal Heart* [1985],
William Hoffman's *As Is* [1985], and Harvey Fierstein's *Torch Song Trilogy*
[1981] and *Safe Sex* [1987].) On the other hand, the second generation

plays, which include *Angels*, have both elements of anger and humor, and have a message to resist against society without falling into sentimentalism. (Along with *Angels*, important works include Terrence McNally's *Lips Together, Teeth Apart* [1991] and Paul Rudnick's *Jeffrey* [1993].) In these, the disease tends to be abstracted and the plays are entertaining in the Broadway tradition. Compared to other second generation plays, Kushner's play extraordinarily suggests "fabulous politics." Terrence McNally's *Love! Valour! Compassion!* (1995), one of the most important works among the second generation of AIDS plays, has eight male characters, who are enjoying their vacations in a suburb. Though they are different from each other (one is Latin American and another is blind), they all have rigid gay identities. "I'm sick of straight people" (McNally 58), says one, showing the dichotomy of homosexuality and heterosexuality inherent in the play and, in fact, in many of the works in this category of gay plays.

This essay will particularly focus on the depiction of the *Angels* character Roy Cohn, modeled after the actual Roy M. Cohn, who was Senator Joseph McCarthy's right-hand man and the prosecutor for the Julius and Ethel Rosenberg trial for espionage. Through the depiction of Roy, Kushner changes Cohn's stereotypical image constructed by homophobic discourses. This depiction is the basis to explore Kushner's fabulous politics.

First, it is important to understand some basic facts about Cohn's life. Born in New York in 1927, Roy Marcus Cohn became well-known as a result of his participation in the case of Ethel Rosenberg, who, along with her husband, Julius, was accused of spying for the Soviet Union and revealing atomic secrets at the height of the Cold War. The Rosenbergs were consequently found guilty and executed in 1953. Subsequently, Cohn was appointed chief counsel of the McCarthy committee and gained notoriety as McCarthy's closest ally and aide. Though McCarthy fell from grace during the Army-McCarthy hearings in 1954, and died from alcoholism three years later, Cohn survived and became a high profile New York City attorney with famous clients including Donald Trump, Andy Warhol, and Cardinal Spellman. Cohn died from an AIDS-related disease shortly after being disbarred in 1986.

The historic Cohn is an undeniably notorious figure. Sydney Zion, who interviewed Cohn and wrote his biography, says about the response from his friends when he decided to write about Cohn:

> I was surprised by the vehemence of a number of my friends. "Why would you want to help out that sonofabitch?" "How could you put your name next to his?" It was the same song and dance I heard twenty years earlier when I first invited Roy to a party [Zion 10].

The press for Cohn was similarly vehement. Shortly before Cohn's death, an anonymous writer in *The Nation* (5/12 July 1984: 4) compares him to Iago in Shakespeare's *Othello*.

Historical Facts and Depiction

Kushner writes in his introductory notes for *Angels* that the depiction of Roy is based on historical facts:

> Roy M. Cohn, the character, is based on the late Roy M. Cohn (1927–1986), who was all too real; for the most part the acts attributed to the character Roy, such as his illegal conferences with Judge Kaufmann during the trial of Ethel Rosenberg, are to be found in the historical record [*Angels* 1:5].

Kushner's depiction of Roy exposes what McCarthyism did; it is connected to a criticism against the Reagan Administration for having failed to take action soon enough against the AIDS epidemic. Reagan referred to AIDS for the first time in public in 1987 after 25,000 people had already succumbed and scores of others were infected with HIV. In his book, *And the Band Played On* (New York: St. Martin's Press, 1987), Randy Shilts illustrates that it was difficult for the CDC to study the disease because of the small budget they received from the government. Larry Kramer's *Reports from the Holocaust* (New York: St. Martin's Press, 1989) similarly provides information on the slow response of the U.S. government to the AIDS crisis. This leads Kushner to condemn the Reagan administration for its failure to respond to the obviously deepening AIDS crisis.

Roy Cohn, however, does not appear as a completely evil person in *Angels*. He is notably portrayed as a forgivable person, too. Why would Kushner do this? Comparing some scenes in the play with historical facts, it can be seen how Roy, the character, is delineated, particularly in regard to the Rosenberg case and the Army-McCarthy hearings. Speaking to Joe, his designated "Roy Boy," about the Rosenberg case, Roy says:

> If it wasn't for me, Joe, Ethel Rosenberg would be alive today, writing some personal-advice column for *Ms. Magazine*. She isn't. Because during the trial, Joe, I was on the phone every day, talking with the judge... [*Angels* 1:107–108].

He continues:

> Every day, doing what I do best, talking on the telephone, making sure that timid Yid nebbish on the bench did his duty to America, to history

> ... she came this close to getting life; I pleaded till I wept to put her in the chair. Me. I did that [*Angels* 1:108].

Shocked, Joe answers:

> You can't possibly mean what you're saying. Roy, you were the Assistant United States Attorney on the Rosenberg case, ex-parte communication with the judge during the trial would be ... censurable, at least, probably conspiracy and ... in a case that resulted in execution, it's... [*Angels* 1:108].

Cohn finishes the sentence: "What? Murder?" Cohn's illegal communication with the judge is part of the historical record (Hoffman 99–101; Zion 65–70). Ethel Rosenberg was judged guilty on evidence that was almost exclusively her brother's testimony. In a book by Sam Roberts, published in 2001, the brother, David Greenglass, confesses that his testimony was false. Cohn, who was only 23 years old at the time of the trial, advanced his career rapidly with this case. McCarthy appointed him as chief counselor for the Communist "witch hunt" he had embarked on, destroying many people's careers and lives.

Although a lot of gay men and lesbians were a target of this witch hunt, Cohn, McCarthy, and G. David Schine, who worked for the committee, were rumored to have had an intimate relationship. Lillian Hellman, who was also a target of the accusation, ridiculed them as "Bonnie, Bonnie and Clyde." The Army-McCarthy hearings, which were held as a result of pressure Cohn had put on the army in order to secure an exemption for Schine's military service, were televised for thirty-five days. During these hearings, McCarthy named a young man as a possible communist; the man had been a member of the National Lawyers Guild, which was listed as a communist group then. Joseph Welch, the attorney of the army, accused McCarthy of wrongly and unfairly naming this young man. Since this naming would surely destroy the young man's future, Welch criticized McCarthy with tears in his eyes:

> Little did I dream you could be so reckless and so cruel as to do an injury to that lad.... I fear he shall always bear a scar needlessly inflicted by you.... Have you no sense of decency, sir, at long last? Have you no sense of decency? [Hoffman 237].

This line, "Have you no decency," became the headline of newspapers all over the country the next day and essentially put an end to McCarthy's command of public attention. Kushner uses this line is used in the second of the *Angels* plays, *Perestroika*. Louis, who left his lover, Prior, after finding out that Prior had full-blown AIDS, is shocked to discover that his new lover, Joe, works for Roy Cohn:

> Louis: *"Have you no decency, at long last, sir, have you no decency at all?"*
> Joe: I DON'T KNOW WHO SAID IT! WHY ARE YOU DOING THIS TO ME! *I LOVE YOU. I LOVE YOU.* WHY...
> Louis: JOSEPH WELCH, THE ARMY/McCARTHY HEARINGS. Ask Roy. He'll tell you. He knows. He was *there* [*Angels* 2:109].

In contrast to McCarthy's dramatic fall from power, Cohn rebounded and became even more powerful as a lawyer working behind the scenes. Based on these facts, Roy is frequently depicted as an evil figure in Kushner's play. He is called "killer queen," by his nurse Belize (*Angels* 2:22), whereas Louis, informed that Joe works for Roy, says: "I don't believe you. Not Roy Cohn. He's like a polestar of human evil, he's like the worst human being who ever lived, he isn't *human* even" (*Angels* 2:93).

Anti-Homophobic Pinklisting

It is risky for Kushner, who wants to present his political message in terms of the liberation of gay people and failure of the government AIDS policy, to depict Cohn as an evil. It is not Kushner's intention to link Cohn's wickedness with his homosexuality. With regard to the pinklisting of Roy Cohn and homophobic discourse, Michael Cadden points out:

> As a rule, when Cohn is subjected to the phenomenon of pinklisting, the performance is not produced by gay writers interested in community pride. The standard pinklisting of Roy Cohn appears in what passes for the liberal press in the United States. Both homophobic and heterosexist, liberal pinklisting usually has far more to do with blacklisting, a genre Cohn understood well, than with the celebration of a gay presence in history [Cadden 79].

As Cadden implies, to present Cohn as homosexual opens this depiction to a typical strategy of homophobes who would suggest that Cohn's evil is connected to his sexual preference. It is convenient to keep a dichotomy of normal heterosexuality and abnormal homosexuality by suggesting Cohn, who is known as a homosexual and a notorious person. Why, then, does Kushner risk using him in his play as a character? What is the difference between the pinklisting of Roy Cohn by homophobes and the one used by Kushner? Roy's failure to claim his identity in the play provides a clue to Kushner's purpose. Roy analyzes his identity for Henry, his doctor:

> Like all labels they tell you one thing and one thing only; where does an individual so identified fit in the food chain, in the pecking order? Not ideology, or sexual taste, but something much simpler: clout. Not who fucks me, but who will pick up the phone when I call, who owes me favors. This is what a label refers to. Now to someone who does not understand this, homosexual is what I am because I have sex with men. But really this is wrong. Homosexuals are not men who sleep with other men. Homosexuals are men who in fifteen years of trying cannot get a puissant antidiscrimination bill through City Council. Homosexuals are men who know nobody and who nobody knows. Who have zero clout [*Angels* 1:45].

Later on, he claims that he has liver cancer (when, in fact, he has AIDS) because, as he describes himself, he is not a homosexual. This claim is also based on Cohn's actual assertion (see, for example, an article on Cohn's disbarment in *Newsweek* 9 December 1985: 7879). In *Angels*, admitting having sexual relationships with men, Roy rejects his sexual identity, which is based on his sexual taste, and claims his political identity, which is based on how effective he is in the world. However, Henry does not accept Roy's claim on identity. Henry regards Roy as a homosexual because Roy has had sexual relationships with men, a fact Henry knows for certain since he diagnosed a sexually transmitted disease in Roy's past. Roy's identity, after all, is decided by whether his sexual orientation is toward men or women; his sexual identity is prior to the political identity he claims. Though he argues that identity is just a label, it is compulsory and he cannot chose it. The identity circulating more persuasively in society is not a political identity that Roy claims, but a sexual identity that society has forced on him. Roy's identity as a gay man is recognized by other characters in *Angels*; similarly, the actual Cohn was known as being gay by his inner circle of friends and especially after his AIDS became public. (As an example to link Cohn's AIDS with his homosexuality, see an obituary by Albin Krebs in the *New York Times* 3 August 1986.) Roy's claim of his identity and its failure to supercede actuality show how sexual identity comes to have excessive meaning as a more important element than others like political identity.

Cohn's sexual identity is skillfully linked with his notorious career through the pinklisting by homophobes. Writing an article in *The Nation* called "King Cohn," Robert Sherrill, refers to the reasons Kushner wrote this play (*Village Voice* 20 April 1993), something Roy also refers to in the play (*Angels* 1:108). In his article, Sherrill looks back at Roy's infamous career, including the Rosenberg case, the McCarthy Communist witch hunt, his debt owed to one of his clients, and his forcible way of winning cases through bribes and threats. He focuses on Roy's homosexuality in the last page, beginning with this line: "As everyone knows, Cohn, 'the best-known non-show-business homosexual in the country,' died of AIDS" (Sherrill 724). After Sherrill introduces a Cohn friend's testimony on his "nasty" sex life, the article ends with: "It's said that the one true love in Roy Cohn's life was his spaniel, Charlie Brown" (Sherrill 725). It illustrates Cohn in the typical homophobic image especially during the AIDS epidemic, which is, "gays cannot build long-lasting relationships because they have unspecified and plural sexual relationships."

Kushner, as a gay and as a Jew, should hate Roy who persecuted gay people and Jews in the McCarthy era. Roy, however, is depicted with some forgiveness in various scenes in which Roy's weakness and occasional gentleness are shown. Though Belize, Roy's nurse who calls him a "killer queen," recognizes what Roy has done in his life and suffers verbal abuse from Roy because he is black, gives Roy gentle words and advice about a remedy of AIDS:

> BELIZE: ... So tell the doctor no thanks for the radiation. He won't want to listen. Persuade him. Or he'll kill you.
> ROY: You're just a fucking nurse. Why should I listen to you over my qualified, very expensive WASP doctor?
> BELIZE: He's not queer. I am.
> ROY: You hate me.
> BELIZE: Yes.
> ROY: Why are you telling me this?
> BELIZE: I wish I knew.
> (Pause)
> ROY (Very nasty): You're a butterfingers spool faggot nurse. I think ... you have little reason to want to help me.
> BELIZE: Consider it solidarity. One faggot to another [Angels 2:26–27].

Belize also recommends that Roy should get AZT, a brand new medicine for AIDS, which was still in FDA trials at this point. There is another scene that attracts sympathy from the audience. Roy is getting weaker because of the disease and medications and, delirious, he mistakes Belize for the embodiment of death:

> BELIZE: You awake? Can you see who I am?
> ROY: Oh yeah, you came for mama, years ago. You wrap your arms around me now. Squeeze the bloody life from me. OK? [Angels 2:75].

Ethel Rosenberg appears as a specter to expose what Roy did to her. Speaking to Roy, the only one who can see her, she says:

> I came to forgive but all I can do is take pleasure in your misery. Hoping I'd get to see you die more terrible than I did. And you are, 'cause you're dying in shit, Roy, defeated. And you could kill me, but you couldn't ever defeat me. You never won. And when you die all anyone will say is: Better he had never lived at all [*Angels* 2:112–113].

However, even she shows compassion for him and, to a certain degree, almost forgives him. They call each other by their first names as if they were old friends. Ethel calls an ambulance for him when his condition gets worse. Mistaking her for his mother, Roy asks her to sing a lullaby. Ethel, singing it to Roy, the man who once made certain she was executed, seems to sympathize with him as his last moment is coming. Finally he seems to die, but before he actually does, he slips in a final invective: "I fooled you Ethel, I knew who you were all along, I can't believe you fell for that ma stuff, I just wanted to see if I could finally, finally make Ethel Rosenberg sing! I WIN!" (*Angels* 2:114). Roy is not the kind of person who dies peacefully, or accepts sympathy when it is offered. Then he says, "Next time around: I don't want to be a man. I wanna be an octopus. Remember that, OK? A fucking..." (*Angels* 2:114) and he finally dies. He wants to be an octopus to deal with incessant calls with eight arms, to have a reach that extends everywhere. His last line shows the vanity of his life. Being deprived of his status as a lawyer, which was the only thing that mattered to him, he is dying with only Ethel, his historic enemy, and Belize, his social opposite, by his side.

After Roy's death, Belize asks Louis, who is Jewish, to chant the Kaddish, the Jewish prayer for the dead, for Roy:

> He was a terrible person. He died a hard death. So maybe ... A queen can forgive her vanquished foe. It isn't easy, it doesn't count if it's easy, it's the hardest thing. Forgiveness. Which is maybe where love and justice finally meet. Peace, at least. Isn't that what the Kaddish asks for? [*Angels* 2:122].

To forgive such a person as Roy is not easy. Louis says the prayer reluctantly, and Ethel joins him. Louis dislikes Roy so much that he cannot even call Roy a human being, while Ethel has deep hatred against Roy for destroying her life. This scene shows forgiveness to Roy most conspicuously. However, it should not be overlooked that they end their chanting of the Kaddish by calling him a "son of a bitch." Although Kushner in

Angels, to a certain degree, forgives Roy, what he did and the dark sides of American history depicted in the play cannot be forgiven easily.

The depiction of Roy's gentle aspect also seems to forgive Roy. His fatherly love toward Joe is expressed:

> It's OK that you hurt me because I love you, baby Joe. That's why I'm so rough on you ... Prodigal son. The world will wipe its dirty hands all over you ... I'll always be here, waiting for you... [*Angels* 1:109].

Roy says that he wants to look after Joe because he owes his current prosperity to elders who mentored him. The real Roy Cohn actually made use of connections with powerful figures to attain success (Many provided favorable comments on Cohn's behalf; see *The Nation* 19/26 July 1986: 48–51.) Though Roy tries to send Joe to Washington to make him clear up the mess caused by his ethics violations, it proves Roy's affection because he has risen in the world in the same way and believes that was right. Whether his way of expressing affection is morally right or not, the depiction of his affection shows a gentler aspect of his character; Kushner is compassionate in his depiction of Cohn.

Why is Roy depicted as a forgivable person in *Angels*? Roy is dying after he has lost his power — if that is taken into consideration, a certain amount of compassion is natural even for this most notorious of historical figures. Furthermore, since Roy is a victim of AIDS, at this point in time a certain death sentence, he becomes a victim, and, as such, a forgivable person. Roy Cohn's sheet of the famous AIDS Quilt which commemorates AIDS victims, calls him not only a bully and a coward, but also a victim.

The issue here is to ask why Kushner uses Cohn as a character in *Angels*. Kushner's intention in using such a complicated figure as one of his main characters, and to depict that character dying of AIDS, is a detail which inevitably attracts the sympathy of his audience. Kushner does not suggest the notoriety of Cohn by linking it with his homosexuality as a lot of homophobic discourses have previously done. Instead, he focuses on aspects of Cohn beyond the stereotypes and questions the homophobic discourses that strengthen those stereotypes. After reading Sherrill's article about Cohn in *The Nation*, Kushner might have felt it a necessity to rewrite Cohn in order to resist the heterosexist discourse. The criticism should have been against only what Cohn did and not what he was, and had to look back at problems in the structure of society that made him do what he did. However, focusing on Cohn's homosexuality, Sherrill changes subjects. Because of the prevailing view against homosexuality in society, Cohn's homosexuality and political persona, morals, and actions are connected expediently, though these elements should be regarded as incidental.

This false connection conceals the real problem that should be discussed and invents the new target that is actually irrelevant to the issue. Kushner reveals that connecting Cohn's evil deeds with his homosexuality is wrong. While illustrating Cohn's crimes as unforgivable, Kushner, in his play, forgives gay Roy Cohn in order to cut the connection. Actually, what he did is not forgivable, but Roy Cohn should be forgiven in the play in order to claim that this kind of pinklisting is odious.

Queer to Fabulous

The pinklisting of Roy Cohn in *Angels* reveals the heterosexism of the hegemonic culture, which too often strives to connect homosexuality with evil. It illustrates how homosexuality is constructed in hegemonic culture and the homosexuality reflexively keeps the dichotomy of homo and heterosexuality rigid to oppress gay people. Roy's failure in the denial of his gay identity shows how gay identity is forcefully assigned to a person and how the identity constructs a subject.

The homophobic discourse repels what is not convenient for the continuation of hegemonic culture into a margin as culturally unintelligible. Cohn's homosexuality and evilness are convenient for hegemonic culture. As particularly in the Western world under heterosexism, gay people have been punished as perverts or studied as sick; categorizing gay people as a group under a bad image enables others to claim a wholesome heterosexual identity. Heterosexual identity, based on a negation of homosexuality, repels any questions to its position as if it were the original. Political practices, however, have been operated by and for the people who are categorized in this obscure heterosexual identity. The hegemonic culture and system should be questioned by focusing on people who have been ignored or represented with a homophobic bias.

The notion that identity is a construction is one of the important arguments of queer theory. However, some criticize queer theory because it destroys the solidarity of minorities, which was obtained after a long struggle. (The Stonewall uprising in 1969 was a turning point that marked the change of the gay movement from a homophile movement to gay liberation though various movements before it should not be neglected. Since Stonewall various activist groups have been formed and gay people have moved toward a more positive identity.) Others claim that the theory is consumed by academism and that it became too theoretical to be politically effective. Judith Butler writes in *Gender Trouble* that the "deconstruction of identity is not the deconstruction of politics" (Butler 189).

Importantly, Butler looks into how identity has been formed genealogically. Queer theory, based on deconstruction, suggests an attitude of analysis by a close reading of history on what has been ignored and fails to be represented. Although analyses by this process are necessary as a theoretical base for actual political practices, queer theory is not directly political by itself. The only significant thing this analysis can do is give necessary ideas to political practices.

The importance of practices is articulated in the new preface to the tenth-anniversary edition of *Gender Trouble*. Butler says that the book owes its basis not only to the academy but also to social movements of the gay and lesbian community which she had joined. Again, deconstructive analyses are not political by themselves. Rather, deconstruction of identity gives a critical point for activism; practice needs theory in order to be careful of what the practice inevitably excluded through their process of representation, as Butler argues:

> [T]he genealogical critique of the queer subject will be central to queer politics to the extent that it constitutes a self-critical dimension within activism, a persistent reminder to take the time to consider the exclusionary force of one of activism's most treasured contemporary premises [*Bodies* 227].

Another criticism on queer theory is the substantialization of queer. Gay people started to use the word, "queer," which is used by homophobes to insult them, in their own terminology. They used the name for self-affirmation in order to express their diversity. If queer represents a stable identity, homophobes can use it to abuse and to categorize gay people again. (In his *Saint = Foucault*, David M. Halperin points out this problem in terms of "the marketing of queer identity" and "queer commodification.") Butler, arguing that queer should not have a stable meaning, also implies a possibility for employing a new word:

> If the term "queer" is to be a site of collective contestation, on the point of departure for a set of historical reflections and futural imaginings, it will have to remain that which is, in the present, never fully owned, but always and only redeployed, twisted, queered from a prior usage and in the direction of urgent and expanding political purposes, and perhaps also yielded in favor of terms that do that political work more effectively. Such a yielding may well become necessary in order to accommodate — without domesticating- democratizing contestations that have and will redraw the contours of the movement in ways that can never be fully anticipated in advance [*Bodies* 228].

Kushner refers to queer politics and suggests the notion of "fabulous," which, this paper argues, can be an alternative to queer. Kushner defines *Angels* as "The Theatre of the Fabulous," and shows two senses of "fabulous" that come from queer politics and the AIDS epidemic. *Angels* shows the new senses of "fabulous" in addition to its textual demonstration of queer politics. A possible answer to the limits of queer theory is found in Kushner's remarks about the idea of "fabulous."

In an interview titled "The Theatre of the Fabulous," Kushner defines *Angels* as "a change from the Theatre of the Ridiculous to the Theatre of the Fabulous," replying to a question, "How do you see *Angels* in relation to the development of queer politics?" Kushner explains two senses of "fabulous" in the above. One of them is a historical viewpoint which the word has in reference to one of its meanings: "legendary." Kushner says of "the Theatre of the Fabulous": "It's incumbent upon us to examine history and be aware of history, of where we've come from and what has given us the freedom to talk the way we do now" (Brask 140). As Kushner says in the same interview, "you have to be constantly looking back at the rubble of history" (Brask 140), it is directly from Walter Benjamin's idea of history. In his "Theses on the Philosophy of History," Benjamin gives his interpretation of an angel in Paul Klee's painting, "Angelus Novus" (Benjamin 257–258). The storm of progress is blowing against the Angel, who is facing the wreckage of history. Though the Angel wants to reconstruct history by collecting the debris, or history of the defeated, it is difficult because the storm, or human desire for development, is so strong that the Angel can no longer close his wings.

During the AIDS epidemic, particularly in its first decade, gay people who had AIDS were discriminated or even ignored. The history of the defeated people had to be dug up from the forgotten debris. *Angels* realistically relates the historical situation as of 1986 and before. Kushner illustrates how people fought against AIDS and struggled with their gay identity. His play focuses on what is not culturally intelligible and reveals it to society.

The other meaning of "fabulous" that Kushner explains is what is opposed to "ridiculous." He argues: "what AIDS forced on the community was the absolute necessity ... of maintaining a queer identity and still being able to talk seriously about treatment protocols and oppression" (Brask 140). It is necessary for gay people facing AIDS to be more politically active; waiting for subversion of hegemony by deconstructive analyses and performances is not enough.

Although identity politics had revealed the situation of oppressed gay people and improved it, gay people found that it was not enough when they faced the reality that the government did not take any effective step for stemming the tide of the AIDS epidemic, and friends and lovers died one after another. Acquisition of limited rights as a minority did not mean actual liberation for them, as Louis claims:

> [W]hat I think is that what AIDS shows us is the limits of tolerance, that it's not enough to be tolerated, because when the shit hits the fan you find out how much tolerance is worth. Nothing. And underneath all the tolerance is intense, passionate hatred [*Angels* 1:90].

The hatred, connecting homosexuality with evilness, keeps the liberation impaired. To have society admit gay rights means only to have it endure the existence of gay people. The endurance has limits; homophobia is hidden just under the cover. As Louis says, AIDS exposed the limits of identity politics. Prior further says at the end of *Angels*: "We won't die secret deaths any more. The world only spins forward. We will be citizens. The time has come" (*Angels* 2:146). Gay people who died from AIDS had to die in the margins of society. The politics of gay people has to take the next step in order not to repeat the tragedy. Gay people need to become "full citizens," as Kushner stresses:

> To be tolerated is worth nothing. Because if you're merely tolerated and you get in trouble, you're going to die. Only by having the status of full citizen, guaranteed by law, are you protected [*Speaks Out* 24].

Then, how can it be possible to become a full citizen? In his *Homos*, Leo Bersani points out a defect of queer theory; deconstruction of identity would lead to the disappearance of gay community, which is a goal of homophobes. The notion of "mobile community," which works for avoiding a further exclusion of minorities that identity politics inevitably falls into, becomes a possible response:

> Rather than deny or apologize for such exclusions, we might more profitably acknowledge them and then try to see the unexpected ways in which an unavoidably limited "I" or "we" also speaks outside its particular perspective.... This mobility should create a kind of community, one that can never be settled, whose membership is always shifting [9].

Bersani admits that identity is exclusive and suggests a community that seeks to cooperate with what it could not accept once, without shutting its gate against it. Although gathering under some identity is inevitable for any community, members have to be aware of the possibility for exclusion and search for a connection with the outside. Identity should not be understood as a final or substantial categorization but as a label that is constructed in the hegemonic culture; mobile solidarity should be pursued without sticking to these labels. While identity politics shows its limits, *Angels* tries to suggest politics that accepts every person as its citizen without oppressing or ignoring his/her differences.

In the epilogue of *Angels*, four years after the rest of the two plays, characters discuss politics beside the Bethesda Fountain in Central Park. There are Prior, who has had AIDS for four years, Louis, a Jew and an ex-lover of Prior, Belize, a black man and former drag queen, and Hannah, a Mormon whose son is gay. They are different in religion, sex, race, and sexuality and this group shows a new model of community, which is not based on exclusive identity but on a mobile solidarity that Bersani suggests.

The positive sense of being alive is privileged in the idea of "fabulous." Prior repeats that he wants to live more. He declares to Angel, "I still want ... My blessing. Even sick. I want to be alive" (*Angels* 2:131). He recognizes the "habit": "the addiction to being alive" (*Angels* 2:133). By depicting AIDS and suffering characters, *Angels* overcomes the limits of queer theory. "Fabulous" covers a wider area than queer since it includes a practical point of view after the AIDS epidemic as well as what queer theory argues. Kushner explains what is "fabulous" for gay people. It can be a political strategy after queer theory and politics:

> I think that there is a way in which people take hatred and transform it into some kind of a style that is profoundly moving to me because it shows people's enormous capacity, or the enormous power of the imagination to transform suffering into something powerful and great. For Jews, it's called menschlikeit and for African Americans it used to be called soul and now I think for younger African Americans it's called badness, and for gay people it's fabulousness [*Thinking*, 75].

He believes that "fabulous" comes from anger and transforms itself into a power of change. Keeping truly queer, ever-changing identity, "fabulous" is able to adapt itself to the world that "spins forward (in Belize's words, 2:44, and then Prior's, *Angels* 2:146)" in the storm of progress. It is based on life and politics as well as theory. In the epilogue, characters talk about the connection of life and theory:

> BELIZE: The world is faster than the mind.
> LOUIS: That's what politics is. The world moving ahead. And only in politics does the miraculous occur.
> BELIZE: But that's a theory.

> HANNAH: You can't live in the world without an idea of the world, but it's living that makes the ideas. You can't wait for a theory, but you have to have a theory [*Angels* 2:144].

Emphasizing the importance of living, these lines suggest a necessity to discuss two issues in different levels, theory and practical politics, together. The pinklisting of Roy Cohn in *Angels* is done in order to forgive him by depicting his more sympathetic aspects which have been intentionally ignored by homophobes, and to reveal the hatred in the heterosexist discourse which invents a negative homosexual image. It enables this play to suggest a fabulous politics, a new politics by gay people after AIDS, which provides a field where one can argue theory and engage in practical activism at the same time.

Works Cited

Benjamin, Walter. "These on the Philosophy of History." *Illuminations*. Edited by Hannah Arendt. Translated by Harry Zohn. New York: Schocken Books, 1968.

Bersani, Leo. *Homos*. Cambridge, MA: Harvard University Press, 1995.

Brask, Per, editor. *Essays on Kushner's* Angels. New York: Blizzard Publishing, 1995.

Butler, Judith. *Gender Trouble: Feminism and the Subversion of Identity (Tenth Anniversary Version)*. (1990) New York: Routledge, 1999.

Cadden, Michael. "Strange Angel: The Pinklisting of Roy Cohn." *Approaching the Millennium: Essays on* Angels in America. Edited by Deborah R. Geis and Steven F. Kruger. Ann Arbor: University of Michigan Press, 1997.

Hoffman, Nicholas von. *Citizen Cohn: The Life and Times of Roy Cohn*. Garden City, NY: Doubleday, 1978.

Jones, Therese, editor. *Sharing the Delirium — The Second Generation of AIDS Plays and Performances*. Portsmouth, NH: Heinemann, 1994.

Kushner, Tony. *Angels in America, Part One: Millennium Approaches* (revised edition). New York: Theatre Communications Group, Inc., 1992.

_____. *Angels in America, Part Two: Perestroika* (revised edition). New York: Theatre Communications Group, Inc., 1994.

McNally, Terrence. *Love! Valour! Compassion!* New York: Plume, 1995.

Roberts, Sam. *The Brother — The Untold Story of the Rosenberg Case*. New York: Random House, 2001.

Sherrill, Robert. "King Cohn." *The Nation* 21 May 1998: 719–725.

Vorlicky, Robert, editor. *Tony Kushner in Conversation*. Ann Arbor: University of Michigan Press, 1998.

Zion, Sidney. *The Autobiography of Roy Cohn*. Secaucus, NJ: Lyle Stuart, Inc., 1998.

7

Two Illusions
Cultural Borrowings and Transcendence
FELICIA HARDISON LONDRÉ

On the title page of the published text of *The Illusion*, Tony Kushner has the grace to keep Pierre Corneille's name above the title as the author of the work while the smaller-font phrase "freely adapted by" serves to disclose his own part in it. The phrase scarcely hints at the creative contribution that lies like the bulk of an iceberg, ninth-tenths submerged beneath the surface text. Even a simple literal translation from French to English involves a daunting degree of cultural transference. An adaptation implies finding more radical equivalencies that can render a seventeenth-century sensibility comprehensible to contemporary audiences. A "free adaptation" might be understood as an admission that some equivalencies simply cannot be made and thus the adaptor must create anew.

In his Acknowledgments, Kushner notes: "This version of Corneille's *L'Illusion Comique* [sic] contains several scenes and many speeches which do not appear in the French original. There are virtually no lines directly translated from the French." Kushner also takes liberties with characters, motivations, thematic emphasis, dramatic structure, and the ending. Yet the source percolates recognizably through the new piece.

There is no doubt that Kushner has given Corneille a place on the American stage of our time that Corneille was not about to achieve on his own. Indeed, very few seventeenth-century neoclassical tragedies or comedies (other than a small selection from Molière) make it into contemporary professional production in the United States. The constraints of neoclassicism — breathtakingly effective in their own place, time, and language — are completely alien to our own sense of the theatrical. That disconnection is often implicit in reviews of *The Illusion*, a number of which are quoted in James Fisher's *The Theater of Tony Kushner*. For example:

the play's "cosmic touch springs from Mr. Kushner's fecund imagination, not Corneille's"; "Kushnerized Corneille is a much better deal than the genuine article" (quoted in Fisher 119–120). My examination of *The Illusion* and its source proceeds from two contentions. First, Corneille's original is better than you think it is. Second, Kushner's play must stand on its own merits without value judgments based upon comparison with the original. And here I find myself in a bind: in order to support both premises, I will have to violate the second. But first, an acknowledgment of my own bias: during my year on a Fulbright study grant at the Université de Caen in 1962–63, I designed the lighting for a production of *L'Illusion comique* at the Lycée Malherbe in Caen. We rehearsed one afternoon a week for the entire academic year, and I came to love the play (even as I developed a crush on the university student who played Matamore). In rereading Corneille's text for this article, I marveled afresh at his trailblazing edginess and often found myself chortling out loud at lively bits of dialogue. Thus I take issue with the sweeping generalization that "Kushnerized Corneille is a much better deal than the genuine article." A better deal for contemporary American audiences (and benighted drama critics): perhaps so. But a better deal as an aesthetic absolute? No. Not better, just different.

Pierre Corneille (1606–1684) was born, educated, and admitted to the bar in Rouen. Substantial colonies of both Spanish and English residents formed part of the city's social fabric. Corneille's ability to read Spanish is certain. His familiarity with Elizabethan drama, either by exposure to English traveling players or English texts available at the time, is a possibility. Corneille probably began his long association with the *théâtre du Marais* in Paris in 1629, the year of the company's founding by the actor Mondory, when it is probable that they performed Corneille's first play, the comedy *Mélite* (published in 1633). Because Corneille's place in theatre history is linked primarily to the 1637 production of *Le Cid* as the (flawed) standard-bearer of neoclassical form that swept away the messy tragicomedies popularized by Alexandre Hardy a generation earlier, he tends to be regarded simply as the progenitor of tragedies about second-tier Roman politicians and generals who rant in long monologues. That view fails to take into account Corneille's wonderful experiments in comic form in the years leading up to the 1636 production of what he called his "odd monster" *(un étrange monstre)*, *L'Illusion comique*.

In his retrospective analysis of his journeyman piece *Mélite*, Corneille notes that it abounds with irregularities because at that time he had no idea there were any rules of the drama. His purpose was to provoke laughter without resorting to the stock character types of the farce players who followed Italian models: clownish servants, parasites, braggart soldiers, and pedants (*Oeuvres* 28). Corneille's first published play, *Clitandre* (originally designated as a tragicomedy and later as a tragedy), was performed by Mondory's troupe in 1631. Corneille's retrospective commentary on it (1660) reveals that he clearly geared his writing to considerations of performance, complicating certain characterizations in order to attract the best actors (*Oeuvres* 55) and, in this play, making his monologues "too long and too frequent," because the audience of that time enjoyed them and the players wanted them as a means of showing off (56). In *La Veuve* (*The Widow*, 1631–32), Corneille consciously avoided overblown rhetorical effects in favor of dialogue that would resonate truthfully for each character and situation. He playfully indulged his antipathy for the aside by giving two characters pretended asides, each aware that the other would hear it (IV.vi). G.J. Mallinson sees *La Veuve* as a refinement of "the juxtaposition of role and reality, detachment and commitment to a degree which has no parallel in the works of his contemporaries," adding that Corneille uses language to convey humor rooted in the very notion of theatrical performance and in "the actor who is constantly visible beneath the persona he embodies" (72).

La Galerie du Palais (1632) continued Corneille's success in expanding the comic forms or winking at the comic conventions he had inherited. Not only do we see a pair of young lovers removed from French comedy's generic quasi-pastoral setting and actually interacting with merchants in their boutiques, but young love itself is deconstructed, shown to be full of hesitations, with latitude for the ego. Referring to Célidée's monologue (II.vii), Mallinson finds that "Corneille suggests not now the temporary replacement of passion with indifference, but the subtle coexistence of the two" (Mallinson 85). This sounds very much like Tony Kushner's own sense of the dramatic value of contradictions, "the idea that a thing can be both one thing and its opposite, that two opposites can exist simultaneously and not cancel each other out. Or they can transform one another through conflict into something new" (Lahr 47). Indeed, Mallinson's description of *La Galerie du Palais* as "the careful investigation of the heart in search of itself" (105) could well apply to Kushner's *The Illusion*.

The audacity of Corneille's *La Suivante* (*The Maidservant*, 1633) is evident in the title: making a servant girl the protagonist. That character's machinations adumbrate those of the servant Lyse in *L'Illusion comique*. Again, in *La Place Royale* (1634), the leading character, Alidor, is both anti-heroic and comic, even sharing some traits with Matamore of *L'Illusion comique*. *L'Illusion comique* (1636) was Corneille's last comedy before *Le Cid*, the success of which propelled him into writing mostly tragedies for the rest of his career. The notable exception was *Le Menteur* (*The Liar*, 1644), his "free adaptation" of Juan Ruíz de Alarcón's *La Verdad sospechosa* (*Truth under Suspicion*). While the foregoing survey of Corneille's early plays has emphasized innovative aspects of his work, influences must also be acknowledged. In preparation for *Le Cid*, Corneille was already embarked on intensive reading of Spanish literature as he worked on *L'Illusion comique*. One stimulus to Corneille's thinking about illusion and reality, not to mention depictions of capricious manifestations of love under the sway of pride, could have been Pedro Calderón de la Barca's *La Vida es sueño* (*Life Is a Dream*), produced in Madrid in 1635 and published in 1636. Lope de Rueda's *Armelina* has been cited for the similarity of its premise and that of *L'Illusion comique*: a father searching for his son with the help of a sage. In Corneille's treatment, the son Clindor's adventures—some recounted by the magician Alcandre and some re-enacted for the father, Pridamant— evoke Spanish picaresque novels like the ones cited by Alcandre (I.iii):

> Enfin, jamais Buscon, Lazarille de Tormes,
> Sayavèdre, et Gusman, ne prirent tant de formes [*Oeuvres*196].

That is: not even a pícaro like Buscón (created by Quevedo in 1626), nor Lazarillo de Tormes (the earliest of the genre, 1544), nor Sayavedra (a character along with the title figure in *Guzmán de Alfarache*, 1599) appeared in so many guises.

The possibility that Corneille also read English may account for similarities between Alcandre's denunciation of false conjurors and the first speech by the Conjuror in John Webster's *The White Devil* (1611). Alcandre says:

> Les novices de l'art, avec tous leur encens
> Et leurs mots inconnus, qu'ils feignent tout-puissants,
> Leurs herbes, leurs parfums, et leurs cérémonies,
> Apportent au métier des longeurs infinies,
> Qui ne sont, après tout, qu'un mystère pipeur
> Pour se faire valoir et pour vous faire peur [*Oeuvres* 196].

Webster's Conjuror expresses similar irritation on the subject of charlatans:

> ..... some there are,
> Which by sophistic tricks, aspire that name
> Which I would gladly lose, of nigromancer;
> As some that use to juggle upon cards,
> Seeming to conjure when indeed they cheat;

....
Fellows indeed that only live by stealth,
Since they do merely lie about stol'n goods—
They'd make men think the devil were fast and loose,
With speaking fustian Latin [Webster 42–43].

Corneille's Matamore has direct origins, of course, in Matamoros and other *capitanos* of the Italian *commedia dell' arte*, and yet he often uncannily echoes Don Armado of Shakespeare's *Love's Labour's Lost*, which also employs the device of the play within the play. Finally, Shakespeare's *The Tempest* offers obvious analogies: the magicians who conjure illusions, the father-daughter relationships, and *The Tempest's* famished courtiers who perhaps prefigure Matamore's emerging weak with hunger after four days in hiding in *L'Illusion comique*.

Critics seeking literary influences or analogies for Tony Kushner's *The Illusion* readily turn to Luigi Pirandello's plays, with their uneasy negotiations between reality and illusion (Fisher 113). Given Kushner's interest in Russian literature, one might also conjecture that Aleksandr Blok's *Balaganchik* (*The Puppet Show*, 1906) impacted his thinking on theatricality and representations of love. In the little painted stage within the stage of Blok's play, three couples in love appear in quick succession to suggest how love might be portrayed via different literary approaches: idealized, melodramatic, and symbolist. It is worth noting here that in *The Illusion* Kushner adds an episode to the romantic entanglements of Pridamant's son to bring the illusions presented by Alcandre to three. Only two romantic episodes are presented by Alcandre in Corneille's play, the first spanning Acts 2, 3, and 4, the second compressed into Act 5. The names Kushner chose for three of the characters in his added episode — Calisto, Melibea, and Elicia — are taken from Fernando de Rojas's magisterial novel in dialogue, *Celestina* (1499), as is the opening of their story. Kushner altered the fourth character's name from Pleberio to Pleribo, which is appropriate since he also alters that figure's dramatic function. *Celestina* begins with Calisto entering a garden in pursuit of a falcon, finding Melibea there, and falling in love with her, and this is how Kushner introduces the first illusion in his play. It is a subtle tribute to a work with which Corneille must have been familiar.

Corneille's retrospective commentary (1660) on *L'Illusion comique* suggests that he considered his play a throwaway caprice that surprised him with its runaway success and quarter-century staying power. He called Act 1 a prologue, the next three acts a self-contained play showing a serious action played in comic style, and Act 5 a tragedy depicted with deliberate brevity to avoid the grandeur that Aristotle demands of tragedy. The seriousness of Clindor's apparent death in Act 5 is pushed to the extreme in order to heighten Pridamant's subsequent joy by contrast. Kushner's two-act structure dispenses with the prologue, substituting the Calisto and Melibea story as a farrago of clichés about romantic comedy. The more psychologically grounded story of Clindor and Isabelle begins in Act 1 and continues in Act 2, which segues into the weeping tragedy (think of weepers like *A Woman Killed with Kindness* or *The Tragedy of Jane Shore*) of Theogenes and Hippolyta.

Corneille ends *L'Illusion comique* quickly and joyfully, savoring the humor and irony of the revelation that Clindor is an actor and that the adventures we have seen are not life, but art. In contrast, Kushner represses the joy that Pridamant should feel upon learning that his son is alive; instead the father (whose characterization proceeds from Kushner's identification of him as a lawyer) reverts to his original embarrassment verging on antipathy toward spells and make-believe. And then Kushner adds what might be called an "epilogue" of ambiguity, a mere half-page that unites the poetic lyricism of the moon and stars with the pathos of Matamore gone completely mad and the Sisyphean cycles of victimization and hope endured by the Amanuensis.

The Amanuensis is Kushner's invention. He replaces Corneille's Dorante whose sole function in *L'Illusion comique* is to serve as confidant to Pridamant in a scene of exposition; after introducing Pridamant to Alcandre, Dorante disappears from the play. Kushner cuts to the chase, allowing Alcandre to appear right away after Pridamant's entrance and hear the exposition for himself. As Alcandre's servant, the Amanuensis appears at intervals throughout the action, sometimes deaf and dumb, but able to hear and speak when the action warrants it. Although Kushner's text offers no indication about the character's physical appearance, his outburst between the second and third love-story illusions (Kushner 67) hints at qualities resembling Caliban in *The Tempest*.

A great appeal of both *L'Illusion comique* and *The Illusion* is their authors' passion for the theatre, awareness of the power of the imagination, and commitment to the necessity of art in human life. Corneille stays close to those underlying concepts, though he does not hold back from treating them with irony, burlesque, and mockery. It should be noted that his title is correctly translated as *The Theatrical Illusion*, for illusion is not confined to comedy, and the standard word for "actor" in seventeenth-century French was *comédien*. Corneille offers numerous delightful turns of phrase with both literal and theatrical meaning. For example, when Dorante is warning Pridamant of Alcandre's powers, he says:

> Que de ses mots savants les forces inconnues
> Transportent les rochers, font descendre les nues ... [*Oeuvres*195].

We can visualize the stage machinery in these and surrounding couplets that ostensibly extol wizardry. Alcandre speaks and huge boulders are set in motion, and the clouds (cloud borders) descend. Kushner's most striking moment of homage to theatre comes near the end when Alcandre exults in having elicited — using his "gumstuck machinery" and "rickety carpentry" — a tear from Pridamant's eye (Kushner 79).

In Corneille's prologue, Alcandre gives a preview of the wonders to come when he waves his wand to open a curtain behind which are displayed sumptuous costumes. He says:

> Jugez de votre fils par un tel equipage [*Oeuvres* 196].

Pridament is suitably impressed at this admonition to judge his son's success by the quality of those garments. In an era when most people wore the same clothing day after day for as long as it lasted, the show of costumes was highly theatrical, and perhaps it even softened the skeptic's scorn for mere players. Kushner retains the device with slight alteration: "Figures appear, dressed beautifully, frozen in tableau. Calisto stands at center." And Kushner finds a clever way to punch up the economic significance of the vision for a modern audience; he gives Pridamant some lines to speak *before* the visual effect, which then trumps his comment: "I want to make him sick with guilt. I want to make him heir to my fortune. He must be very poor..." (Kushner 6).

Both Corneille and Kushner allow — even hint at — the possibility that the Clindor and Isabelle episode is one that really happened, for the backstory in each is compatible with the frame story told by Pridamant, even to the son's name. And yet even that assumption is undercut when we hear in Theogenes and Hippolyta's episode hints of a backstory that is compatible with the action we saw in Clindor and Isabelle's story. Kushner further clouds the issue when Pridamant becomes confused about his son's name. Both Corneille and Kushner lard their plays with clues to the theatrical conceit, and yet it is entirely possible that the spectator could watch either play and be taken as much by surprise at the denouement as is Pridamant. Corneille notes in his retrospective commentary that the device is one that works once and seems marvelous, but does not bear repeating.

While Corneille keeps his focus on the theatre and its permutations, Kushner loads his version with greater emphasis on generational conflict as well as ambiguous, nuanced, often contradictory manifestations of love. As James Fisher describes it: "Kushner will have none of the traditional theatrical notion of love as a reward, culmination, or happy ending. Rather, he presents love as a process that is not easy — at various points the characters compare it to a sarcophagus or a catastrophe" (Fisher 119). Kushner also expands the range of moods in the play, even into repellent cruelty, as when Alcandre coldly describes the surgery he performed on the Amanuensis to render him deaf and dumb (Kushner 5). But is this "better" than Corneille? No, although it may well be more suited to American audiences.

We have seen that a great deal of cultural borrowing went into Corneille's *L'Illusion comique*, and it takes nothing away from his sources to say that Corneille's play is brilliant. It still gets produced in France nearly four centuries after it was written, and thus it has transcended its sources. Kushner's *The Illusion* is still going strong after more than a decade, and Kushner is right to give Corneille the credit he is due. Yet Kushner too has in some ways transcended his source. *The Illusion* stands on its own merits as a play that speaks to a culture very different from the one that embraced the original. If, as a by-product of its success, *The Illusion* inspires a few to renew acquaintance with our cultural ancestors, that too is a valuable transcendence of limitations.

Works Cited

Blok, Aleksandr Aleksandrovich. *The Puppet Show. Twentieth-Century Russian Plays: An Anthology*. Edited, translated and introduced by F.D. Reeve. New York: W.W. Norton and Co., 1963: 163–175.

Corneille, Pierre. *The Illusion*, freely adapted by Tony Kushner. New York: Theatre Communications Group, Inc., 1994.

_____. *Oeuvres completes*. Preface by Raymond Lebègue; presentation and notes by André Stegman. Paris: Editions du Seuil, 1963. Quotations translated into English by Felicia Londré.

Fisher, James. *The Theater of Tony Kushner: Living Past Hope*. New York: Routledge, 2002.

Lahr, John. "Profiles: After *Angels*: Tony Kushner's Promethean Itch," *The New Yorker* 3 January 2005: 42–52.

Mallinson, G. J. *The Comedies of Corneille: Experiments in the Comic*. Manchester: Manchester University Press, 1984.

Rojas, Fernando de. *Celestina*. Translated by Mack Hendricks Singleton. Madison: University of Wisconsin Press, 1962.

Webster, John. *The Selected Plays of John Webster*. Edited by Jonathan Dollimore and Alan Sinfield. Cambridge: Cambridge University Press, 1983.

8

Reading Corneille with Brecht

The Comedy of Illusion and the Illusions of Citizenship

STEFKA MIHAYLOVA

"the audience are so used to it that it does not worry them" —
Pierre Corneille

Theatre artists who approached Pierre Corneille's *L'Illusion comique* (1636) in the last two decades of the twentieth century speak about their experience with perplexed amusement. Italian director Giorgio Strehler, who staged the play at the Théâtre de l'Europe in 1984, found himself bedridden by *proteus mirabilis*: two words that, were they not the name of a rare virus, would be an apt description of the play's protagonist — the histrionic and deceitful Clindor. The belated opening coincided with the 300th anniversary of Corneille's death (Kerr 48). Tony Kushner attributes the numerous technical problems throughout the 1989 Hartford Stage production of his adaptation *The Illusion* to "professional jealousy from beyond the grave" (Gold H5).

L'Illusion comique tells the story of Pridamant — a repentant father looking for his son Clindor alienated by paternal severity. The play opens in front of the cave of the magician Alcandre who conjures spirits to show Pridamant a play-within-the-play about Clindor's adventures. Pridamant's displeasure grows as he learns that throughout the long years of his absence Clindor has pursued many shady occupations ending up as an actor in Paris: another profession of dubious decency in seventeenth-century France. At the end of the vision Clindor pays for his deceitfulness with his life.

The curtain falls over the magical theatre-cave and then is raised again

135

to reveal the participants in the death scene exchanging money. The grief-stricken Pridamant exclaims, "What, are they counting money in death's realm?" (Corneille 117). Alcandre then reveals that Pridamant has not seen his son's death but a theatrical illusion. The characters in the play-within-the-play are traveling actors. Clindor, too, has become an actor and is currently playing in Paris. Pridamant's relief is mixed with disappointment. In seventeenth-century France, acting is a profession of dubious decency. In response, Alcandre pronounces his famous apology for theatre. He points out to Pridamant, who stands for the play's intended audience, that theatre has become a respected art, popular with the court for its civilizing influence. In the end, *L'Illusion comique* turns out not to be about a father in search of his son, but about theatre's relation to reality (Dort 10). Theatrical magic and illusion, the play argues, should be used to moral ends.

The insistent metatheatricality of the play and the meditation on theatre's social significance has intrigued Strehler and Kushner who share a fascination with theatrical magic and a commitment to socially-responsible theatre. Kushner's 1987 adaptation *The Illusion* transforms Corneille's story into a fable about consumerism: a social ill in which he implicates the theatrical institution. Strehler, on the other hand, was stirred by Corneille's "poetic and staggering" use of theatre to demonstrate the relativity of the protagonists' relations and feelings in the drama of humanity (Strehler 3). In Strehler's words, it was not he who chose Corneille; Corneille chose him (Kerr 46). Though this romantic formulation does not strike as immediately political, the special status of Strehler's production provokes questions about the political implications of his choice and reading of Corneille's text.

In 1983 the French Minister of Culture Jack Lang, with the support of President Mitterrand, founded the Théâtre de l'Europe at the site of the Odéon. This multilingual theatre was conceived by Strehler himself as a forum where European plays would be presented or co-produced "to help assert the cultural identity of Europeans as a multi-faceted, complex and contradictory identity, which can, despite this, be recognized as the red thread weaving our history" (*The Odeon and Europe*; The official decree of June 1 1990 modified the mission. The theatre now aims "to foster joint work by stage directors, actors, writers and other European practitioners of the dramatic arts for the purpose of presenting new, original works and bringing life to the artistic heritage of Europe"). Strehler's *L'Illusion comique* was the theatre's inaugural production. The symbolic charge brought by this context was reinforced by Strehler's own artistic and political position. Brecht's loudly-proclaimed applause for Strehler's 1956 staging of the *Threepenny Opera* helped establish him as an exemplary Brechtian director (Böhme-Kuby 33), one who strove to put into practice his political ideals not only trough theatre but also as a socialist member of the European parliament and the Italian senate (Delgado and Heritage 266). It is thus not surprising that critics have sought evidence for Brechtian influence in Strehler's production (Kerr 66). Kushner's adaptation, on the other hand, has received little scholarly response and the political implications of his take on Corneille's text have not been given much attention in spite of the adaptation's numerous productions (Fisher 218–219; in his monograph on Tony Kushner, James Fisher names 33 productions as of 2001) and Kushner's widely acknowledged indebtedness to Brecht. Evaluating the implications of their approaches as well as Strehler's particular application of Brechtian dramaturgy in *L'Illusion comique* is necessary because Brecht's name is typically used as a guarantee of socially-progressive art and the Brechtian urge for critical thinking is at the core of theories of political theatre.

Drawing a line between his work and consumerist productions, Strehler defines his "social theatre with human face" as theatre which enables the construction of a rational world and a critically thinking community (Kerr 45). Likewise, to theatre scholar Baz Kershaw theatre is politically-progressive if it enables "the practice of citizenship through common critique" (Kershaw 32). What, then, does it mean to be a citizen of united Europe or of consumerist America? How do Kushner's and Strehler's readings of Corneille construct citizenship and to what effect? Does their use of Brecht counter or confirm Kershaw's harsh judgment that no critical theatre can be produced on the mainstream stages in traditional theatre buildings: disciplinary machines which suppress "disruptive agencies, oppositional voices and radical voices for progressive social change"? (Kershaw 32, 54). Kershaw's approach suggests that the political bent of a performance may be made explicit by looking at ideological controversies raised in the process of production (Kershaw 33, 35) and by analyzing the positions of spectating that it opens through architectural, textual and other conventions (Kershaw 38, 50–51). Corneille himself wondered at spectators' willingness to submit to convention and suspend their disbelief, regardless of what meets their eye.

The setting for neo-classic plays was often "a street with one or more houses and a central playing area." (Muir 16) Almost all acting took place in the central area: a convention which helped solve the neo-classic requirement for unity of place. Changing the setting—from one private home to another or to the street—would be against the rule. Therefore, characters would have intimate conversations in the street. To Corneille's amazement, this blatant violation of verisimilitude did not disturb spectators: "the audience are so used to it," he observed, "that it does not worry them" (quoted in Muir 16). Playing center stage was also necessitated by the narrow visual perspective and limited stage technology in seventeenth-century theatre houses in Paris (Golder 190; John Golder admits the possibility that, in an attempt to achieve greater verisimilitude, some private scenes might have taken place in the compartments around the central area as well. Compartments could represent a house or a prison, for instance. "Placed inconveniently in blind positions around the stage," the compartments, would have obstructed vision). The Théâtre de Marais, where *L'Illusion comique* was first produced, was built on the site of an indoor tennis court. The distribution of boxes and pit within this rectangular structure limited considerably spectator's view. In spite of this, the Théâtre de Marais set the architectural model for all major theatres in Paris at that time, even for theatres not built on the site of tennis courts: a paradox that reinforces Corneille's observation about spectators' uncritical acceptance of convention (O'Regan 125; Michael O'Regan writes, "Only two theatres were purpose-built in Paris between 1630 and 1680: the one inaugurated in 1641 at the Palais-Cardinal, later renamed the Palais Royal, and the "Salle des Machines" in the Tuileri, opened in 1662. Both were built as private Court Theatres, yet both took the rectangular shape of the tennis court of the Old Hotel de Bourgogne, rather than more convenient shapes which had already evolved in Italy and England").

Corneille's own flexible approach to neo-classical conventions in *L'Illusion comique* has intrigued artists and scholars alike. It has been widely accepted, for instance, that Corneille strove to establish comedy as a high-art genre. Hence, it is unusual that he created a protagonist whose shaky moral qualities never meet the criteria of *bienséance*: the norms of propriety that seventeenth-century French theatre had to display so that it could qualify as art of value. It is even more unusual, that he made the secondary characters bearers of morality.

Courting Isabelle for her riches and noble rank and her servant Lyse for her looks, Clindor finds himself at an impasse, when, driven by jealousy, Lyse reveals to Isabelle's lawful fiancé Adraste that the lowly valet Clindor is his rival. In the ensuing duel, Clindor kills Adraste and is sentenced to death. Repentant, Lyse seduces the jailor and promises to marry him in order to save Clindor. Until then, Lyse has been a one-dimensional comic stock character: a type frequently encountered in commedia dell' arte or in Elizabethan drama. By contrast, her decision to save Clindor confers unusual depth on her:

> LYSE: So, Clindor, I alone decide your fate;
> the chains I put on you I now remove
> and can decide whether you live or die.

Their vengeance on you has gone too far.
I only wished to end your pleasuring,
and your too bitter fate has changed my mind
...
I hope, too, Clindor, that in gratitude,
your court of me will now be innocent,
and since a husband will possess me now
his presence should defeat your mad desires [Kushner 97].

It is through the servant's moral reversal that the play meets the criteria for *biénséance*. Clindor's status of a heroic protagonist is thus challenged not only by the contrast between Lyse's attainment of morality and his irreparable moral deficiencies, but also because his escape has been enabled by a woman, who is, moreover, his social inferior (Marpeau 35). Lyse's monologue is also significant in terms of its narrative status. Because, according to Corneille's own rules for high comedy, servants should not be allowed heroic acts, in *L'Illusion comique* and in other works, he introduces hors-scène narration. Inferior characters are not shown accomplishing heroic deeds but are allowed to narrate them and to comment on the actions of their superiors. The hors-scène does not offer objective commentary but hypotheses subject to the characters' peculiarities. Their truth value is thus undecidable (Marpeau 34–36). Nevertheless, the contradiction that results from the subversive juxtaposition between the hors-scène and the principal actions is worth exploring if the play is approached through a Brechtian lens.

The violation of character convention is coupled with a radical transgression of genre purity. Referring to the unusual combination of tragic, comic, and pastoral elements and to the use of tragic meter within comic acts, Corneille calls this early work a "monster" and "caprice." Culminating with the final coup de théàtre, the persistent exposure of theatrical rules and the perceived social significance of this exposure has resulted in comparisons between Corneille and Brecht. "*L'Illusion* is in some way Corneille's *Threepenny Opera*," writes Brechtian scholar Bernard Dort. Even if Corneille did not manage to critique spectators' desires to the degree to which Brecht did, Dort continues, the sustained incertitude in *L'Illusion* mars its happy resolution (Dort 14–15). Gay McAuley, on the other hand, sees as Brechtian not so much Corneille's technique as "the measure of social and moral utility" that Corneille claims for theatre at the end of the play (McAuley 73). However, while in Brecht's work the concept of socially-committed theatre and the method for such a theatre are inextricably related, in *L'Illusion comique*, the relation between theatrical method and social utility does not result in Brechtian critique. Also, Corneille's awareness and transgressions of convention turn out to be less scandalous on second reading.

When the coup de théâtre shows that the story of love intrigues that Pridamant has just witnessed is but an illusion, the immoral protagonist Clindor, too, turns out to be nothing but a role. And just in case this would not be enough to meet the criteria of *biénséance*, by the time of the coup de théâtre Clindor's character has been killed by the virtuous Prince Florilame. The risky mixture of genres is ultimately tamed as well. By means of the external frame of Pridamant's search for his son, which confines the genre impurity to the play-within-the-play, the neo-classic requirements of unity snap back into place (Peureux 26). The social function accorded to theatre reinforces rather than challenge the political status quo: "And those whose profound wisdom we behold/ ruling the world in peace by careful art/ find in a spectacle such sweet delight/ they can lay down their burden for a while," Alcandre says (Kushner 118). Theatre offers itself as an entertainment in the monarch's service. Hence, with *L'Illusion comique*, Corneille, who also served in the royal administration, targeted a very specific elite patron. Even the potentially subversive tension between principal action and hors-scène narration is reduced by the play's final resolution. This tension, too, remains confined to the illusionary play-within-the-play. While Brechtian dramaturgy requires that the audience should be divided over contradictions (Willett 60), *L'Illusion comique* is invested in smoothing them out. Not incidentally, Bernard Dort calls Corneille "a poet of legitimacy, a subject convinced in the virtues of absolutism" (Dort 23).

In his 1984 production at the Théâtre de l'Europe, Giorgio Strehler emphasized the metatheatricality of Corneille's text by making several choices that bear affinity to Brechtian techniques. Pridamant and his friend Dorante entered from behind the audience and crossed the entire auditorium before they climbed on stage, thus drawing attention to the conventional separation between spectators and performers in the realist tradition. The wise magician Alcandre and the braggart soldier Matamore (a comic stock character) were both played by Gérard Desarthe who would change his costumes in front of the audience without interrupting his conversation with Pridamant. Nada Strancar was double-cast as the servant Lyse and the Princess Rosine. The substitutions invited a reflection on the arbitrariness of wisdom and folly and of social hierarchy (Kerr 51–52). The scene preceding the coup de théâtre, when following Clindor's death the characters of the play-within-the-play gathered to count their money, was gestically treated as well. It was staged as a silent pantomime interrupted only by the tinkling of a bell, as the troupe's leader gathered the actors to distribute the profit, and the tinkling of coins. Strehler used the sound of the bell to evoke the sacred mystery of theatre, while the sound of coins was to suggest theatre's material aspect. Pridamant, who, distressed to see his son die, had looked away from the stage, was to turn to the sound of the coins rather than the bell because, in Strehler's interpretation, it was the possibility to make money through theatre that changed his attitude to Clindor's profession (Trousdell 70–71). It is only the end of the production, much like Corneille's text, that makes it hard to sustain a Brechtian reading.

Strehler, who believed that the intentions of a playwright are recoverable regardless of historical and/or cultural distance, upheld the "fundamental principle" that a director should remain true to the playwright's original meaning. "When I stage Corneille I try to be the best of all Cornellians," he said in an interview (Kerr 46). In the case of the 1984 production of *L'Illusion comique*, being more Cornellian than Corneille translated into adding a sequel to Corneille's text. While Corneille closes on the suggestion that Pridamant is going to Paris to find his son, Strehler's production actually staged their happy reunion. This stated belief in the recoverability of authorial intention alerts that Strehler's approach to Brecht differs from the historicist awareness central to Brechtian theory. Nevertheless, drawing on her conversations with Strehler, Cynthia Kerr calls his resolution Brechtian because, in her view, it calls for solidarity and "illustrates the union between the two dramatic spaces, the stage and the auditorium, [showing] that theatre and reality are the same thing." The privileged spectator Pridamant is now summoned to participate. Like Pridamant, Strehler's spectators were supposed to leave the theatre "better prepared to face the adversities and dilemmas of existence" (Kerr 61). Is this final urge for solidarity, based on supposedly universal values such as the love between father and son, politically progressive? Or does it preclude social critique under the guise of solidarity?

According to Janelle Reinelt, a play can be considered epic "*if* some sense of what might be done next is suggested but not spelled out" and "*if* it does not let spectators off he hook by allowing too much psychological investment in particular characters or too much good feeling of resolution at the end" (Reinelt 36). Strehler's production seems to me both to spell out what is to be done next and to allow "too much good feeling of resolution." Taking into account Brecht's approval of Strehler's work, it is safe to assume that Strehler understood the concept of epic theatre. Did he then purposefully choose to deviate from Brechtian dramaturgy in this production and, if so, to what ends?

In his essay on the production, Strehler defines as its major theme the controversial human identity. "Everything else," he writes, "the historical context, the legitimation of theatre, the defense of theatre, of its moral nature are for us secondary themes and points. They are, perhaps, themselves misleading traps set for the most naïve." In the same vein, he explains his choice of double-casting the magician and the braggart not as intended to provoke critical viewing but "so that *L'Illusion* should be even more illusory" (Strehler 3). This attitude to historical context as a trap for the naïve sounds dangerously conservative, but, paradoxically, in view of Europe's history of nationalist hostility and of using history as a bag of facts justifying confrontation rather than as a way to understand and overcome it, the old humanist appeal to forget and embrace each other sounds more tempting than ever at the time of Europe's unification. Yet, no matter how alluring a humanist approach may seem, Strehler's solution to ignore history is symptomatic and unsatisfactory both artistically and socially.

Such a solution repeats the unhappy French liaison between Brecht and Corneille which started in 1951 when Jean Vilar staged the first French production of *Mother Courage*. Countering attacks that he was staging a communist work, Vilar presented Brecht as a classic author concerned with the universal human situation; not with politics in a narrow sense. Accordingly, Vilar staged *Mother Courage* along with Corneille's *Le Cid*. He would offer the same package to the audience for four subsequent years (Ubersfeld 199–210). While Vilar's approach to Brecht is not the only French approach and did not remain uncontested, his "undialectized" Brecht received considerable currency (Ubersfeld 203). In Italy as well, Susanna Böhme-Kuby writes, "the broad appeal of Brecht's theatre ... was accompanied by a two-fold degradation and reduction of Brecht's intentions. The inclination to depoliticize, on the one hand, and to ideologize, on the other" (Böhme-Kuby 230). Strehler's life project for "a theatre of humanity" synthesizing Stanislavski's and Brecht's methods (Hirst 28, 102), too, threatens to reduce epic theatre to a set of formal techniques in his production of *L'Illusion*. It also threatens to reduce Strehler's vision of a Europe "of diversity and particularity" (Delgado and Heritage 268) to a Eurocentric reality. In view of the increasing racial violence in Europe since the 1980s, the resurfacing of racist discourse particularly after the attacks of September 11, and the growing popularity of some neofascist parties (Williams 127–128) it is not too much to ask whether, in 1984 and since, the vision of solidarity derived from this western reading of a seventeenth-century French classic, would have conferred political agency upon the non-white and/or non–European-born residents of Europe. Is there room for their particularity in the idyllic reunion of father and son?

Or is this metaphor for solidarity beyond the pains of history another haunting illusion?

Though Brecht's reception in America has gone through the same pitfalls that it went through in Italy and France, reviews of Tony Kushner's 1987 adaptation *The Illusion* give evidence that he did not succumb to the un-epic temptation of allowing spectators "too much good feeling of resolution at the end." Director Diana Fajrajsl feared that, if sustained, the metatheatricality of Kushner's text makes the play too cynical (Lawson E6). Theatre critic Jeffrey Wainwright notes appreciatively that the decision not to show the reunion between father and son in Matthew Lloyd's production results in "the comedy's most unsettling absence and one which points to its deeper questioning of the existence of reality" (Wainwright 12). Wainwright's colleague Naomi Doudai, on the other hand, sets out to seek "eternal truth" in the Kahn theatre production and ends her review by complaining about the unrealist set design (Doudai 24). Even just these three of the many reviews on productions of *The Illusion* demonstrate that Kushner's adaptation suggests divided rather than unified audience response: a prerequisite for critical viewing.

Noting the decreasing possibilities for critical viewing in mainstream theatre which, under the guise of choice and pluralism, "masks a deadening cultural conformity," Baz Kershaw suggests that the focus of analyses of the politics of theatre should shift from the commodification of production to the commodification of consumption, a method developed by feminist cultural critics (Kershaw 32, 38). In *The Illusion*, Kushner does just that. The major strategy he employs to engage in a critique of the commodification of viewing is shifting the emphasis of Corneille's text from the magical vision itself to its spectator Pridamant.

In striking contrast to Corneille's repentant father full of respect for the wise magician, Kushner's Pridamant is a personification of the modern consumer who knows how to get the value for his money. "I'm looking for the sorcerer Alcandre they told me lives in this dismal pit," Pridamant says. Alcandre's reply follows suit: "What do you want? ... my time is precious to me; your business, or go away" (Kushner 79). If Pridamant's disrespectfulness is not enough to construct him as unreliable, his explanation why his son left home strips him of any credibility: "I destroyed my son, he acknowledges, "He seemed uncontrollable, wild, dangerous to me ... I loved him so much I wanted to strangle him. I wanted to snap his spine sometimes in a ferocious embrace" (80). The allusion that Pridamant might have been homoerotically attracted to his own son is at least as scandalous as any of Corneille's challenges to *bienséance*. Propriety, however, matters little to Kushner's characters. Instead, they are on the lookout for coherent stories that fit their requirements and for which they are prepared to pay. Act One of Kushner's *The Illusion*: Alcandre has just shown Pridamant the first glimpse of his son. Overwhelmed with excitement, Pridamant complains that what Alcandre is showing him is bad for his heart. "What did you expect?" Alcandre asks. "Information. Memory restored," Pridamant says, "But safely, painlessly. Crystal balls and tea leaves, not this ... resurrection" (80–81). Pridamant's attitude is mirrored by that of Elicia: one of the servant's impersonations in the play-within-a-play. In Corneille's text, when Isabelle first appears, she has already fallen in love with Clindor. Kushner's Melibea, who only changes to Isabelle in the second act, is initially hostile to Calisto (later Clindor). Elicia who slyly manipulates Melibea into looking favorably on Calisto is unsure of her motives for doing so.

> ELICIA: So I'm helping out and why should I care?
> I find him attractive; and intrigue is fun,
> And a *surrogate* love affair's better than none [85; my emphasis].

In striking contrast to Corneille, the interactions among Kushner's characters focus around the supply and demand of safe surrogate experience, not truth; of meanings bought rather than painfully fought for. The theatrical apparatus is mercilessly implicated in the exchange.

Throughout the magical vision, its characters change their names three times. At first this inconsistency confuses Pridamant. "Concentrate on the general outline, leave the details to me," the magician says. Kushner thus subtly draws attention to the suspension of disbelief central to the passive viewing and vicarious experience, which Brecht critiques. By the time characters have changed names for the third time, Pridamant has become used to the inconsistency: "I see they've changed the names again. This time I won't let it upset me" (120). In search for coherence at any price, Pridamant willingly concedes to the normalizing effect of repetition, and becomes a disciplined spectator. Alcandre, on the other hand, modifies the visions several times to meet his customer's preferences.

The story of theatrical supply and demand takes an explicit Marxist turn when through the addition of the amanuensis, a character not present in Corneille's text, Kushner emphasizes the labor of theatrical representation. An intermediary figure, the amanuensis moves back and forth between Pridamant and the "specters" performing the magic vision under Alcandre's command. Deaf and dumb for most of the time, the amanuensis is unable to comment on either the visions, in which he himself occasionally participates, or on the exchanges between Pridamant and Alcandre.

When he finally speaks, the ramifications are serious. Alcandre, he reveals to Pridamant, has never crossed over to the world of specters himself (119). Why, then, does Alcandre run this business of illusions?

The magical vision ends and all that is left is a stage covered with corpses, including that of Pridamant's son. The devastated father becomes aware that he has been crying. Alcandre plucks a tear from Pridamant's eye and pronounces a lofty apology for vicarious feeling:

> ALCANDRE: This, this jewel. This precious leaded crystal pendant ... for this
> infinitesimal seepage, for this atom of remorse, for this little
> globe ... in which loss, love, sorrow, consequence dwell in
> miniature ... [I] erect the rickety carpentry of mine illusions.
> For this, to see your granite heart softened just a bit [127].

Alcandre, too, is on a quest for painless satisfaction. He sells illusions for illusions. Like Pridamant, he is a consumer of the amanuensis' effort.

The exposure of theatrical representation as a relation among unequally-positioned social actors accomplishes not just a successful materialist reading of *L'Illusion comique*: the kind of reading that Brecht developed throughout his life. By choosing to focus on spectating rather than any other aspect of the theatrical relationship, *The Illusion* establishes a unique connection between Corneille's text and Brecht's writings on theatre. Brechtian concepts are not simply informing Kushner's reading; a particular Brechtian text, intentionally or not, is turned into a performance script:

> Bursting out of the underground station, eager to become as wax in the
> magicians' hands, grown-up men, their resolution proved in the struggle
> for existence, rush to the box office. They hand in their hat at the cloak-
> room, and with it they hand their normal behavior: the attitudes of every-
> day life [Willett 39].

In both Brecht and Kushner, the center of histrionic ambiguity shifts: from the actor to the spectator.

The structural modifications to the primary text that Kushner undertakes to highlight its original metatheatricality further reinforce the possibility for critical viewing. The central conflict — a love triangle resulting in murder — is played and replayed three times in the adaptation. The function of this repetition is twofold. On the one hand, it reveals the resolution of the play-within-the-play in advance. Hence, spectators will hopefully shift their attention to the apparatus of representation. On the other hand, the repetition draws attention to the labor of representation behind the satisfactory illusions, vicarious feelings, and invented memories of commercial theatre once again. The engagement with representation as labor is what prevents either a cynical or an idealistic blurring of illusion and reality in Kushner's text. Strehler, too, touches upon the labor of representation by exposing the constructedness of images through double-casting. However, Strehler's happy end deprives this exposure from political significance.

Finally, Kushner refuses to promise any hope of happy father-son reunion. While in Corneille's text, Pridamant sets off to Paris as soon as he learns that his son is there, in Kushner's rewriting, it becomes clear that Pridamant will never go to Paris. "I may, if health permits, go to Paris this spring, providing that they've put straw down on the muddy roads and made them passable," he says unconvincingly (Kushner 129) confirming yet again that what he has been searching for is neither truth, nor his son, but a convenient story. The continual emphasis on this distinction is one of Kushner's most radical interventions.

Kushner's Brechtian rewriting of a play offering theatre to the service of absolute monarchy into a critique of the commodification of the artist-spectator exchange is undeniably pertinent in a present reality ruled by media illusions. But as a text alone, it cannot transform the spectator-artist exchange into social critique. The mixed reviews of productions of *The Illusion*, range from admiration for Kushner's exploration of audiences' willingness to succumb to fiction to frustrations that actors dared subvert the illusions they initially proffered and to dismissal of the play's "Zen-like, New Agey appeal and an occasional incantation." More often than not reviewers foreground the themes of imagination and love rather than of consumerism. Though it satirizes the disciplining effect of the theatrical apparatus, Kushner's text seems to have fallen victim to this same apparatus on more than one occasion. Shall we, then, together with Baz Kershaw abandon all hope of bringing social critique into traditional theatre? Brecht himself struggled with this dilemma. He was aware that mainstream theatres would easily reduce his radical plays to formal innovations; at the same time he insisted that formal innovation cannot be accomplished autonomously but within institutions and, in the best case, may constitute a challenge to those same institutions (Kruger 24–25). Figuring out the conditions of theatrical exchange that can enable the practice of critical citizenship remains a challenging and pressing necessity.

Works Cited

Böhme-Kuby, Susanna. "Brecht in Italy: Aspects of Reception." *Modern Drama* 42 (1999): 223–33.

Corneille, Pierre. *The Comedy of Illusion (L'illusion Comique)*. Translated by Lynette Muir. Ottawa: Dovehouse Editions Inc., 2000.

Delgado, Maria M., and Paul Heritage. *In Contact with the Gods? Directors Talk Theatre*. Manchester: Manchester University Press, 1996.

Doudai, Naomi. Review of *The Illusion*, by Tony Kushner. Directed by Yossi Israeli. Khan Theatre, Jerusalem. *The Jerusalem Post* 28 October 2003: 24.

Dort, Bernard. "Pierre Corneille, son inscription sociale." Playbill for *L'Illusion* by Pierre Corneille. Directed by Giorgio Strehler. Théâtre de L'Europe, Paris, 1984.

_____. "Une vis sans fin ou le vertige de 'L'Illusion.'" Playbill for *L'Illusion* by Pierre Corneille. Directed by Giorgio Strehler. Théâtre de L'Europe, Paris, 1984.

Fisher, James. *The Theatre of Tony Kushner: Living Past Hope*. New York: Routledge, 2002.

Gold, Sylviane. "Today's Big-Name Playwrights Are Busy Translating the Past's." *New York Times* 3 August 1997: H5.

Golder, John. "The Stage Setting of Corneille's Early Plays." *Seventeenth Century French Studies* 7 (1985): 184–197.

Hirst, David L. *Giorgio Strehler*. Cambridge: Cambridge University Press, 1993.

Kerr, Cynthia B. "Rencontre autour d'une *Illusion*." *Corneille a L'affiche: Vingt and De Creations Theatrales, 1980–2000*. Tubingen: Gunter Narr Verlag Tubingen, 2000.

Kershaw, Baz. *The Radical in Performance: Between Brecht and Baudrillard*. London and New York: Routledge, 1999.

Kruger, Loren. *Post-Imperial Brecht: Politics and Performance, East and South*. Cambridge: Cambridge University Press, 2004.

Kushner, Tony. "The Illusion (1988)." *Plays by Tony Kushner*. New York: Broadway Play Publishing Inc., 1999.

Lawson, Catherine. Review of *The Illusion*, by Tony Kushner. Dir. Diana Fajrajsl. Theatre. *Ottawa Citizen* 24 July 2003: E6.

Marpeau, Elsa. "L'illusion narrative ou les mondes possibles de *L'Illusion comique*." *Lectures du jeune Corneille: L'Illusion comique et Le Cid*. J.-Y. Vialleton. Rennes: Presses Universitaires de Rennes, 2001.

McAuley, Gay. "Cave and Prison: Corneille's View of the Social Function of Theatre." *From Page to Stage: L'illusion Comique*. Sydney: University of Sydney, 1987.

Muir, Lynette. "Introduction." *The Comedy of Illusion (L'Illusion comique)*. By Pierre Corneille. Translated by Lynette Muir. Ottawa: Dovehouse Editions, 2000.

The Odeon and Europe. Odéon, Paris. 10 January 2005 <http://www.theatre odeon.fr/english/europe/ft_eu_00.htm>.

O'Regan, Michael. "Playhouses and Companies." *French Theatre in the Neo-Classical Era, 1550–1789*. Edited by William D. Howarth. Cambridge: Cambridge University Press, 1997.

Peureux, Guillaume. "*L'Illusion comique*, une 'pièce capricieuse': les ruses du dramaturge." *Lectures du jeune Corneille: L'Illusion et Le Cid*. J.-Y. Vialleton. Rennes: Presses Universitaires de Rennes, 2001.

Reinelt, Janelle. "Notes on *Angels in America* as American Epic Theatre." *Approaching the Millenium: Essays on* Angels in America. Edited by Deborah R. Geis and Steven F. Kruger. Ann Arbor: University of Muchigan Press, 1997.

Strehler, Giorgio. "L'Illusion." Playbill for *L'Illusion* by Pierre Corneille. Dir. Giorgio Strehler. Théâtre de L'Europe, Paris, 1984.

Trousdell, Richard. "Strehler in Rehearsal." *The Drama Review* 30.4 (1986): 65–83.

Ubersfeld, Anne. "Mother Courage in France." *Modern Drama* 42 (1999): 198–206.

Wainwright, Jeffrey. Review of *The Illusion*, by Tony Kushner. Dir. Matthew Lloyd. The Royal Exchange Theatre, Manchester. *The Independent* 23 June 1997: 12.

Willett, John. *Brecht on Theatre: The Development of an Aesthetic.* New York: Hill and Wang, 1964.

Williams, Fiona. "Contesting Race and Gender in the European Union: a Multilayered Recognition Struggle for Voice and Visibility." *Recognition Struggles and Social Movements: Contested Identities, Gender and Power.* Edited by Barbara Hobson. Cambridge: Cambridge University Press, 2003.

9

When Worlds Collide

The Kushner-Lamos *A Dybbuk* at Hartford Stage

PAULA T. ALEKSON

February 12, 1995, marked the world premier of Pulitzer Prize and Tony Award winning playwright Tony Kushner's adaptation *A Dybbuk; or Between Two Worlds* at the Hartford Stage Company in Hartford, Connecticut. Regarded as "one of the highest profile projects of Hartford Stage" (Rizzo, "Kushner's *Dybbuk*" G1), the opening night performance saw the culmination of five years of thought, work, and planning, initially inspired by the suggestion of artistic director Mark Lamos that Kushner consider adapting S. Ansky's 1914 *The Dybbuk*, the most celebrated and adapted tradition of the Yiddish theatre — a play which Harold Bloom drolly refers to as "Ansky's Yiddish warhorse" (109). Lamos not only provided the impetus for Kushner's *A Dybbuk* project, but also proved to be the greatest influence upon the final form the new script took on stage. What follows is an examination of published accounts regarding Lamos and Kushner, preliminary production notes, the production prompt book, rehearsal and performance reports, theatrical reviews, and interviews with members of the production team at the Hartford Stage Company which reveals how Lamos's directorial vision for the play, his directing style, and his struggles with the realities of production at a regional, nonprofit theatre greatly shaped Kushner's original adaptation of *The Dybbuk*. In addition, the following exploration assesses the strengths and weaknesses of the Kushner-Lamos collaborative product and considers the textual and aesthetic modifications made to *A Dybbuk* by Kushner and his subsequent collaborator for the play's Off Broadway incarnation at the Joseph Papp Public Theatre.

Between Two Worlds— amid the opposing forces of light and darkness, life and death, wealth and poverty, and the holy and the demonic — is the place occupied by Shloyme-Zanvle ben Aaron Hocohen Rappoport's (later S. Ansky) main character in *The Dybbuk*. It was also the liminal space occupied by Ansky, born 1863, during his journey away from Judaism. "Broken, severed, [and] ruptured," are words he used to describe the period of his life when he abandoned the world of his Hasidic-Jewish upbringing and education along with Yiddish culture and language for the world of the enlightened, Western-reaching Russian intelligentsia and Russian language. Reflecting on this chaotic time, Ansky remarked, "Many years of my life passed on this frontier, on the border between two worlds" (quoted in Roskies xix; for more on S. Ansky's life and work see David J. Roskies "Introduction" to *The Dybbuk and Other Writings*.) Ansky's dramatic legend tells the story of Khonen, a poor yeshiva scholar who is in love with Leah, the daughter of a wealthy merchant. Ignored by Leah's father as a suitable suitor, Khonen attempts to win her through the dangerous and mystical powers of the Kabbalah. When it is announced in the shul that she is betrothed to another man, Khonen dies. Three months later, on her wedding day, Leah invites not only the ghost of her mother to the celebration, as is the tradition, but also welcomes the spirit of Khonen. As her marriage ceremony begins, the disturbed soul of Khonen enters and possesses Leah's body as a dybbuk: "a cleavage of an evil spirit to the body" (Fishman 44). Leah is taken by her father to the city to be examined by the great wonder rabbi or tzaddik, Rabbi Azriel, who prepares to exorcise the dybbuk but questions the reasons for the possession. The dybbuk divulges that he was wronged by Sender, Leah's father, and through mystical dreams, the impaneling of a rabbinical court, and its ghostly witness, it is revealed to Rabbi Azriel that Sender's transgression was a broken, long-forgotten oath with Khonen's father — an oath that pledged that their children would one day marry one another. Rabbi Azriel and the court pass a judgment to restore harmony between the earthly and spirit worlds, but the dybbuk still refuses to leave. An exorcism is performed and the dybbuk is threatened with excommunication. As Khonen's weakened spirit leaves Leah's body, Rabbi Azriel rescinds the anathema, and quickly orders the marriage of the freed Leah to her earthly groom. As the wedding is prepared for, Leah dies and is united with her destined bridegroom in the spirit world.

The most celebrated production of *The Dybbuk* was mounted under the direction of Evgeny Vakhtangov in 1922, for the Habimah Theatre in Moscow. Habimah was founded in 1917, with a mission to stage professional productions of plays in Hebrew — an attempt to introduce the sacred to the secular world. Sensitive to their mission and repertoire, Konstantin Stanislavsky sent them not only Ansky's *The Dybbuk* — which had been translated into Hebrew by poet Hayyim Nahman Bialik — but also his student Vakhtangov to direct it. The project was a curious mix of ethnicities: Ansky's Yiddish folk tale; the Hebrew Habimah company; the Armenian, Russian-speaking Vakhtangov; Bialik's Hebrew translation; and Vakhtangov's working copy of the script in Russian, penned by Ansky.

The rehearsal period for *The Dybbuk* became a three-year theatrical experiment in expressionistic performance and design modes. Uncharacteristic of his mentor's theatrical aesthetics, Vakhtangov's approach to the play's performance "removed superficial realism and replaced it with theatrical freezes, silences, chanting, singing, ghostly makeup, and grotesque formalized movements" (Fishman 44). In a similar way, the scenic design attempted a visually grotesque version of reality. Nathan Altman's set and costume designs for the production exhibited a fantastic theatricality reminiscent of the psychic-distortions of Marc Chagall. Chagall's connections to Ansky and *The Dybbuk* are quite interesting; not only was the artist born in the same village as Rappoport-Ansky (indeed, the images of his Hasidic upbringing in Vitebsk made up a large body of his early work), but Chagall also claimed that he was originally approached to design the sets for the Habimah production. Although Altman's work appeared on stage instead of Chagall's, the Chagallesque influence is certain; the latter explained, "...it turned out, as someone told me afterwards, that a year later, Vakhtangov was spending hours in front of my murals in Granovsky's theatre" (Bohm-Duchen 153). Fantasy and distortion also made their way into Ansky's script, which Vakhtangov tailored to suit his highly theatrical impulses. Vakhtangov's vision for the production, in many ways, altered Ansky's concept of dramatically preserving the Jewish-Yiddish culture and aesthetic, yet the Armenian's concept for the production truly influenced the Jewish theatrical art of the future.

The Dybbuk became Habimah's most renowned production; it solidified and conventionalized the "Habimah" fantastic-grotesque performance style (á la Vakhtangov), which the company eventually took to Israel in 1928; ultimately their mode of performance became the Israeli National Theatre style. Between 1922 and 1980, *The Dybbuk* was mounted at least 1,100 times (Fishman 43), a figure which suggests that the play was either mounted or performed an average of nearly nineteen times a year for over fifty-eight years — an impressive number for a mystical play set in an Eastern European shtetl.

The history of notable, professional American productions of the play may not be as remarkable, numerically speaking, but is, nevertheless, quite varied in its scope. New York's Yiddish Art Theatre is reported, in 1920, to have produced Ansky's "second degree translation" (Neugroschel,

Translator's Note)—that is, the "translation" the playwright made from Bialik's Hebrew translation of his original Yiddish manuscript after it was seized in 1918 by the Bolsheviks with the rest of the contents of the Jewish Ethnographic Museum—while Vakhtangov was only into his second year of rehearsals. The first American production in English was mounted at the Neighborhood Playhouse in New York City in 1926; it is noted to have borrowed greatly from the Habimah-Vakhtangov production. In 1959, Paddy Chayefsky appropriated Ansky's legend for his Broadway bound production of *The Tenth Man*. The story was also adapted, in 1961, as *The Play of the Week*, directed by Sidney Lumet, for the Public Broadcasting System. John Hirsch, Hungarian-Jewish émigré to Canada, survivor of the Nazi occupation of Budapest, and director, translated his own version of *The Dybbuk* in 1974, and presented it first at the Manitoba Theatre Center and then at the Mark Taper Forum in Los Angeles. A staging in the late 1970's, at the Public Theatre in New York City, was directed by Joseph Chaikin and utilized his adaptation with Mira Rafalowicz. The National Theatre for the Deaf also produced the play in their 1987–88 season. Bruce Myers, colleague of Peter Brook and cast member in Chaikin's Public Theatre production adapted his own *Dybbuk* "for two actors" which was first presented in 1989 by the Traveling Jewish Theatre, and which offered a "stunning new adaptation" in 2004, to celebrate its twenty-fifth anniversary (TJT). These few examples from the North American theatre suggest the diverse appeal of the drama. Even in the specificity of Ansky's legend, there lies a broad attraction, perhaps best characterized as either a fascination with the theatricality of the piece, or with its inherent universality.

The seed that ultimately sprouted into the Kushner-Lamos production of *A Dybbuk* in 1995 was first planted by Lamos in late 1989–early 1990. The occasion was the collaboration of the two on Kushner's 1988 adaptation of Pierre Corneille's *The Illusion* at Hartford Stage. At some point in the creative process, Lamos's passion for *The Dybbuk* was conveyed to Kushner, who has an equal passion for writing adaptations—as is evidenced by his comprehensive adaptation bibliography: *Stella. A Play for Lovers* (1987; based upon J. W. Goethe's lesser tragedy of the same name), *Widows* (1991; adapted in collaboration with and from the novel by Ariel Dorfman), *The Good Person of Setzuan* (1994; adapted from Bertolt Brecht's play), *Grim(m)* (1995; an unproduced screenplay inspired by the Brothers Grimm's tale of "The Two Journeymen"), and *St. Cecilia, or The Power of Music* (1997; a operatic libretto adaptation of Heinrich von Kleist's story *Die Heilige Cäcilie)* (For a more detailed exploration of all of Kushner's adaptations, including *A Dybbuk*, see Chapter 5, "Transformations and Convergences," of James Fisher's *The Theatre of Tony Kushner: Living Past*

Hope.) Although Lamos had never been directly involved with a production of *The Dybbuk*, he had been a close friend of its adapter and director John Hirsh, whose mountings of the play at the Manitoba Theatre Center (1974), Mark Taper Theatre and Arena Stage (1975) garnered Hirsch accolades as well as the Los Angeles Drama Critics Circle Award in 1975. Perhaps it was Hirsch's recent and untimely death from AIDS in 1989 that reminded Lamos of the play and urged him to suggest its adaptation and production to Kushner during rehearsals for *The Illusion*. Persuaded by "Mark's enthusiasm" (Staton 1) and inspired by spirits from his own past, Kushner embraced the idea:

> I was haunted in a way. I've always been attracted to pictures and photographs of the Yiddish theatre of the teens and twenties and the thirties. I've heard lots of stories and hard phonograph recordings. Vanessa Redgrave did a benefit for a group called Memorial for the Victims of Stalin's Oppression in New York about four or five years ago, and one of the people that performed was an eighty-five year-old actress from the original Jewish theatre in Moscow, who was this beanpole of a woman in this fabulous black velvet dress, and white face paint. She did a Yiddish poem about the Holocaust [....] [It was] incredibly elegant, and fluid and melodious [...] I became very fond of hearing [Yiddish], and decided that I'd be interested in working on a play, and *The Dybbuk* seemed like the obvious place to start, and it's a great play [Cohen 222–224].

With his creative juices stirred by Lamos's enthusiasm, visuals from the Yiddish theatre, and the Habimaesque performance of the Yiddish actress, all Kushner needed for his *Dybbuk* project was time and a fitting translation to adapt.

Time was one of the greatest forces that held the *Dybbuk* project back for nearly five years—time and Kushner's finally-realized success with *Angels in America, A Gay Fantasia on National Themes* plays, *Part I: Millennium Approaches*, first produced in 1992 (1993 Pulitzer Prize for Drama, the Tony Award for Best Play, Drama Desk Award, etc.) and *Part II: Perestroika* produced in 1993 (1994 Tony Award, Drama Desk Award, etc.). Also, between 1990 and 1995, Kushner premièred his play *A Bright Room Called Day* and his adaptation of *The Good Person of Setzuan*, wrote *Slavs!*, and mounted various national and international productions of *Angels in America*. Additionally, Kushner was occupied with matters of both personal and extra-artistic significance in those five years:

> He took his first trip to Israel; participated in the watershed ACT UP action-protest at New York's St. Patrick's Cathedral in December 1990; was named 1993 "Man of the Year" by the *Advocate*; spoke at many college

campuses, public readings and demonstrations [...] and published numerous essays, poems, commentaries, and a book *Thinking About Longstanding Problems of Virtue and Happiness* [...] [Vorlicky 3].

Lamos's time as Artistic Director at Hartford Stage was equally occupied.
Beyond his administrative duties and all of the pressures these entail —
planning and pitching four exciting and artistic seasons to a board, theatre subscribers, and the greater Hartford community — Lamos also
directed eleven shows for the institution. On and Off Broadway, he directed
Our Country's Good (1991) at the Nederlander Theatre, for which he
received a Tony nomination, and *The End of the Day* (1992) at Playwrights
Horizons. In addition, Lamos added directorial credits to his opera résumé,
which included a total of ten productions at Glimmer Glass Opera, Portland Opera, the Metropolitan Opera, Seattle Opera, and the Munich Biennale. Artistic enthusiasm aside, both Kushner and Lamos were busy in
their individual careers, and scheduling time — which in Lamos's case often
includes booking jobs sometimes three years in advance (Rizzo, "A Curtain Falls" F1) — for script development and research proved an insurmountable hurdle. Ironically, scheduling difficulties ultimately worked in
Kushner's and Lamos's favor in terms of their *A Dybbuk* collaboration.

The starting point of any adaptation of a foreign language play, ideally, begins with an appropriate translation; a suitable text was needed for
the Kushner-Lamos *Dybbuk* project. According to Joachim Neugroschel,
translator of over one hundred and eighty works, including those of Franz
Kafka, Anton Chekhov, Sholem Aleichem, Thomas Mann, and Albert
Schweitzer, Kushner approached him to create a new English language
translation of S. Ansky's *The Dybbuk* for adaptation — the translation was
completed in 1992 (*Yiddish Imagination* xi). Neugroschel's *Ansky['s] The
Dybbuk, or Between Two Worlds: A Dramatic Legend in Four Acts*, as a literal or "curatorial" (xii) translation of the original, closely adheres to the
primary author's work, that is, liberties are not taken with the play's structure, nor with the basic characterizations. For any translation, however, a
style of poetic license, borne out of artistic necessity, often influences the
translator's final product. In his Translator's Note, which accompanies his
self-published treatment and is bound into the Hartford Stage Production
Stage Manager's promptbook, Neugroschel discusses the obstacles for the
English translator presented specifically by Ansky's text:

> In the tradition of Yiddish melodrama, the overwrought language of *The
> Dybbuk* tends to be grandiloquent and melodramatic, reaching a gushing
> intensity that was perfectly acceptable to, indeed demanded by its audi-
> ence, but that would sound almost comically overcharged in English [n.p.].

Neugroschel offers the following approach to such obstacles:

> Given all of these peculiar problems, I have steered the English version toward a blend of normal and slightly elevated speech [...] In addition, though Ansky incorporates no other poetic passages, aside from the rhyming "rap" chant in the Nanny's monologue to Leah, I have used a fusion of free verse and blank verse for most of the prose dialogue of the more mystical characters— the Messenger, Leah, and Khonen — especially in the amorous parts, which in a culture that was very buttoned-up about public utterances of love, sex, and even affection, and an intensely erotic effect that would otherwise be lost in English [n.p.].

In his Introduction to the 1998 published version of the translation, Neugroschel qualifies his work further: "My efforts may look like adaptation — and they are. But they focus on arousing the same emotions, the same reactions, that the original drama, in its fashion, touches off in readers and spectators" (xv). Neugroschel's efforts provided Kushner with a translation sensitive to "the emotional fullness and the melodrama and the poetry" of the playwright's beloved Yiddish (qtd. in Rizzo, "Kushner's *Dybbuk*" G1). According to Lamos, Kushner's subsequent adaptation based upon Neugroschel's translation "energized the turgid dramaturgy" of Ansky's original (quoted in Rizzo, "Kushner's *Dybbuk*" G1).

Kushner describes his adaptation of Ansky's *The Dybbuk* as "fairly straightforward" (Staton 1), despite *New York Times* critic Ben Brantley's estimation that "those who haven't read [*The*] *Dybbuk* recently may not realize just how much Mr. Kushner has altered it" ("Talking to the Dead" C9). The changes he did make— beyond his attention to carefully crafting the characters' dialogue into comfortable colloquial speech in the more mundane exchanges and artfully sculpting beautiful, spiritually poetic verse for the play's more mystical moments— are for the most part dramaturgical in nature. Kushner explains his choice to retain the basic plot and structure of the original thusly: "I did a few things structurally [...] There's a lot of storytelling in *The Dybbuk* and I added a few things that I liked and I took out a few. I think the conclusion of the play is terrifically moving and I didn't want to change it at all" (Staton 1). Kushner altered the title to *A Dybbuk* according to Lamos, "Partially [...] to differentiate it from all the other translations [...] But also because there's so much of the supernatural in the play, this indicates there are a lot of dybbuks in the world. It gives a sense there may be many spirits lurking that could jump into a body at any given moment" (Rizzo, "Kushner's 'A' Not 'The' *Dybbuk*" E3).

Kushner's omissions from Ansky's original become evident in a comparison of Neugroschel's literal translation with the working script for

Hartford Stage, dated January 12, 1995; these elimination include a few
Hasidic legends told by both the batlonim in Act I and Rabbi Azriel in Act
II and many of the tzaddik's directives for Act IV's exorcism/ excommunication. Dramaturgical tinkering also saw the restructuring of Act III. In
Ansky's version, the Act begins with the introduction of Rabbi Azriel and
his delivery of a lengthy mystical discourse to the Hasidim and the mysterious Messenger. In Kushner's script, Sender enters immediately with
Leah/the Dybbuk and pleads for help; later the playwright weaves the mystical discourse from the original as dialogue between the tzaddik and his
spiritual associate, the Messenger.

Overt additions to the play include: (1) A new opening; Act I, Scene
1 opens with the discovery of Khonen washing himself in a mikvah, or ritual bath, as the "Mipney Ma" from the Song of Songs is chanted; (2) Khonen's death comes not with the announcement of Leah's betrothal, but
appears to be the direct result of his whispering the Unutterable Name of
God three times into the ear of the Messenger; (3) A mikvah scene with
Fradde and Leah ritually preparing for her wedding day begins Act II; (4)
Khonen's ghost becomes part of the Beggar's Dance; and (5) The character of a Scribe becomes crucial to the plot in Acts III and IV — he is caused
to be spiritually distressed during the supernatural rabbinical court pro-
ceedings. Although these alterations by Kushner seem quite detailed and
different, his mind's eye was always on Ansky's "warhorse."

It is obvious from Kushner's changes that his dialogue deletions and
structural shifts were executed to tighten and intensify the dramatic plot,
and his artistic insertions were meant to deepen the star-crossed connection between Khonen and Leah and to increase other supernatural elements. However, his adapted text, beyond the nuts and bolts of dramaturgy
and the artful sculpting of dialogue and poetic images, seemed to lack a
personal vision or an emotional center for the playwright. When asked to
describe his concept for the drama in 1995, he intellectualized: "The play
is very much about gender and crossing of boundaries and transgression
[...] I added a few things in about gender to sort of remind people about
these issues, but I think Ansky had already got it in there" (Staton 1).
Ansky's alleged and anachronistic gender-consciousness notwithstanding,
it was few years later — that is, following Kushner's revising of A Dybbuk
for its Off Broadway premiere in 1997 — that the playwright began to more
programatically assert his adaptation's transgressiveness in relation to both
gender and sexuality:

> I would really like to have people see A Dybbuk as a gay play, not because
> I've done things to make it gay, but because there are all sorts of ways this

is a play about gender transgression and the refusal of love to obey moral strictures. But also I want homosexuals to come watch Rabbi Azriel the exorcist wrestling with God, because I feel that's part of the gay project [Goldstein 59].

In addition to projecting queerness onto *A Dybbuk* for its Public Theatre production, as will be explored below, Kushner would eventually discover his personal vision in and the emotional center to his adapted text. However, prior to entering rehearsals at Hartford Stage — rehearsals being the crucible in which new plays are melted down and reworked by a director and his team of collaborators— Kushner's conception of the play and its issues resided on a mostly cerebral, yet mystical, plane. With the commencement of the rehearsal period and through the directorial vision of Mark Lamos, a compelling emotional core for *A Dybbuk* was discovered and visually and physically manifested in the play's staging.

Before delving into Lamos's specific vision for *A Dybbuk*, the director's approach to theatre and his artistic strengths warrant brief investigation. Before choosing to make theatre his life's work, the Illinois native pursued a career in musical performance. He attended Northwestern University on a music scholarship and trained as a classical violinist; his musical training from youth to university spread across thirteen years. However, his love for the arts and performance went beyond the world of music, and not long after his graduation at Northwestern in 1969 he began a professional acting career. Lamos's Broadway acting debut came in 1972, in Romulus Linney's *Love-Suicide at Schofield Barracks*. That same year he appeared as Christian to Christopher Plummer's Cyrano in the Broadway musical version of Rostand's classic, and then in Arthur Miller's *The Creation of the World and Other Business*. Work at the Guthrie Theatre in Minneapolis put him under the tutelage of director Michael Langham, who had been trained by Tyrone Guthrie himself. No doubt with Langham's professional clout and recommendation, Lamos went from the position of Artistic Director at the Arizona Theatre Company in 1978, to Associate at the California Shakespearean Festival (under Langham) in 1979, to joint positions as Artistic Director at the Hartford Stage Company and the California Shakespearean Festival in 1980.

Beyond the connections his mentorship provided, Langham's directorial style greatly influenced Lamos as both an actor and as a burgeoning director. According to Lamos, "[...] my understanding of the rhythm of a whole play, my sense of a play's architecture — these came from Michael, who learned them from his mentor Tyrone Guthrie" (quoted in Bartow 176). Indeed, all three directors in this artistic lineage specialize

or specialized in classical drama (primarily Shakespeare) and each approaches a play as a conductor approaches a symphony—the musicality of
the play is a key consideration. Lamos's concept of what directing is, however, is decidedly more psychological than that of his predecessors; he
moves beyond Guthrie's "producer as coordinator" approach and Langham's intellectualized director as "humanist" position:

> Directing is psychology. It's about how to work with other human beings.
> It's also the art of inducing a psychological effect on a group of people who
> have come into a theatre to experience that effect. In your mind you're say-
> ing to yourself, "What do I want the audience to feel?" From there it's a
> process of moving toward that feeling with actors, designers, etc. [...]
> [quoted 180].

Lamos's belief that one goes to a theatrical performance to see "moments
of real passion and tenderness," clearly correlates with his artistic concep-
tualizations for the plays he directs (quoted 178). This is especially obvious in his directorial vision for *A Dybbuk*.

Lamos's initial attraction to Ansky's original work was an interest in
the otherworldly love story it contained, which he describes as "the romantic theme of love after death, of love being stronger than death" (Rizzo,
"Kushner's *Dybbuk*" G1). As he began working on the play, Lamos became
equally interested in the Hasidic shtetl, a world of "ecstatic, fantastical
religion," a world in which, "people danced their way to God and lived life
as great beating hearts" (G1). With Kushner's adaptation, however, Lamos
became more interested specifically in the concept of possession, and how
the love story related to Leah's possession by her lover. According to Artistic Associate and Production Dramaturg Amy Stevens:

> Mark wanted to explore the idea of possession as being sexy. He wasn't inter-
> ested in politics. He wasn't interested in the methodology of exorcism. He
> was interested in what was happening in Leah's body. He wanted to explore
> the idea of her being filled up, of being taken over by this male force.

These ideas, united with Lamos's visceral reaction to the seductive, dark,
and fantastical elements of the play, were pitched during pre-production
to the design team of John Conklin (sets), Pat Collins (lights), Jess Goldstein (costumes), and David Budries (sound)—theatre artists with whom
Lamos frequently works.

Lamos believes that his love and desire for collaboration stems from
his early work as an actor. To him, it is both a "generous" and "*regenera-
tive*" process: "Collaboration is saying, 'I understand certain potent feelings

I have about the work, but I don't understand everything" (quoted in Bartow 189). The role of the production team, according to Lamos, is to find "a way into the project" (quoted 189). Early on in discussions between Lamos and Kushner, they decided that the play, despite its historic "expressionistic baggage," was better suited, in Lamos's wording, to "the tone of realism [...] with only moments of expressionism" (quoted in Staton 1). Kushner related this leaning specifically to the text: "I think we both, even with our various interests in the avant garde [*sic*] and in experimentation, are working with the tradition of narrative realism. I think we're both interested in a marriage of that genre and techniques that come from other genres" (1). A marriage of genres and techniques accurately defines the overall visual and aural design collaboration for *A Dybbuk*, which included Conklin's geometrically abstracted and distorted sets, influenced by "expressionistic baggage" and Lamos's own interest in Chagall; Collins lighting collaboration with Conklin which featured translucent white and black velour screens, backlighting and projections which played with the visual theme of the opposition of darkness and light, black and white; Goldstein's relatively realistic approach to period costuming, which utilized contemporary tailoring techniques to heighten the shape and form of the historical clothing; and Budries' layered sound design featuring layered realistic music and sound with supernatural elements and effects, and the music specifically composed for the play by four members of the six-member klezmer group, The Klezmatics (musicians/composers Frank London, Paul Morrissett, Lorin Sklamberg, and Alicia Svigals).

Lamos's pre-production work — in addition to the task of becoming expertly familiar with Kushner's adaptation, further focusing his vision for the play, and finding effective ways to express it — included the casting of the show. At odds going into audition were the demands of the script (i.e., twenty-five actors to play forty characters) and the reality of a not-for-profit resident theatre's budget. A member of the League of Resident Theatres (LORT), Hartford Stage Company is without a resident company of artists and therefore must hire its acting talent on a show-by-show basis. Personnel needs are balanced against Actor's Equity Association and LORT B requirements for every given season. For *A Dybbuk*, seasonal provisions allowed for sixteen professional Equity actors and nine non–Equity extras; these restrictions necessitated the double — and sometimes triple-casting of the Equity actors.

Lamos brought with him to the casting sessions his concept of possession, and the related themes of sexuality, power, and the ecstatic and fantastical. These themes were made manifest in the overall youth of the cast, and most specifically in the actors he chose to play the leads. In collaboration with Bernard Telsey Casting, Lamos selected Michael Hayden for the role of Khonen and Julie Dretzin for Leah. The casting of these particular young actors was a coup for the Hartford Stage Public Relations department, as both had just completed successful Broadway runs: Hayden as Billy Bigelow in the revival of Rodgers' and Hammerstein's *Carousel,* and Dretzin in Wendy Wasserstein's *The Sisters Rosensweig,* both at Lincoln Center. For the production of *A Dybbuk,* however, Hayden's and Dretzin's bodies would become as important as their talent and résumés. On stage, Hayden's tall, muscular build complimented Dretzin's petite, seemingly delicate frame. With the casting of these physical opposites, Lamos's concept of possession as sexy began to take shape as a convincing visual reality.

Rehearsals for *A Dybbuk* began in the Hartford Stage rehearsal room on January 12, 1995. Script revisions started streaming in from Kushner's computer the next day, January 13. (The following description and characterization of the *A Dybbuk* rehearsal process is based upon rehearsal and production reports generated by Production Stage Manager Deborah Vandergrift, as well as on interviews with Vandergrift, Artistic Associate and Production Dramaturg Amy Stevens, and Production Assistant Myra Hope Bobbitt.) The stage manager's promptbook indicates that dated script replacements and revisions also occurred on January 15, 19, and February 3 and 7. Production Assistant Myra Hope Bobbitt, who was responsible for photocopying script changes for the production, noted that Kushner would sometimes submit fresh revisions as often as three times in one day; occasionally last minute revisions would delay the rehearsal. This is nothing new to Kushner, perhaps best described by *Washington Post* staff writer Peter Marks as a "replaywright" (C1). An obsessive rewriter, Kushner tinkered with *Angels in America, Millennium Approaches* from its inception in 1988, through its workshop production at the Mark Taper Forum in May 1990, for its world premiere at the Eureka Theatre Company the following year, again on the occasion of its London premiere in January 1992, and throughout rehearsals for its Broadway production in spring of 1993 — the same year a version of the play won the Pulitzer Prize. Kushner began *Homebody/Kabul* as the one-act monologue in 1997 and it was staged as such in London in July 1999. In December 2001, a two-act political drama was added to the monologue for the play's American premiere at the New York Theatre Workshop. Mel Gussow reported for the *New York Times* in September 2002, that Kushner was continuing, in the playwright's own words, with "tinkering and tightening and tweaking and trying to get it right," for a run at the Mark Taper Forum (E1), and on May 12, 2004, David Finkle of TheatreMania.com, noted that Kushner was working on *Homebody/Kabul*'s seventeenth draft for a mounting of the three and a half hour play at the Brooklyn Academy of Music. On a more modest and compressed scale, the early modifications Kushner made to *A Dybbuk* during its rehearsal period attempted to clarify dialogue and character relationships, as well as tighten the dramatic action. Subsequent script changes were made during previews. As Ben Brantley noted in his opening night review in the *New York Times*, "Mr. Kushner, true to form, was adding to and deleting from the text until the very last minute" ("Talking to the Dead" C9), a fact corroborated by Bobbitt who provided further backstage detail: "We were indeed making changes until the very last minute. There was an Equity vote to rehearse during dinner break. Michael Hayden missed his dinner plans because we were rehearsing the final moments of the play."

According to *A Dybbuk* Production Stage Manager Deborah Vandergrift and Artistic Associate and Production Dramaturg Amy Stevens, the rehearsal period for the production was extremely tense. Vandergrift, who worked with Lamos for about ten years, said it was the most difficult Lamos show she had ever worked on. She explained: "Producing a new show is always a very hard process. It is very emotional." For *A Dybbuk*, Vandergrift indicated that both Kushner and Lamos were so passionate about the project that production meetings became electric. Vandergrift's assistant, Bobbitt, who did not attend weekly production meetings, however, felt that any artistic differences between Kushner and Lamos expressed during those meetings were never brought into the rehearsal room. Bobbitt said of rehearsals that "they were about as stressful as any other production."

Daily rehearsal reports from Vandergrift indicate that the design process continued throughout regular rehearsals and right into technical rehearsals: the sizes and shapes of set pieces and furniture were debated and changed, properties were added and cut, and costumes and costume pieces were constantly being added and altered. For Conklin and his crew, the design and placement of the mikvah was a major discussion point. Lamos wanted the mikvah to allow for the full immersion of Khonen in Act I and Leah in Act II. Conklin designed a four foot watertight trap in the raked floor which could be covered quickly. The original set design for the show included a cantilevered "graveyard platform" suspended over the raked stage and the heads of the actors. It was designed specifically for Act II, with the intention that it could be lowered and able to support the weight of an actor (most likely Dretzin). This idea, however, was scrapped at some point in the build period, possibly due to budgetary and safety considerations. A smaller version of the "graveyard platform" was retained and utilized as a spooky effect during the "Beggar's Dance."

Of special concern to Lamos and his design collaborators during the rehearsal period were the aural and visual manifestations of the dybbuk and how the possession could be rendered technologically. Rehearsal reports note that Lamos and Collins considered using a laser or moving light to represent the dybbuk, and even a shadow effect was discussed. The idea of a visualized dybbuk was quickly scrapped, though the dybbuk as aural phenomenon continued to be debated. Budries and Lamos came up with the idea of molding two voices into one. It was considered that both Hayden (offstage) and Dretzin (onstage) could be miked, their voices joined, and then transmitted through a speaker placed somewhere on Dretzin's person to create the effect that Khonen was, in essence, inside of Leah. A speaker small enough to be sewn into a costume or undergarment was discussed, but quickly vetoed, perhaps for fear that a tiny speaker would produce only a tiny voice — eliciting laughs from the audience instead of inducing terror. It was eventually decided that both would be miked, their joined voices would be specially effected, and then fed out of stage speakers. As a result of the adoption of this technical effect, Lamos toyed further with his concept of possession. Two dybbuk lines from Act III were assigned to Hayden's voice only; these are the lines when the dybbuk specifically accuses Sender for his suffering.

Vandergrift opined that the most difficult phase of the rehearsal period from a stage manager's point of view involved the Beggar's Dance in Act II of *A Dybbuk.* "It was the hardest thing to rehearse," she commented, and then added that it entailed a number of compromises between actors, director, choreographer, and costume designer. Lamos desired for the first phase of the dance a continuous, cyclical interweaving of rich guest with poor guests. Although almost all of the twenty-five actors were involved, the desired number of wedding guests and beggars Lamos wanted was triple that number. To achieve this, Lamos asked for quick and mostly full costume changes so that actors could go from guest to beggars and back again. Goldstein was concerned with his budget, the build time and the crew and time needed to affect such quick changes. Their compromises consisted of the use of costume pieces (hats, large scarves, and masks) to distinguish between guest and beggars. Choreographer Mark Dendy utilized contrasting dancing styles to distinguish between the wedding guests and the beggars: the former were assigned a style similar to folk dancing, while the latter were coached in grotesque and modern movements.

When *A Dybbuk* finally went into technical rehearsal — on stage with full sets, lights, costumes and sound — two major problems were revealed. The first problem was that Lamos didn't like Leah's mikvah scene which Kushner had created to open Act II. Neither Vandergrift, Stevens, nor Bobbitt remembered what the director found disagreeable, but he cut it from the production, and in doing so removed two full pages of dialogue from the performance. One might speculate that Lamos found the scene too repetitive, visually unsatisfactory, or unimportant or impeding to the dramatic flow of the play. [Note that Leah's mikvah scene is preserved as Act II, Scene 1 in the published 1998 versions of Kushner's adaptation, which the playwright dedicates to Mark Lamos "with love and gratitude" (viii).] The second problem involved the actor portraying Rabbi Azriel, Sam Gray. Having made it through the difficulties of the rehearsal process, compounded by the cuts and changes to the script by Kushner, Gray began to have great trouble remembering his lines. According to Bobbitt, during regular rehearsals Gray seemed on par with the rest of the cast, "Everyone was calling for lines once we went off book." However, once the cast was put into the theatre and on the stage, Gray had serious problems. Publicly, Lamos assigned members of the company to assist the actor in working on his lines and, in private, discussed the matter with his production team. It was decided that Gray should be "wired" and fitted with an earpiece so that lines could be fed to him whenever he had difficulty. When the solution was discussed with the actor, he refused and assured Lamos that he would have his lines memorized by previews.

The first preview of *A Dybbuk*, scheduled for February 11, was canceled by Lamos who wanted another technical dress rehearsal before putting the show in front of an audience. Bobbitt comically recalled, "It's not that anything in particular was wrong, it was just that everything was wrong." February 12 saw the first "official" preview. Vandergrift's performance report notes a number of technical problems that needed to be addressed by cast and crew for the next day's rehearsal and evening performance, and it also included commentary on the continued difficulty Gray was having with his lines. Gray's problem was so grave and debilitating — to both the actor's confidence and the production as a whole — that Kushner cut more than five pages of dialogue from Act III and three and a half pages from Act IV following the first preview performance. It should be noted that not only Gray's lines were cut; the Messenger and the Scribe each had large monologues removed, monologues which were never restored in the published script. Interestingly, these excisions tightened the action of the play and emphasized the dybbuk in his plight over the concerns of the Rabbi and his followers; they also diminished the uncanny spiritual connection Kushner had developed between Azriel and the Messenger and excised some of the urgent, mystical, and frightening — not to mention highly theatrical —(stage) business of exorcism (some of which was later returned in the published version). In addition to these cuts, Lamos asked Kushner for a restructuring of the four acts in relation to the intermissions. Originally, the breakdown was:

Acts I and II
Intermission
Act III
Intermission
Act IV

With acts distributed in this manner, the three month leap from the death of Khonen to Leah's wedding is confusingly compacted, and the exorcism, rabbinical trial, and excommunication are drawn out. Lamos suggested a new breakdown:

Act I
Intermission
Acts II and III
Intermission
Act IV

Within this change, Lamos increased the dramatic tension and further focused the drama on Khonen's death, his possession of Leah, and the play's final resolution.

The Kushner-Lamos *A Dybbuk* officially opened on February 17, 1995, at Hartford Stage. From moment one of the performance, it was obvious that the audience was introduced and transported to another world of sound and sight. As the house lights faded to black, a ripple of eerie music filled the auditorium. In the darkness, a lone male voice chanted in voiceover:

Why did the soul,
Oh tell me this,
Tumble from Heaven
To the Great Abyss?
The most profound descents contain
Ascensions to the height again...

Slowly pale light rose on the lower stage-right side of the raked floor to reveal a naked man chanting and immersing himself in a pool of water set into the stage floor. As he completed a third immersion, the lights faded on the scene and the eerie music faded out. A moment later the lights rose on the entire stage revealing a synagogue filled with piles of sacred tomes, lit candles, chairs, benches and tables, and a clutch of black and white attired yeshiva students and the arguing batlonim. The effect of this sequence was stunning.

The simplistic beauty of the music, poetry, water and naked flesh replaced by the clutter of the books and the chatter of men. It wasn't until well into the scene that Khonen's presence in the synagogue was made clear to the audience, and even then it wasn't certain that he was the ritual bather until he speaks—his erotic intensity (or that of actor Michael Hayden) was recognizable.

Lamos's directorial concept of possession as sexy was effectively drawn bodily from Kushner's script. His physical and emotional direction of Hayden in the first act set the vision in place. Every interaction Khonen has with other characters was filled with an intense, almost palpable, passion: from his brief interrogation of the Messenger, to his debate with Henekh over the Kabbalah, to his erotic recitation of the "Song of Songs," to his one sentence conversation with Leah. In one act, Kushner, Lamos, and Hayden make Khonen such a memorable figure that the audience is virtually unaware by the fourth act that he has been physically removed from the stage for more than two and a half acts (save for his brief and effective appearance in the "Beggar's Dance"). Credit for this theatrical feat is also due Dretzin who "embodied" both Leah and Leah's beloved and to sound designer Budries who gave them their supernatural voice.

The exploitation of the supernatural through the elements of design was a memorable achievement of the entire artistic collaboration, especially in Act II in which the Beggar's Dance and the actual possession occur. The expressionistic distortions of the set pieces— Sender's house, the picket fence, the skewed chairs set out for the beggars—combined with the abstracted projections, light and shadow, the crooked-sounding tune of a hurdy-gurdy, and crooked bodies of the actors in motion, effectively set the mood for the fantastical possession. However, the build-up in energy was somewhat diffused by Kushner's dedication to Ansky's script. By retaining the comical introduction of the frightened bridegroom, he inadvertently lessened the dramatic tension.

Act III in Ansky's original script relied heavily on Rabbi Azriel to expound on the powers of God and the supernatural abilities of the tzaddikum before the introduction of the dybbuk. Kushner freed the script of *A Dybbuk* from the exposition and presented Rabbi Azriel with the problem of the dybbuk immediately. This restructuring worked in Lamos's favor by focusing attention on the possession and the possessed and not on the exhaustive details of the Hasidic legends. Instead a possessed Leah becomes the center of attention: she writhes about on the floor in front of the Rabbi, pants when agitated, and speaks in a voice broken with the passion of Khonen. The additional cuts made by Kushner to aid Sam Gray's performance further directed the play's action on possession. Notwithstanding the difficulties the actor had in technical rehearsals, and despite the fact that performance reports note that he was forced to wear a wire, Gray's Rabbi was reasonably strong and successful — though a few theatre critics who reviewed the opening night performance (e.g., Ben Brantley, Iris Fanger of the *Boston Herald*) made note of his obvious lack of line confidence. Still, the juxtaposition of the older, spiritually powerful Azriel with the younger, petite, yet demonic Leah made the struggle excitingly strange.

The ending of the play was perhaps the most memorable of its moments. Khonen's reunion with Leah is actually the first time in the play that the lovers touch, and Lamos crafted a "symphonic" conclusion of music, light and dance to celebrate their spiritual wedding.

A Dybbuk at Hartford Stage was essentially well-received by audiences and local reviewers. Given Kushner's recent and "sudden" post–*Angels* fame, much was made of his relationship to the project — he was lauded as a celebrity-in-residence in Connecticut. A number of out of town critics, proved to be a little less star-struck, a lot more cynical, and expecting of a remounting on Broadway, and considered the play, like *Variety's* Markland Taylor, to be a "work-in-progress" (83), while Iris Fanger suggested that "the production has not yet found its center" (47). Nevertheless, most critiques of *A Dybbuk* emphasized both the playwright's "incomparable ear and his vaulting language" — which, according to the *Boston Globe's* Richard Dyer, was Kushner's "great gift to the play" (65) — as well as the director's comparable visual gift: "Lamos has an eye equal to Kushner's ear; the first image of *A Dybbuk* is unforgettable — a panel opens in the stage and Khonen rises, moon-pale and dripping from the waters of the ritual bath" (65). This moment of the play was consistently commended by reviewers regardless of a their ultimate assessment of the overall merits of the production. Of Khonen's mikvah scene, Fanger wrote, "Lamos adds a rich and erotic prologue of the Yeshiva student Khonen, naked in the ritual bath" (47). Ben Brantley observed for the *Times*, "...the action [of the play] is persistently and tellingly physical. The play's first image is of a nude Mr. Hayden performing ritual ablutions with a viciousness that would seem to eradicate flesh" ("Talking to the Dead" C9). Succumbing to Lamos's emphasis on the play's love story and his project of possession as sexy, Brantley noted, "The dominant physical motif in the play is an embrace that expresses infinite, frustrated longing," and later added: ... The contained sexual presence of Mr. Hayden, which was used to such piquant advantage in his performance as Billy Bigelow in *Carousel*, lends a pervasive eroticism to the other students' timid discussions about the otherness of women. And when the beautiful Leah (Julie Dretzin), the object of Khonen's unspoken desire, enters this masculine sanctuary with three other women, all dressed in contrastingly rich colors, it is viscerally shocking. Improbably enough, the sexiest scene I've witnessed onstage since, well, *Carousel,* involves Leah lingeringly kissing the Torah as Khonen watches from a distance. Brantley likewise commented that "the extraordinary accomplishment of this production" was "its discovery of a pulsing core that humanizes both the play's obvious sensationalism and its drier academic elements" (C9).

Less enthusiasm was offered *A Dybbuk* for its competing plot of the powerful tzaddik and his pains to exorcise the restless soul of the forsaken Khonen. "In the production at Hartford Stage," Fanger opined, "the simple story of the beshert — the lovers destined for each other — is nearly obscured by the torrent of mystical musings, glorious images and circular explanations of meanings within meanings." Fanger furthered, "The strengthening of the subplot about Rabbi Azriel [...] is a mistaken notion, diverting attention from the fate of the lovers" (47). Yet Fanger, in her assessment of the acting in *A Dybbuk,* adjudicated Sam Gray's performance as Azriel as "problematic," charging that the actor "needs to take command of the play but does not"; a paradoxical statement, to be sure, given that she chides Kushner for strengthening Azriel's presence in the play and Gray's performance as Azriel for not being strong enough. However, it seems that Fanger's critical inconsistency points to the realities of production and rather accurately highlights the artistic tension and contention from which the Kushner-Lamos *A Dybbuk* sprung — that is, from out of the colliding worlds of a playwright's conception, a director's vision, and an actor's challenge.

Following the Hartford Stage production, Kushner reworked *A Dybbuk* for its Off Broadway premiere at the Joseph Papp Public Theatre. For this November 1997 remounting, directed by the Public's Artistic Associate Brian Kulik, the "replaywright" added an entire (albeit brief) new scene to Act III which highlighted the clash of the shtetl ways with modern notions and foreshadowed the horrors of the Holocaust. In addition, Kushner returned much of what was cut in the Hartford Stage production and added to Rabbi Azriel's lines, further emphasizing the tzaddik's spiritual uncertainty and re-exploring the mystical and kindred relationship between Rabbi and Messenger. In this incarnation, *A Dybbuk* became less about possession and more about historical collisions, as Kushner explained to Patrick Pacheco of *Newsday:*

> It's very much a drama between two worlds, not just of the living and dead, but also between the worlds of tradition and modernity, of structure and divine mystery [....] There is a sense of an ancient community on

the brink of tremendous change, and the struggle to maintain one's bearings is what the play is about [B3].

It seems that Kushner's intellectual reconceptualization of the play in its broader, post–Ansky, post–World War II, AIDS-current, pre–Millennium history allowed the playwright to focus on a more personal vision for the piece, and from this reviewing and rethinking of the play, a true emotional center emerged for him. Kushner's revisions indicate a shift in dramatic interests, away from the Leah-Khonen love story and possession toward the personal and spiritual struggles of the tzaddik "wrestling with God" in an uncertain time and place — the kind of chaotic world familiar and of greatest interest to Kushner, as is evidenced by his body of dramatic work. James Fisher best captures the true complexity of Kushner's dramatic grapplings "between two worlds" in the newly focused *A Dybbuk*:

> While the play's time period and ethnic specificity matter to Kushner, especially in the social, historical and sexual connotations he draws from folklore, his late-twentieth-century sensibility is also critically important. As he struggles to create an uneasy truce between fundamental religious faith and the secular world, Kushner strives to make the invisible visible on the stage as his focus touches on the historical ravages of the past and the future, on the order of the universe, on the need for atonement and the possibility of spiritual redemption, on honoring the dead, on celebrating the living, and on rebirth in a hauntingly atmospheric setting [147–48].

This describes *A Dybbuk* of a different color — a hue on the other side of the dramatic spectrum from possession as sexy.

It seems clear, from critical reaction to the Public's production, that Brian Kulik completely embraced Kushner's new vision for the play in his capacity as director. In comparison with press for the Hartford Stage production, for which critics chiefly dedicated column space to the Leah-Khonen love story, the content of Off Broadway reviews concentrated mostly on the exorcism and Kushner's historical juxtapositions, as is exemplified, first, in Linda Winer's report for her *Newsday* readership:

> The play — which opened last night with Ron Leibman in Brian Kulick's seriously fantastical and exuberantly musical production — is ostensibly about an exorcism in a shtetl in eastern Europe, about a dead rabbinical student who takes possession of his beloved's body on the night of her arranged marriage. As filtered through Kushner, however, the play has a deep wistfulness abut a flawed but rich culture on the precipice of apocalyptic change, about technology poised to tear through ancient truths and the seductions of assimilation ready to devastate whatever culture is left after the slaughters of the 20th Century [B2].

Michael Feingold of *The Village Voice* cut more to the quick, if not to the bone:

> Tony Kushner couldn't merely retell the myth or leave it alone: He has to shoot it down with post–Holocaust consciousness, and simultaneously overload it with superstition, an unbeliever trying frantically to recapture roots he knows to have been wiped out. As a result, what once was magical becomes soggy and muddled [111].

"It impresses on an intellectual level," offered *Daily Variety*'s Charles Isherwood, "without engaging the emotions" (n.p.). The only New York critic to review both the Hartford Stage's *A Dybbuk* as well as the Public's, Ben Brantley, essentially agreed with Isherwood's estimation, and what's more, offered his sense of scope of the production history of the play:

> Three years ago, Mark Lamos directed an earlier production at the Hartford Stage Company on which Mr. Kushner had worked with the same translator, Joachim Neugroschel. The results, while imperfect, were undeniably stirring, rich in a troubled, questing sensibility that tore at the heart [E5].

And he wrote of the Kushner-Kulick collaboration,

> A dark, soul-sapping force seems to have taken possession of Tony Kushner's adaptation [....] And it's not the sad supernatural creature of the play's title, a homeless spirit that seeks refuge in the bodies of the living. Actually, it is more as if an intellectual vampire had sunk its teeth in S. Ansky's eternally fascinating tale of a ghostly lover in a [*sic*]Eastern European shtetl in the late 19th century. For this "Dybbuk," as staged by the stylish young director Brain Kulik [*sic*], seems perversely drained of the passion that was always its hallmark. [...] the forlorn, aching communion with the dead that has traditionally informed this singular drama has been muted. And the work's dominant voice now seems to be as pedantic as that of the play's intense, insular scholars who ponder the arcane of the Talmud with furrowed brows. What on earth happened? [E5].

Brantley answers his own question in the course of his review, speculating that Kushner's and Kulick's "overall intention" was the dramatic reduction of a "sense of individual relationships for the broader historic picture" (E5).

This shift in director's conception of *A Dybbuk*, according to Brantley was further evidenced in the difference in casting of the central character of Khonen. Whereas the Lamos-Hartford Stage production offered Michael Hayden, a hunky "actor of intense sensual presence," the Kulick-Public version put forth Michael Stuhlbarg, "a mannered performer of an

other worldly, slightly androgynous mien"; Brantley chided, "This Khonen appears to have drifted into the great beyond long before he actually
dies" (E5). Stuhlbarg — who, incidentally, portrayed the Messenger in the
Hartford Stage production — as Khonen was likewise described by Winer
as having the "febrile energy of Dennis Miller mixed with Charlie Manson" (B2), while Feingold criticized the actor's "usual frenetic lack of con-
viction" in the role (111). With the choice of Stuhlbarg, it appears that
Kulick played more into Kushner's queering of *A Dybbuk*. By de-
emphasizing the physical tension and love of the beshert and presenting
a softer, intellectually passionate and distant Khonen, Kushner clarified
his gay project: "Here, all the eros is in the longing" (Goldstein 59). For
Kulick's production, the opening mikvah scene was cut; this worked to further maximize Kushner's revisioning and to minimize the sexual and erotic
power intrinsic to Lamos's. The resulting effect of a less physical Khonen,
was reportedly an absent, or, at least, nonreactive chemistry between Stul-
hbarg's Khonen and Marin Hinkle's Leah; Brantley observed that while
Hinkle "gives a vital, affecting performance, the sexual current flows only
one way" (E5). Note, however, that it was not Kushner's nor Kulick's project to make Khonen gay *per se*— though the Public production did feature
a deliberately "faygeleh" Sender (portrayed by Robert Dorfman)— instead,
it appears the intention was to inject a sense of Kushnerian ambivalence,
flexibility, restlessness (i.e., queerness), into the world of *A Dybbuk*— a
world apart from the "possession as being sexy" *A Dybbuk* of Lamos.

Works Cited

Bartow, Arthur. "Mark Lamos." *The Director's Voice: Twenty-One Interviews*. New York:
    Theatre Communications Group, 1988. 175–193.
Bloom, Harold. "Afterword." *A Dybbuk*. Adapted by Tony Kushner. New York: The-
    atre Communications Group, 1998: 109–112.
Bobbitt, Myra Hope. E-mail to the author 1 June 2004.
_____. Personal interview 12 December 1998.
Bohm-Duchen, Monica. *Chagall*. London: Phaidon Publishers, 1998.
Brantley, Ben. "A *Dybbuk* Foresees 'The Martyred Dead.'" *New York Times* 17 Novem-
    ber 1997: E5.
_____. "Talking to the Dead, Yearning for Answers." *New York Times* 20 February
    1995: C9.
Cohen, Rabbi Norman J. "Wrestling with Angels." *Tony Kushner in Conversation*.
    Edited by Robert Vorlicky. Ann Arbor: University of Michigan Press, 1998: 217–230.
Dyer, Richard. "Kushner Gives Dybbuk New Life." *Boston Globe* 15 March 1995: 65.
Fanger, Iris. "Ghost Story from the Shtetl." *Boston Herald* 23 February 1995, second
    edition: 47.
Feingold, Michael. "Spectacle and Spirit." *Village Voice* 25 November 1997: 111.

Finkle, David. Review of *Homebody/Kabul* by Tony Kushner. TheatreMania.com. 12 May 2004. <http:// www.theatermania.com/content/news.cfm?int_news_id=4715>.

Fisher, James. *The Theater of Tony Kushner: Living Past Hope.* New York: Routledge, 2001.

Fishman, Pearl. "Vakhtangov's *The Dybbuk.*" *The Drama Review* 24.3 (September 1980): 44–58.

Goldstein, Richard. "A Queer *Dybbuk*: Tony Kushner Dares to Speak the Name." *Village Voice* 2 December 1997: 59.

Gussow, Mel. "Write It, Stage It, Tweak It: Tony Kushner Continues to Tinker with *Homebody/Kabul.*" *New York Times* 9 September 2003, late edition: E1.

Hartford Stage Company. *A Dybbuk* Production Stage Manager's prompt book and additional production materials. Hartford, CT: Hartford Stage Company, 1994–1995.

Isherwood, Charles. Review of *A Dybbuk, or Between Two Worlds* by Tony Kushner. *Daily Variety* 18 November 1997, review section.

Kushner, Tony. *A Dybbuk.* Directed by Mark Lamos. Performed by Michael Hayden, Julie Dretzin, Sam Gray, et al. Hartford Stage Company, Hartford. 17 Feb. 1995.

_____. *A Dybbuk, or Between Two Worlds: A Dramatic Legend in Four Acts.* Hartford Stage Company prompt book with revisions. Hartford, CT: Hartford Stage Company, 1995.

_____. *A Dybbuk ; and, The Dybbuk Melody and Other Themes and Variations.* New York: Theatre Communications Group, Inc., 1998.

Kushner, Tony, Joachim Neugroschel and S. An-Ski. *A Dybbuk and Other Tales of the Supernatural.* New York and London: Theatre Communications Group, Inc.; Nick Hern, 1998.

"Mark Lamos." *Contemporary Theatre, Film and Television*, Volume 43. Gale Group, 2002. Reproduced in *Biography Resource Center.* Farmington Hills, MI: The Gale Group. 2004. http://galenet.galegroup.com/servlet/BioRC.

Marks, Peter. "Tony Kushner, Replaywright." *Washington Post* 8 March 2004: C01.

Neugroschel, Joachim, editor and translator *The Dybbuk and the Yiddish Imagination: A Haunted Reader.* Syracuse, NY: Syracuse University Press, 2000.

_____. "Translator's Note," *Ansky['s] The Dybbuk or Between Two Worlds: A Dramatic Legend in Four Acts.* Belle Harbor, NY: Joachim Neugroschel, 1992.

Pacheco, Patrick. "Caught Between Different Worlds: Kushner Adaptation Probes a Crisis of Faith." *Newsday* 18 November 1997: B3.

Rizzo, Frank. "A Curtain Falls: Two Impresarios of Regional Theatre Reminisce." *Hartford Courant* 15 November 1997: F1.

_____. "Kushner's 'A' Not 'The' *Dybbuk* for Hartford Stage Production." *Hartford Courant* 30 December 1994: E3.

_____. "Kushner's *Dybbuk* Ready for the Stage." *Hartford Courant* 12 February 1995: G1.

Roskies, David G. "Introduction." *The Dybbuk and Other Writings.* New York: Schocken Books, 1992. xi–xxxvi.

Staton, David M. "Playwright Tony Kushner Adapts *A Dybbuk* for Hartford Stage." *Scene: News from Hartford Stage* Feb. 1995: 1–2.

Stevens, Amy. Telephone interview 6 Dec. 1998.

Taylor, Markland. Review of *A Dybbuk, or Between Two Worlds* by Tony Kushner. *Variety* 27 February–5 March 1995: 83.

Traveling Jewish Theatre (TJT). Dybbuk. 7 June 2004. <*http://www.atjt.com/Archives/04_dybbuk.htm*>.

Vandergrift, Deborah. Personal interview 12 December 1998.

Vorlicky, Robert H., editor "Introduction." *Tony Kushner in Conversation.* Ann Arbor: University of Michigan Press, 1998: 1–10.

Winer, Linda. "Revisiting Spirits and Mystery." *Newsday* 17 November 1997: B2.

10

Repairing Reality

The Media and *Homebody/Kabul* in New York, 2001

JACOB JUNTUNEN

Coming out of the subway onto Fourth Street on my way to see *Homebody/Kabul* at the New York Theatre Workshop (NYTW), the evening was cold but clear. The crime-filled mass transit system I heard about growing up on the West Coast in the 1980s was not the subway I took in 2002. This was a post–Giuliani, post–9/11 subway: clean, friendly, and with a car that had a recorded voice telling me the next stop instead of a static-filled and unintelligible announcement from the driver. Walking East on Fourth Street, I passed Washington Square, NYU, and the innumerable coffee shops, record stores, boutiques and restaurants of the upscale East Village. The neighborhood increased my feeling of being a sophisticated and literate person going to see what was being billed as the first major work by playwright Tony Kushner since his 1993 epic *Angels in America* (New York Theatre Workshop, "Press Release").

I knew *Homebody/Kabul* had already been extended twice (once before even opening), and that every evening was either selling out or coming close to it. There were only six articles about the planned New York production before the World Trade Center attacks of 2001, and their main concern was how *Homebody/Kabul* would compare to *Angels in America* (Hall; Hartigan; Bornstein; McKinley; Hurwitt; Beck), but after the World Trade Center attacks the media coverage of *Homebody/Kabul* was amazingly extensive. Over seventy articles would eventually be written about the 2001 NYTW production. These reviews ranged from "celebrating" the play by calling it the most "important drama in the last decade" (Heilpern) to criticizing the play as propaganda written by a "Taliban playwright" (Phillips). Depending on what paper(s) they read, audience members could enter the NYTW expecting to see dangerous terrorist propaganda, the latest work to restore political and artistic relevance to U.S. theatre, or any number of positions in-between. In fact, considering there were seventy-seven separate articles written about the NYTW production of *Homebody/Kabul* (see appendix 1), it is quite likely that audience members had extremely different expectations about the play they were about to see. Susan Bennett writes that

> multiple horizons of expectations are bound to exist within any culture and these are, always, open to renegotiation before, during, and after the theatrical performance. The relationship then between culture and the idea of the theatrical event is one that is necessarily flexible and inevitably rewritten on a daily basis [Bennett 106].

This is even more the case with *Homebody/Kabul* because of the sheer number of potential articles and points of view to which an audience member could have been exposed before the performance. Due to the number of ideological frames through which audience members could be viewing the play, this production in particular is a likely spot for cultural "renegotiation." Ric Knowles considers theatrical performances "cultural productions which serve specific cultural and theatrical communities at particular historical moments as sites for the negotiation, transmission, and transformation of cultural values" (Knowles 10). Since the NYTW production of *Homebody/Kabul* came so soon after the World Trade Center attacks of 2001 and during the U.S. invasion of Afghanistan, the play was a perfect site for cultural negotiation, for the "transmission, and transformation of cultural values." But this did not merely occur in the production.

Marvin Carlson argues that "both theatre organizations and public have come to accept reviewers as 'official' readers of productions, giving to their reactions a particular authority" (Carlson 1990, 23). So the reviews of any production carry a "particular" weight in the cultural negotiation surrounding it. And, in the fall of 2001, *Homebody/Kabul's* relation to current events made it a site of intense cultural negotiation. Rarely has a small, non-profit, Off Broadway production received such extensive media attention. This makes the NYTW production of *Homebody/Kabul* an ideal case study for examining the role of the media in the political work of popular U.S. theatre in the early twenty-first century. By analyzing the reviews of *Homebody/Kabul*, one can view what Carlson calls the "official" discourse surrounding the play which, in this case, relates to the "official discourse" surrounding the World Trade Center attacks and the emerging discourse from Washington about the "war on terror." The seventy-seven

articles about *Homebody/Kabul* are material evidence of public discourse
writing and rewriting the meaning of both the play and recent events.
When the World Trade Center was attacked in September of 2001 and
the U.S. responded by invading Afghanistan, suddenly the U.S. media was
full of stories about burqas, hijab, and other cultural aspects of Afghanistan,
particularly its treatment of women (who the U.S. was supposedly liberating while at the same time exacting "justice"). This changed the view of
Homebody/Kabul— which deals with some of these same cultural aspects of
Afghanistan —from one where the artists involved with the production
expected the typical American audience member to be ignorant of Afghan
culture to one where the artists expected the audience to have a certain basic
knowledge of Afghanistan. As NYTW artistic director Jim Nicola put it, "It's
almost impossible to not encounter [the play] through the lens of our common experience of the last three months and see that as the major element
of it" (Nicola). Theatre scholar James Fisher writes that "Kushner has seen
his newest play, *Homebody/Kabul*, which he began writing nearly four years
ago, become, as his two-play epic *Angels in America* did a decade ago, a
lightning rod for social and political debate on questions of immediate
import." (Fisher ix) An important difference, though, is that when Kushner wrote *Angels in America* he was looking back at events that had already
happened and was commenting on them. In *Homebody/Kabul*, a coincidence
of world events made his play appear to comment on the present.

The publicity and reviews for the production invariably noted that the
play had been in the works for several years and that no one involved was
deliberately capitalizing on the recent tragic events. Nevertheless, it was
impossible to walk towards a theatre in New York in the fall of 2001 to see
a play partially set in Kabul without thinking about the current historical
moment. In mid–September, when George W. Bush literally used "dead or
alive" rhetoric in his "crusade" against Osama bin Laden, 4,000 Afghans fled
into Pakistan each day (Bush, 9/17/2001; Bush, 9/16/2001). The Taliban
offered to turn in bin Laden if given some evidence of his guilt, but the Bush
Administration was not interested in negotiating. Also in mid–September,
"the League of American Theaters and Producers quickly hammered out an
agreement whereby performers in suddenly imperiled [New York] shows
would accept pay cuts for a month to minimize financial damage that came
from drastically reduced attendance" (Pressley). There was also a "new look
for entertainment in a terror-conscious world" (Leland and Marks). Movies,
television shows, plays, books, popular music, video games, and the internet all voluntarily toned down anything that might be seen as inappropriate. Stephen Sondheim's musical, *Assassins*, was pulled from the 2001–02
Broadway season; Arnold Schwarzenegger and Tim Allen both had movies

pulled due to terrorist connections (one an action movie, the other a comedy); Jon Stewart began his normally irreverent show after a week off the air by saying, "I'm sorry to do this to you; it's another entertainment show beginning with an overwrought speech of a shaken host"; and even the satirical internet magazine *Modern Humorist* which regularly published scathing satires of Bush wrote, "You probably wouldn't guess that the creeps behind *Modern Humorist* are the sort who wave flags and sing 'America the Beautiful' with strangers on the street.... But that is what we have been doing, in unity with others" (Leland and Marks).

In contrast, the NYTW production of *Homebody/Kabul* was produced as planned. Reporting on the production, *Newsweek* wrote, "Surely Kushner wouldn't dare go ahead with *Homebody/Kabul*, a play set in Afghanistan that features a Taliban mullah, women in burqas and at least one reference to Osama bin Laden. Or would he?" (Peyser). Of course, whether to go ahead with the production was not entirely the playwright's decision, and artistic director Jim Nicola and Kushner had "some discussion about it" (M. Phillips, "After the Attack"). But in the end they "didn't consider the possibility of postponing for very long" (Michael Phillips, "After the Attack").

Even though *Homebody/Kabul* is decidedly not "about" the events of 2001, the reaction to it in the media made it seem like it was by combining Kushner's views on world events and the play. In particular, an interview published first in the *Los Angeles Times* in September and then in the *Chicago Tribune* in October (M. Phillips, "After the Attack"; "Art Imitates"), and an interview from *Newsweek* in December (Peyser), quote Kushner's political views as if they are part of the play. These interviews collapse Kushner's comments on current events and his play into one conversation. This created a frame through which the play was seen in every review after them: that the play is a liberal comment on the events of fall 2001.

In the interview published in September and October 2001, Kushner described being in Ireland when the World Trade Center was attacked, and how the British and Irish press was incredibly sympathetic to the suffering in the United States. But he went on to state how the British and Irish press

> was also full of a kind of European horror at the American cowboy mentality so stunningly embodied by our president. It created an impression that frightened me — the impression that America could only respond to this by talking like this was the shootout at the OK Corral. A depressing number of people think this is truly a war, which it is not, in any sense [M. Phillips, "Art Imitates"; "After the Attack"].

This criticism of both President Bush and a more general "American cowboy mentality" went against the Bush Administration's "crusade" rhetoric

(Bush, 9/16/2001). And by actively questioning whether the attacks on the World Trade Center truly constituted "a war," Kushner also blatantly interrogated the Bush Administration's "war on terror" rhetoric first used on September 16th and then used non-stop (Bush, 9/16/2001). Neither of these liberal critiques of the Bush Administration and a particular brand of U.S. conservatism had anything to do with the play *Homebody/Kabul*, but the interview was explicitly about the play and so Kushner's liberal take on the events of fall 2001 was associated with the play he wrote before those events took place.

In the *Newsweek* interview that began by suggesting that "certainly Kushner wouldn't dare go ahead with *Homebody/Kabul*" after the World Trade Center attacks, Kushner stated that he knew "a lot more about the situation than a lot of the people [he heard] on talk shows, which is not always reassuring because some of them are generals" (Peyser). Regardless of the veracity of that claim, it again had nothing to do with the play *Homebody/Kabul*, but was again in an interview explicitly about the play. Thus the comment critiqued the generals running the "war on terrorism" and became associated with the production in a way that framed the play as a liberal critique on the events of 2001.

In October 2001, the United States began a ground assault against the Taliban, and in November the U.S. began to take cities previously held by the Taliban. On December 1, the National Endowment for the Arts delayed a $60,000 grant for a production of *Homebody/Kabul* scheduled to take place later that season at Berkeley Repertory Theatre (Pogrebin, "Arts Agency"). *Newsweek* commented that "some people"—meaning, in this case, the U.S. government—"still don't love the idea [of *Homebody/Kabul*]" (Peyser). Nevertheless, on December 5, 2001 *Homebody/Kabul* had its first preview performance at the NYTW, and on that same day Hamid Karzai was chosen to head the interim government of Afghanistan. On December 16, the United States declared that al-Queda was destroyed in Afghanistan, and three days later *Homebody/Kabul* had its official New York opening while the NEA approved funding for the Berkeley production (Pogrebin, "Split Decision"; Trescott).

All these events effected what Susan Bennett calls "selection." The selection process begins with a theatre's selection of plays to produce, and ends with an audience member choosing a play to see on a particular evening. Bennett writes that "where groups are reliant on government grants, self-imposed censorship may well result." It is interesting that even though the NYTW is a non-profit theatre dependent upon many grants, it nevertheless chose to go ahead with the production of *Homebody/Kabul*. This decision was partly based on Kushner's attitude that there was nothing controversial in the play, and partly based on artistic director Jim Nicola's willingness to take a risk that no other New York theatre was willing to take: to produce a play that could potentially offend in fall of 2001. But this gamble ultimately paid off with sellout crowds, two extensions, and eventually three separate U.S. productions and one U.K. production in the 2001–02 season alone (Snyder).

It is undeniable, however, that world events and the controversy surrounding the production effected audience members' decision to buy tickets. Bennett points out that "the audience member is always buying another's ideology" and that reviews often "determine a very specific set of expectations in the audience and thus determine how that audience will receive the play" (Bennett 118, 22). As Marvin Carlson puts it, "Even a reader who does not believe that a new play is likely to truly be 'the wittiest comedy since Noel Coward' will be unlikely, having read such a comment, to see the play without Coward's becoming a more or less conscious intertextual element in the reception" (*Theatre Semiotics* 23–24). The ideologically charged articles responding to Kushner's play that collapsed his liberal critique of the events of fall 2001 with *Homebody/Kabul* could not help but become part of the audience's reception of the play.

For instance, beyond saying "Kushner wouldn't dare" allow *Homebody/Kabul* to be produced, the *Newsweek* interview from mid–December stated that, "While *Homebody* is clearly anti–Taliban, Kushner allows his most radical creations to speak their minds in a way that may feel uncomfortable now that any criticism of America is deemed unpatriotic," and quotes Kushner saying, "You're not going to see a four-hour play about Afghanistan because you're looking for an easy night" (Peyser). These types of comments, along with the NEA controversy and Kushner's political comments during interviews, created a relatively specific (if perhaps mistaken) horizon of expectations for audience members: this play is a liberal critique of America that is related to current events.

However, an audience's horizon of expectations is not based solely on the media reception of the play; it is also based on material elements of the experience like the neighborhood, the theatre's architecture and amenities, the pre-show scenery, and the program. Carlson writes that beyond "providing a space for a public to watch a performance, [a theatre] will provide many additional connotative meanings to the culture of which it is a part" (*Theatre Semiotics* 43), and Bennett adds that "the milieu which surrounds a theatre is always ideologically encoded and the presence of a theatre can be measured as typical or incongruous within it" (Bennett 126). Seeing *Homebody/Kabul* at the NYTW was entirely typical of the space surrounding it. Surely there was no better place to see a play framed as oppositional to conservative U.S. policy than the East Village, famed for housing generations of rebellious artists and intellectuals among its coffee shops and lofts.

Walking along a wide sidewalk littered with the East Village's typical garbage cans and parked bicycles, and passing the art galleries and coffee shops that surrounded the theatre space, the audience reached two sets of plain, glass doors. The façade of the NYTW was unimposing and fit right into the shops surrounding it. Indeed, one might walk by it without noticing the theatre. Its under-statedness meant that the excitement of seeing a performance there did not arise from a marquee proclaiming the stars about to take the stage; instead it came from the East Village milieu and the impending theatre event itself.

Since the lobby is the first space that a theatre audience inhabits after it enters the theatre, it is an extremely important aspect of the framing of the experience. Knowles writes that lobbies "are today perhaps even more significant than entranceways in terms of their impact on the theatrical experience ... particularly in their framing and preparing audience horizons of expectations" (Knowles 71). The NYTW's small lobby, already cramped at 7:30 p.m. from people trying to get out of the cold, had little decoration besides a black and white sign with show times for *Homebody/Kabul* and a few quotes from reviews. There were no concessions being sold in the lobby, no fancy bar, or even coffee. The only amenity the lobby offered was a small, cramped bathroom. Like the unpretentious façade, the lobby without amenities emphasized the theatrical production as the main event rather than integrating the evening with cocktails and making it a "social occasion" connected to activities (such as dinner, etc.) occurring outside the theatrical space.

Likewise the auditorium was quite austere. There were two aisles, left and right, no balcony, unadorned walls made of gray bricks, and red plush seats. Carlson writes, "The possession of a box at the opera has traditionally been regarded in Western society as one of the most dependable signs of membership in the privileged classes" (*Theatre Semiotics* 45), but the NYTW did not have boxes. In fact, the 188 seats were all on the same level (there was no balcony), and they all had more or less the same view of the stage. With this seating arrangement, and with tickets at the uniform price of $60, there was a certain egalitarianism demonstrated in the theatre's architecture.

The stage was a proscenium and appeared to have a black curtain in front of it, so there was no preset to examine. The "proscenium stage (as progenitor of the cinematic and televisual screen) is the closest thing that theatre has to an audience-stage relationship that contemporary English-language theatrical cultures considers to be 'normal,' and that theatre workers and audiences tend to take for granted." (Knowles 63) The lack of pre-show spectacle again encouraged excitement from the impending show rather than from the intricate architecture or stage design.

The program was marked by a tremendous amount of blank space. It was not a glossy production full of ads, but a stapled booklet of white paper and black print. The cover merely said, "New York Theatre Workshop" in a small font with no logo; the inside cover gave the e-mail address of the artistic director, and invited "Questions? Comments? Suggestions?"; the third page simply stated the title and playwright; and the rest of the program was taken up by explanations of the theatre's artistic mission, bios, the artists involved with workshops, and the donors to the theatre (New York Theatre Workshop, "Homebody/Kabul Program"). But the blankness and simplicity of the program were its most prominent features; this was in keeping with the modest façade, the lack of amenities in the lobby, and the austere auditorium architecture.

The last element that can help frame a production is one of the most difficult to quantify: the composition of the audience itself. Any actor or regular theatre-goer knows that shows vary wildly from one night to the next depending on how an audience reacts to the performance. While this reaction cannot exactly be measured, there is one aspect of audience composition that can: the number of seats filled. Bennett writes that "the percentage of seats occupied will inevitably affect reception both through its effect on the quality of the actors' performances and through inter-spectator relations" (Bennett 131). *Homebody/Kabul* sold out nearly every night in New York, and "when a theatre is at capacity, not only can this enhance an audience's confidence to respond to the performance, but it can also reaffirm the spectators' sense of themselves both individually and as a group" (Bennett 131). But what did it mean to be an individual member of a group of people at this particular play?

Repairing Reality

Before September 11, 2001, there were few articles about the upcoming Kushner play, and they concentrated on its relationship to *Angels in America*. They tended to be speculative interviews about "the curse of the sophomore slump" (Beck), and to focus on Kushner's concern about being a "one hit wonder" and having an "Angel on his back" (Beck; Hall). But that all changed after Afghanistan became part of United States' common parlance through extensive media coverage; *Homebody/Kabul* went from being compared to Kushner's previous work to being compared to real life events, from being his "sophomore work" to "eerily prescient" (Marks). After the World Trade Center attacks, a national narrative was quickly created in the media and in the Bush administration akin to a Hollywood action movie. Indeed, even those in New York who witnessed the events with their own eyes rather than mediated through television images "remarked in some way or another that the event seemed not like reality but like a disaster film ... [so] it is hardly surprising that our imaginations should find that the almost inevitable point of reference" (Carlson, "9/11" 3–4). And even if one did not find real life to be like a disaster film, people began to find their "personal images eclipsed by the images that were the only visual source for most of the rest of the world, for whom the 'mediatization' of those images was present from the beginning" (Carlson, "9/11" 4). These observations by Carlson led him to his larger and convincing argument that

> Films like *Independence Day* provided an immediate orienting scenario that almost at once could be seen reflected, if unacknowledged, through the media and certainly in the Bush Government. According to this scenario, a peaceful, peace-loving, and generally admirable and blameless America is suddenly subjected to a vicious and unprovoked attack by some alien power.... The hitherto quiet and trusting United States, however, immediately mobilizes and eventually tracks down and destroys the evil aliens who were so unwise as to awaken this sleeping giant [Carlson, "9/11" 4].

This unconscious but ever-present frame of reference was reflected in television news channel's musical themes first relating to September 11th then the "war on terror," and certainly in President Bush's sudden "conversion" from an unpopular leader to a man on a "crusade" against the "Darth Vader of our times" (Carlson, "9/11" 4), Osama bin Laden.

In this environment hostile to any narrative where the United States was not "blameless," *Homebody/Kabul* became a lightning rod for public commentary about dissent from the action movie narrative. This is not surprising considering that a shift in ideology was clearly happening in the United States and since art is often the focal point of ideological shifts, the places where such social movements are made visible and negotiated. And since *Homebody/Kabul* was the only dissenting voice in popular theatre (and, indeed, in the entertainment media in general as shown by the reluctance to produce or distribute any piece of entertainment that might be deemed "unpatriotic" after the World Trade Center attacks1), *Homebody/Kabul* became the site of cultural negotiation.

Clifford Geertz argues that works of art "bring a particular cast of mind out into the world of objects, where men [and women] can look at it" (Geertz 99). *Homebody/Kabul* allowed audience members to consider a "cast of mind" where the United States was not entirely blameless for the Taliban's existence. But this did not happen in a static environment. Indeed, Raymond Williams argues that such ideological shifts are never static, and that the threshold of ideological change is always in constant motion in what he calls a "structure of feeling." Williams writes that a structure of feeling is

> often indeed not yet recognized as social but taken to be private, idiosyn-cratic and even isolating, but which in analysis (though rarely otherwise) has its emergent, connecting and dominant characteristics, indeed its specific hierarchies. These are often more recognizable at a later stage, when they have been formalized, classified and in many cases built into institutions and formations [Williams 197].

At the moment of *Homebody/Kabul's* production, the "war on terror" hege-mony was clearly becoming dominant, but even as such it was emergent because the country was still making sense of recent events. Therefore, while any expression against it was rare (and considered inappropriate), there was a sense that a competing, more liberal ideology could still pre-vail, especially if the competing ideology attached itself to U.S. actions in Afghanistan during the Cold War which made the U.S. far from a "blame-less" character in the World Trade Center attacks (For a more detailed analy-sis of the self-censorship that occurred after the World Trade Center attacks, see John Leland and Peter Marks, "New Look for Entertainment in a Terror-Conscious World," *New York Times* 24 September 2001, and Linda Win-ter, "What's Appropriate Now?," *Newsday* 23 September 2001).

But, more importantly in the analysis of the media reaction to *Home-body/Kabul*, as the Bush Administration's "war on terror" hegemony was being "formalized" and "built into institutions and formations" in United States government via the Patriot Act and other legislation and speeches, anyone who held an opposing ideology was likely to feel "private, idiosyn-cratic" and, especially, "isolat[ed]" (Williams 197). This made *Homebody/ Kabul* an especially important site of resistance to the Bush Administra-tion hegemony because it allowed 188 people to come together nightly and experience an alternative view. But also, and perhaps more importantly, because seventy-seven newspaper articles and several television and radio spots broadcast Kushner's alternative politics nationwide, this resistant ideology was broadcast nationally. Thus the media coverage of the play is extremely important to analyze because it is a record from that moment of people's reactions to a resistant ideology.

According to media theorist James Carey, there are two ways to analyze a newspaper: using the transmission view of communication or the
ritual view of communication. At the center of the transmission view of
communication is "the transmission of signals or messages over distance
for the purpose of control" (Carey 15). This view posits that the producer
of communication has information, like a good to be transported, that is
sent via the medium to the audience, who receives that information like
a product.

Carey defines the ritual view of communication by saying it "is
directed not toward the extension of messages in space but towards the
maintenance of society in time; not the act of imparting information but
the representation of shared beliefs" (Carey 18). Therefore, according to
the ritual view of communication, the goal is not to disseminate information as far as possible for reasons of control and persuasion, but instead
to make the already existing society as unified as possible. Carey argues:

> This projection of community ideals and their embodiment in material
> form — dance, plays, architecture, news stories, strings of speech —creates
> an artificial though nonetheless real symbolic order that operates to pro-
> vide not information but confirmation, not to alter attitudes or change
> minds but to represent an underlying order of things, not to perform func-
> tions but to manifest an ongoing and fragile social process [Carey 19].

In other words, one can look at "news stories"—in this case, reviews of
Homebody/Kabul—not as "information" that is disseminated to people
outside the community of readers, but instead as "confirmation" to the
already extant community of readers about how the play is related to that
community's view of the "underlying order of things."

Writing explicitly about newspapers, Carey says, "If one examines a
newspaper under a transmission view of communication, one sees the
medium as an instrument for disseminating news and knowledge.... Questions arise as to the effects of this on audiences: news as enlightening or
obscuring reality, as changing or hardening attitudes, as breeding credibility or doubt" (Carey 20). While this methodology is crucial to many
forms of analysis—finding instances of political bias in news reporting, for
instance—it will not help expose how the reviews are a record of the
reviewer's reactions to a resistant ideology. For that, a ritual view of communication is necessary. As Carey writes,

> A ritual view of communication will focus on a different range of prob-
> lems examining a newspaper. It will, for example, view reading a newspa-
> per less as sending or gaining information and more as attending a mass,

a situation in which nothing new is learned but in which a particular view of the world is portrayed and confirmed. News reading, and writing, is a ritual act and moreover a dramatic one [20].

Thus, when examining a newspaper using the ritual view of communication, "news reading, and writing" becomes "a ritual," and, as Geertz suggests, a ritual is a way to "bring a particular cast of mind out into the world of objects" (Geertz 99). This methodology allows the one analyzing the news articles to examine "a particular view of the world," and doing so in the case of *Homebody/Kabul* will make clear its relation to the hegemonic "war on terrorism" ideology.

Of course, neither the transmission nor ritual view is happening exclusively when one reads a newspaper. Carey makes it clear that each must be taken into account. But with regard to theatre reviews, the information transmitted is far from the transmission of "pure" facts about the play, and much closer to transmitting opinions, often, as Carlson argues, opinions which are viewed by the public as "official" and having "authority" (*Theatre Semiotics* 23). So reviews of *Homebody/Kabul* are not merely giving their readers facts which they can acquire, but are allowing the reader to join "a world of contending forces," which in this case were competing narratives about how to make sense of the world after the World Trade Center was destroyed, and, importantly, how to deal with this play's singular dissenting voice from the "war on terrorism" narrative where the U.S. is a blameless character. Carey writes that in general "news changes little from day to day" (Carey 21) but there are times when changes occur. In those moments "reality must be repaired" through ritual communication (Carey 30). The reviews analyzed here represent the scores of reviews written that attempt to "repair reality" and were chosen based on their extremity; their ideologies are remarkably clear because of their rhetorical extremes, but they nonetheless represent larger categories of reviews.

For the reviews of *Homebody/Kabul* that support the nascent "war on terror" hegemony and therefore disagree with the supposedly dissenting ideology of *Homebody/Kabul*, there are two ways to fit Kushner into their narrative: envelope his dissenting view that rejects a "blameless" United States, or excommunicate him from rational thought. The first technique (enveloping) is best represented by an article for *The Weekly Standard* by John Podhoretz, a regular columnist for *The New York Post*. The very title of his stunning review begins the work of incorporating Kushner's play into his world view: "Even an America-hater Has His Limits" (Podhoretz 21). While Kushner may hate America, even he cannot truly doubt America's innocence and right to retaliate. Podhoretz quotes Kushner saying that New Yorkers are "less hawkish" and are not "in lock step behind" Bush (Podhoretz 21), and then contradicts these supposedly out of touch views by invoking scenes of New Yorkers chanting "USA! USA!" at ground zero and Bush's response that "the people who knocked these buildings down will hear from us soon" (Bush, 9/14/2001). Podhoretz calls Kushner "isolated ... in those coffeehouse conversations with the world's oldest living Bolsheviks" (Podhoretz 23). But, says Podhoretz, "Kushner is actually trying to teach the world in *Homebody/Kabul*— that there existed in the world a regime of sadistic barbarity, a fanatical regime that could not be reasoned or negotiated with, that could only be destroyed" (Podhoretz 23). Podhoretz is speaking here of the Taliban, but I think Kushner might well think that sentence best describes the Bush Administration. Nevertheless, Podhoretz clearly spells out what he thinks *Homebody/Kabul* means: "It means that when it comes to the face of evil in Afghanistan, some truths are so obvious even the most determined anti–American leftist can't miss them" (Podhoretz 23). With this review Podhoretz, rightly or wrongly, cast Kushner into the fold of those who thought the Taliban must be destroyed. Iris Fanger mirrored Podhoretz's technique in *Christian Science Monitor* when she wrote, "What gives the play added urgency is Kushner's dramatization of the desperation of people living under a totalitarian regime and how survival comes to supersede any moral laws" (Fanger 19). Fanger finds in Kushner's play the moral that whether it is their fault or not, the residents of Afghanistan lost all respect for "moral laws" under the Taliban, and the "peace-loving" United States has no choice but to destroy them.

The most common way to deal with Kushner's dissenting view of current events, however, is simply to excommunicate him from the world of rational thought, and the easiest way to do this is to charge him with the crime of not making Westerners blameless victims. Mark Steyn in the *New Criterion* writes that "Kushner is inverting the perspective of traditional Imperial drama: the English are the primitive exotics, the Afghans are cultured, educated, artistic, urbane, articulate, poets, and librarians, masters of all the virtues the metropolitan power once claimed for itself" (Steyn 38). And, because of this inversion, Kushner is comparable to "the left's 'peace movement'" which "got nowhere after September 11th ... because they were obvious know-nothings, the lame generalities of their demo placards untroubled by anything so tiresome as a verifiable fact about the region" (Steyn 41). And, while Kushner has "taken the trouble to unearth ten-thousand facts" he still "has as little to say as the ignoramuses [of the peace-movement]" (Steyn 41). Because Kushner does not see the Afghans as alien, and, indeed gives them characteristics that are not only recognizably human but civilized, he has missed the crucial "fact about the region," and therefore his play has nothing to say. Likewise as notable a critic as Robert Brustein writing for *The New Republic* decides that "with the exception of the Homebody, all of the Western characters are singularly unappealing, and the occasional anti–Western sentiments that we overhear suggest that this is deliberate" (Brustein 27). In the end, Brustein argues that "thanks to the Homebody, we leave the theater having learned a lot more about Afghanistan than we knew when we came. But it is knowledge that has not been sufficiently rooted in either the human events of the play or the events of recent history" (Brustein 27). So, again, while the play may have some facts in it, it does not take into account "the events of recent history" and is therefore unimportant in the shaping of ideas about "recent history."

The most dramatic excommunication of Kushner takes place in the *USA Today* review written by Elysa Gardner. She begins the review by describing a dream she had in which she attends the play with Donald Rumsfeld, President Bush's hawkish Secretary of Defense. In her dream, Rumsfeld "bellows" against this "irreverence" and yells that it is "an affront to everything our brave young people are fighting for abroad" (Gardner D9). Upon awakening, her first impulse is to defend Kushner, but after a moment she

> then decided [her] dream date may have had a point ... in trying to illustrate the historical and political complexities behind Afghanistan's suffering ... [Kushner] ultimately makes the Afghan characters more sympathetic, and more interesting, than the Anglos, who are portrayed as nattering, navel-gazing substance abusers and misanthropes [Gardner D9].

Kushner's capital crime, once again, is not making the Westerners central to the narrative, nor portraying them as paragons of righteousness. This offense makes the official view — in this case actually represented by a subconscious internalization of a government official — supersede Kushner's.

For reviews that are sympathetic with an ideology that resists the Bush Administration's "war on terror," the most common strategy is to praise the play (whatever its dramaturgical shortcomings) for its accurate portrayal of the characters. Michael Feingold in *The Village Voice* writes that "as for the nature and causes of that trouble [the World Trade Center attacks], politically [Kushner] has them pegged ... that Westerners (and in particular Americans) don't approach the rest of the world on its own terms or make the effort to perceive it from its own point of view" (Feingold 60). In direct contrast to trying to push Kushner's point of view outside the bounds of rational thought, Feingold embraces it as absolutely correct. Likewise, Julia M. Klein *in The Chronicle for Higher Education* finds that "some of the play's best scenes ... involve the [Westerners] sharing political insights and drugs—another form of traveling" (Klein B20). This is a far cry from the concerns in other reviews that the Westerners are unsympathetic junkies. *The Nation's* review by Elizabeth Pochoda even finds that the Homebody, the one character the more conservative reviews found likeable, is "dangerously charming because the question remains: What exactly does a person do when faced with a calamity of historic proportions? When we are so overwhelmed, she says, we succumb to luxury" (Pochoda 35). This is particularly interesting since Bush's advice to United States citizens after the attacks was to go shopping or to visit Disney World (Bush, 9/27/2001). So, Pochoda finds that the one "charming" Western character represents the exact danger that the official narrative is proposing as the best way to react to "a calamity of historic proportions."

Richard Christiansen directly contradicts the Bush Administration rhetoric of "us versus them" when he writes in the *Chicago Tribune* that "*Homebody/Kabul* is not about good people versus bad people. It is a play about people caught in a clash of cultures that has corroded and corrupted the network of our humanity" (Christiansen 5.3). And Michael Phillips' review in the *Los Angeles Times* states that "Kushner's play is clearly not on the side of the Taliban, though it takes pains to humanize (or at least not demonize) what these bumbling English citizens abroad see as The Other" (Michael Phillips, "Response" A5). He also writes that "this isn't the sort of thing many Americans want to confront right now, as the war on terrorism wears on. And yet, the world premiere's run has already been extended through Feb. 10" (Michael Phillips, "Response" A5). While sympathetic with the play, he does not or cannot explain what he sees as a contradiction: that here is a popular play confronting potential American blame and the Taliban's humanity.

This contradiction is explained, however, when one considers that this play was being treated by the media as the one piece of theatre in the fall of 2001 that was resisting the Bush Administration's "war on terror" rhetoric. Indeed, with the cancellation of movies, TV shows, and the toning down of everything from the internet to late night talk-shows, *Homebody/Kabul* may have been the only popular entertainment to contradict the official narrative.

James Reston Jr., analyzing the play in *American Theatre*, writes that the Afghan characters "speak most pointedly to the situation America now faces in Central Asia" and that because of the play "we see how atrocity is possible, everywhere, by anyone, for any reason" (Reston 50). This, again, goes against the official narrative of Afghans as alien monsters, to be destroyed not understood. Reston also writes that "all fall, the newspapers and news-magazines had been confounded by Arab wrath.... What the theatre can display better than any other medium is passion. This includes the passion of the Arab religious fanatic and the passion of his most immediate victim" (Reston 52). Perhaps *Homebody/Kabul* displayed the "passion" at the heart of "Arab wrath" that so confused the U.S. news media with its countless stories on "Why do they hate us?"

If theatre can indeed portray passion better than CNN and editorial pages, then it makes sense that people would seek out relevant theatre in times of change, especially if that change was caused by people's "wrath." Perhaps timely theatre offers a way to make manifest a "structure of feeling." While theatre that contradicts the official narrative might be uncomfortable for some to watch, it would surely be proportionately comforting to those who struggle against the official narrative. And whichever side of the ideological fence a particular audience member might place him or herself, viewing the "passion" that is missing in the endless news reports might be pleasurable in some other sense, perhaps cathartic. The night I saw the play there was certainly a great deal of crying at emotionally charged moments where the performance text and reality suddenly collided, such as a line spoken by an Afghan woman character that was often quoted in reviews: "You love the Taliban so much, bring them to New York. Well don't worry, they're coming to New York!" (Kushner 85). Moments like that did not occur on CNN. And if you were looking for catharsis, you could cry at that line whether you were liberal or conservative. But if, as Reston describes *Homebody/Kabul*, "we see no American flags fluttering on this stage, hear no macho one-liners from a Wild West American president" and if "this is a play for those who are interested in the root causes that proceeded Sept. 11, for those who can see through the fog of patriotism to the finer distinctions, who are finally ready to ask how on earth do we get out of this godforsaken place, who can bear to contemplate the thought that we have participated to some extent in our own tragedy" (Reston 53), then it was singular in the popular theatre in New York City in the fall of 2001. And that singularity is extremely important in questioning why people chose to see the production.

Phillips states that the sold out run of the play is "surprising" because the play contained views that "many Americans [did not] want to confront" (Phillips, "Response" A5). But its singularity, the fact that *Homebody/Kabul* was the one piece of popular theatre one could see in New York where an opposing ideology was made manifest in art, makes the response quite logical. It was because of these views that people saw the play: views which may or may not be in the text, but were framed by the journalism surrounding the play, by the "liberal" East Village location, by the advertising focusing on the reviews, by the theatre's "blank" architecture and program that did not contradict the horizon of expectations that audiences brought to the play, and most importantly by Kushner's leftist comments during interviews that were collapsed into the play's reviews. Because of all these frames, the audience's horizon of expectation was focused on the play's supposed relation to current events and on its supposedly oppositional ideology. Its success was not in spite of its opposition to the dominant ideology, but because of it.

Works Cited

Beck, John. "Kushner Hopes Early Success Is No Jinx." *Milwaukee Journal Sentinel* 6 February 2001: 01E.
Bennett, Susan. *Theatre Audiences: A Theory of Production and Reception.* Second edition. New York: Routledge, 1997.
Bornstein, Lisa. "Playwright Unleashes Ideas in a Machinegun Fashion." *Rocky Mountain News* 11 February 2001: 7D.
Brustein, Robert. "Angels in Afghanistan." *The New Republic* 18 March 2002: 27.
Bush, George W. *Remarks by the President to Airline Employees O'Hare International Airport 9/27/2001.* 2001. http://www.vote-smart.org/speech_detail.php?speech_id=3523. Accessed 11 December 2004.
_____. *Remarks by the President to Employees at the Pentagon 9/17/2001.* 2001. http://vote-smart.org/speech_detail.php?speech_id=3479. Accessed 11 December 2004.
_____. *Remarks by the President to Police, Firemen and Rescue Workers at Ground Zero 9/14/2001.* 2001. http://www.vote-smart.org/speech_detail.php?speech_id=3468. Accessed 11 December 2004.
_____. *Remarks by the President Upon Arrival at the South Lawn 9/16/2001.* 2001. http://www.vote-smart.org/speech_detail.php?speech_id=3477. Accessed 11 December 2004.
Carey, James W. *Communication as Culture: Essays on Media and Society.* Boston, MA: Unwin Hyman, 1989.
Carlson, Marvin A. "9/11, Afghanistan, and Iraq: The Response of the New York Theatre." *Theatre Survey* 45.1 (2004): 3–17.
_____. *Theatre Semiotics: Signs of Life.* Bloomington: Indiana University Press, 1990.
Christiansen, Richard. "Clash of Cultures; Tony Kushner's *Kabul* Is a Feast of a Play, Spiced with Controversy." *Chicago Tribune* 20 December 2001: 5.3.
Fanger, Iris. "Prophetic *Homebody/Kabul.*" *Christian Science Monitor* 28 December 2001: 19.
Feingold, Michael. "Disorientalism: There's a Lot of Afghanistan in Tony Kushner's Play. Now How About Some Playwriting?" Review. *Village Voice* 1 January 2002: 60.
Fisher, James. *The Theater of Tony Kushner: Living Past Hope.* New York: Routledge, 2002.
Gardner, Elysa. "*Kabul* Take Four-Hours March Down Road of Western Guilt." *USA Today* 20 December 2001: D9.
Geertz, Clifford. *Local Knowledge: Further Essays in Interpretive Anthropology.* New York: Basic Books, 1983.

Hall, Howard. "Angel on His Back." *Time Out New York* 30 August–6 September 2001: 58–59.

Hartigan, Patti. "Playwright Has a Lot on His Mind." *Boston Globe* 2 February 2001: D9.

Heilpern, John. "Kushner's Great *Homebody/Kabul* Is Our Best Play in Last 10 Years." *New York Observer* 7 January 2002: A1, A27.

Hurwitt, Robert. "Kushner, Culture Clash in Berkeley Rep's New Season." *San Francisco Chronicle* 16 May 2001: B5.

Klein, Julia M. "*Homebody/Kabul*: Overtaken by History." *Chronicle of Higher Education* 18 January 2002: B19–B20.

Knowles, Ric. *Reading the Material Theatre*. London: Cambridge University Press, 2004.

Kushner, Tony. *Homebody/Kabul: 8th Draft/NYTW Rehearsal Draft Nov. 18, 2001*. Unpublished, 2001.

Leland, John, and Peter Marks. "New Look for Entertainment in a Terror-Conscious World." *New York Times* 24 September 2001: A1.

Marks, Peter. "For Tony Kushner, an Eerily Prescient Return." *New York Times* 25 November 2001: 2.1.

McKinley, Jesse. "On Stage and Off." *New York Times* 1 June 2001: E3.

New York Theatre Workshop. "*Homebody/Kabul* Press Release." 2001.

_____. "*Homebody/Kabul Program*." 2001.20.

Nicola, Jim. Personal Interview 4 January 2002.

Peyser, Marc. "Tales from Behind Enemy Lines." *Newsweek* 17 December 2001: 68.

Phillips, Barbara D. "Devils in America: Taliban Lunacy Foreshadowed." *Wall Street Journal* 21 December 2001: W9.

Phillips, Michael. "After the Attack: Media/Culture; Tony Kushner: 'It's No Time for Silence.'" *Los Angeles Times* 22 September 2001: F1.

_____. "Response to Terror; Critic's Notebook; *Homebody/Kabul*: Theater of Cultural War; Drama: Tony Kushner's Passionate Play, Written before Sept 11, Premieres in New York." *Los Angeles Times* 20 December 2001: A5.

_____. "Tony Kushner's Art Imitates Strife; Play Set in Afghanistan Sure to Be Controversial." *Chicago Tribune* 3 October 2001: 5.3.

Pochoda, Elizabeth. Review of *Homebody/Kabul*. *The Nation* 4 February 2002: 35–36.

Podhoretz, John. "Tony Kushner's Afghanistan." *Weekly Standard* 7.21 (2002): 21–23.

Pogrebin, Robin. "Arts Agency Delays Decision on Two Grants." *New York Times* 1 December 2001: A15.

_____. "Split Decision on Impounded Arts Grants." *New York Times* 19 December 2001: E9.

Pressley, Nelson. "Theater of the Unnerved; the Stage Took a Hit Sept 11. Is Fearless Programming the Answer?" *Washington Post* 25 November 2001: G1.

Reston, James, Jr. "A Prophet in His Time." *American Theatre* March 2002: 28–30+.

Snyder, Laura. "Homebody/Kabul Gets Three Venues, National Funding." *Show Business* 26 December 2001, Show Business News section: 5.

Steyn, Mark. "Goin' to Afghanistan." *New Criterion* February 2002: 35–41.

Trescott, Jacqueline. "After Holdup, Arts Agency Funds *Kabul* Production; Art, Not Politics, Basic for Decision, NEA Says." *Washington Post* 19 December 2001: C1.

Williams, Raymond. *Marxism and Literature*. Oxford: Oxford University Press, 1977.

Winer, Linda. "What's Appropriate Now?" *Newsday* 23 September 2001.

11

"Succumbing to Luxury"

History, Language, and Hope in *Homebody/Kabul*

JAMES FISHER

> *When we conjure up the past we run the risk of reawakening old nightmares, of being overwhelmed with horror. Conjuring the future is even more treacherous, because to attempt to envision the future we must resort to what is known, to the past, and if the past as past is nearly unbearable, how much more unbearable to look ahead and see only old nightmares staring back at us. Then again, considering the dire present, imagining that we have any future at all has got to be accounted a cause for celebration* [A Bright Room Called Day *183*].—
> Tony Kushner

Tony Kushner, a playwright on permanent heightened alert for periods of historical transition, finds the aftermath of 9/11—and the subsequent and on-going war on terrorism — occasions for national self-examination and for exploring the cultural differences separating us from both the benign and the malignant "other." "Even a country at war has a moral imperative to think about the people with whom they are fighting and ask questions about them" (Poniewozik 112), Kushner proposes, and in *Homebody/Kabul*, he frames possible answers to these questions within the complex context of contemporary international circumstance in the aftermath of 9/11 and the subsequent "war on terror."

Kushner began writing *Homebody/Kabul* as early as 1998 as a one-act monologue for British actress Kika Markham, and it was first produced as *Homebody* at London's Chelsea Theatre Centre in July 1999, prior to its reinvention as a full-length play, *Homebody/Kabul*, first staged at the New York Theatre Workshop in late 2001. Despite an Obie Award as Best Play, and the 2002 publication of the text used for this premiere production, Kushner continues to revise *Homebody/Kabul*, developing new two-act and three-act versions for workshops at New York's Public Theatre in late March 2003 in anticipation of well-received productions at Chicago's Steppenwolf Theatre (under the direction of Frank Galati) and in London during the summer of 2003, and a forthcoming HBO film version. A revised text resulting from some of the initial production has also been published and produced at the Brooklyn Academy of Music.

The full-length *Homebody/Kabul* was about to commence rehearsals for its New York Theatre Workshop production in late 2001 when the tragedies of 9/11 occurred, inspiring critics to proclaim it an "eerily prescient" play, a description firmly rejected by the playwright, who jokes that if he ever becomes a drag queen the stage name he will use is "Era Lee Prescient." Humor aside, Kushner suggests that any dramatist writing about current events is likely to seem prescient on occasion when addressing issues in the contemporary political, social, and moral spheres. In light of 9/11 and resultant events, it seems that Kushner's dramatized concern about the tragedies of Afghanistan under the Taliban — and perennial conflicts throughout the Middle East — provides one of those occasions; once again, one of his plays places Kushner at the center of a national debate, just as *Angels in America* had in the early 1990s. The toppling of Saddam Hussein's regime in Iraq, promoted by the George W. Bush administration as a necessity in order to stamp out Saddam's link to terrorism, is just the latest phase in violence borne of centuries of vast cultural and economic difference, religious fundamentalism, and the West's luxurious predominance in the world. *Homebody/Kabul* is Kushner's dramatic vehicle for participating in the complicated and often contentious debate surrounding these issues.

An over three-and-a-half hour drama exploring a middle-class British woman's fascination with the past and present of Afghanistan might have been instructive for an audience comparatively uninformed about this troubled corner of the world prior to 9/11; after 9/11, *Homebody/Kabul's* intense exploration of the dilemmas facing a United States precariously balanced on the precipice of past, present, and future is instructive in framing many of the momentous questions. Were the tragedies of 9/11 a result of a long history of misguided American foreign policy decisions dating back to the Vietnam era or before? Why did the government fail to fully recognize the powder keg that was Afghanistan prior to 9/11? What other choices were possible and what, if any, difference might they have made? Can America co-exist with other cultures, especially those so alien to our own? Has America, in the George W. Bush era, adopted a new brand of imperialism? Is religious fundamentalism impervious to compromise and peaceful co-existence with different beliefs and values? Is the conversion of other countries to our way of life an inevitable or necessary development for our ultimate survival? Will the world ultimately melt into one culture, one economy, one value system? In focusing on these perhaps unanswerable questions, Kushner examines the profound consequences inherent in every possible choice — political or personal (inextricably linked realms in Kushner's view)—and the simple truth that only more troubling questions spring from each possible answer.

From a position that can only be described as skeptical optimism, Kushner ponders those particular moments in history when the fabric of everyday life unravels. Finding that real and fundamental change may be possible in such dislocations, Kushner, a neo-socialist, invites his audience to recognize and acknowledge the interconnectedness among diverse, seemingly incompatible cultures—a recognition that he believes the 9/11 attacks compel the United States to realize:

> People will always be able to get into this country.... The country really can defend itself only by behaving justly with the rest of the world. If we do that, if we tackle the question of our place in the world, we can begin the new century in a spirit of transformation and justice. And if we ignore that, it'll be at our peril, and the peril of the entire planet [Phillips 1].

Kushner stresses in *Homebody/Kabul*, as in some of his earlier works, that social change can be propelled by the unstable dynamism of a chronically chaotic society or when the acute turbulence of an important transition moment shatters the comfortable illusion of stability:

> Something has definitely ended, and something new has begun. And I can't think of another time when this country has been called upon to examine itself, examine its responses— or rather, to examine how it should proceed in responding, which I believe should be in a circumspect and compassionate and thoughtful manner [Phillips 1].

He believes that a thoughtful, compassionate response has not come from the leadership of the United States. Kushner condemns what he calls Bush's "cowboy mentality" and the notion that the only way to respond to terrorism and the Middle East crisis is a "shootout at the OK Corral" (Phillips 1)— and, to the suggestion that a play on this subject might seem inappropriate in the midst of this troubling moment, Kushner says

> I don't think silence is what we want to ask of artists.... Although God knows there should be a certain degree of caution approaching the subject of this horror. As with Auschwitz, or the slave ships, there are places where art should only proceed with the greatest caution [Phillips 1].

Caution, however, is not Kushner's forte, as vividly demonstrated by the first scene of a new Kushner play. The scene, titled "Only We Who Guard the Mystery Shall Be Unhappy," was published in *The Nation* (24 March 2003), and it depicts First Lady Laura Bush visiting a classroom to read a story to the children. Instead of a teacher, the presiding presence is an angel, and the pajama-clad students are thousands of dead Iraqi children killed in American bombings. Mrs. Bush's story, "The Grand Inquisitor" from Dostoyevsky's *Brothers Karamazov*, is, she says, her favorite, and for Kushner it symbolizes what he sees as the central conflict of Mrs. Bush's life. Her husband sleeps contentedly and soundly — almost too soundly — and she wonders how he possibly can do so. She fears what it means that there are those in the world able to forgive themselves for culpability in death, destruction, and especially the killing of children. Only a "shitty" person could do that, a distressed Mrs. Bush contends. Beginning to understand that she herself has become a representative for values quite different from her own (she was once a Democrat and is believed to be pro-choice and anti-death penalty, for example), she despairs, but seems to be moving toward a new resolve. Kissing the children, she quotes Dostoyevsky: "The kiss glows in my heart. But. I adhere to my ideas" ("Only We Who Guard the Mystery Shall Be Happy" 15). For Kushner, culpability can also result from silence in the face of a great wrong.

Kushner, perhaps the American theatre's most politically engaged major dramatist at present, has closely watched the evolution of the crisis in Afghanistan. During the period of the Soviet Union's attempt to occupy Afghanistan, he was distressed by the actions of the Russians and by the mayhem resulting from the legacy of colonization and, more recently, from the tragic results of Pakistanis, Chinese, and the C.I.A. selling weapons to various factions inside Afghanistan.

In *Homebody/Kabul*, the crumbling city of Kabul provides the background for a wrenching drama of a crumbling, dysfunctional British family forever changed by an encounter with that ancient city. Theatre as a transformative force is in full evidence as Kushner proposes immersion in the culture of the "other" as a fearful yet necessary journey toward a greater compassion he contends is our only hope for redemption. That the family in *Homebody/Kabul* is British matters little — Kushner uses them to explore the particularly American aversion to bad news, discomfort, cultural difference, and, most of all, instability. The Homebody insists that those living in comparable comfort and safety in the Western world are in grave danger of "succumbing to luxury" (*Homebody/Kabul* 1), of allowing the illusion of safety and comfort to make it possible for us to ignore the suffering of others. She concludes that it might be better to live among the suffering than with those around her succumbing to that very luxury, fading into a senescence of ease and security that permits, and even encourages, indifference and inactivity. Despite feeling an understandable pessimism about current international events, Kushner believes that engagement — and a willingness to aid those without luxury — is the sole path by which to avoid this fate.

Kushner is frequently labeled as a "gay" dramatist as a result of the success of the boldly gay-themed *Angels in America*, but his entire canon of dramatic works thus far suggests a more accurate description might be "political" writer (although critic Harold Bloom, focusing on the spiritual aspects of Kushner's plays, has labeled him a "theological playwright.") Prior Walter, one of the central characters of *Angels*, speaking in *Perestroika*, the second *Angels* play, espouses the belief that "We live past hope" (*Perestroika* 136). This line, more than any other to be found in Kushner's theatrical output, embodies the central political philosophy of his drama: a belief that despite centuries of wrong turns, we must continue to resist despair and progressively face the inevitabilities of a future we cannot know while, at the same time, learning from an often tragic past we know only too well. Kushner is inspired, in part, by Walter Benjamin's description of the Angel of History as depicted in Paul Klee's painting, "Angelus Novus." Blown into the unknown future by the winds of progress, the Angel gazes back on the rubble of history; past, present, and future are inextricably linked. Kushner is also influenced by British socialist philosopher Raymond Williams's phrase "thinking about the longstanding problems of virtue and happiness," which he interprets as describing a skeptical faith in progress, in the transformative power of compassion, and in the perhaps unattainable dream of a true world community. He knows that progress costs— the process is painful, even destructive, and its benefits are hard won, but despite it all, progress is necessary and inevitable. Hopelessness breeds inaction; Kushner retains hope as a true activist must.

The purposeful dramatist, Kushner theorizes, is by nature overtly political and is likely to fit into one of two distinct categories: "the ones who ask small questions but give great answers (the traditionalists) and the ones who ask huge questions and often, as a consequence of the ambitiousness of their questioning, fail to give good answers or even any answers at all (the experimentalists, the vessel breakers); both are necessary" (E-mail to James Fisher). There is little doubt as to which category Kushner aspires.

Kushner's political activism is firmly tied to his art — good politics produce good aesthetics, he believes, and Kushner remains alert to the raw edges of contemporary life and to those pressure points of our present international problems. Perhaps most importantly, he respects his audience by challenging it. Speaking specifically of *Homebody/Kabul*, Kushner explains that no theatre-goer attends a play about Afghanistan expecting an easy night, adding that he depends on "an audience really wanting to ask a lot of questions and be asked to do a certain amount of thinking" (Peyser 68). His plays, from *Angels* to *Homebody/Kabul*, have occasionally engendered controversy — and Kushner, a committed political activist and advocate for the arts, also defends other artists caught up in controversy. In response to attempts to censor Terrence McNally's *Corpus Christi*, Kushner even made the Almighty an ally to wonder why would "a God who gave us powers of creation, curiosity and love then command us to avoid the ideas and art these powers produce?" ("Fighting the Arts Bullies" 41). A society too fragile to value a questioning spirit is in danger of losing the best of itself, he believes; Kushner assumes his audience seeks interrogation, even as the inflamed post–9/11 patriotism aims to curtail dissent.

In *Homebody/Kabul*, Kushner expands the private into the public — and back again; the play is rife with grieving ruminations on the fracturing of an ancient and mysterious city once again at the center of international conflict. Melding fact with fiction, he reveals the contradictions and personal tragedies embodied by this devastated society. While visiting a London novelty shop run by an Afghani man, the unhappily married Homebody notices that part of the man's hand has been neatly chopped off, leaving her to wonder about the reasons behind this mutilation. She imagines several possible scenarios, including one in which she makes love to the man under an olive tree after he tells her that his damaged hand may have resulted from stealing. "I stole bread for my starving family. I stole bread from a starving family" (*Homebody/Kabul* 23), the man confusingly confesses, and through the personal possibilities (and probabilities) Kushner indicts the political and economic forces perpetuating injustice and economic deprivation. Perpetrator and victim may, in fact, be one and the same.

History and culture intersect in this epic play, an epic in both the classic and the Brechtian senses. Its theatrical fusing of the past, current events, and Kushner's vivid imaginings demonstrates the theatre's transformative power and its ability to clarify the questions at hand. *Homebody/Kabul*, James Reston, Jr., writes, is for "those who can see through the fog of patriotism to the finer distinctions, who are finally ready to ask how on earth do we get out of this godforsaken place, who can bear to contemplate the thought that we have participated to some extent in our own tragedy" (Reston 53). Kushner can bear to contemplate it — and he asks his audience to contemplate it as well.

As *Homebody/Kabul* moves past the Homebody's dizzyingly imaginative monologue into its more sweeping second and third acts, Kushner's characters are obliged to face the consequences of some critical choices. Moving from the Homebody's cozy living room in London to the dark heart of Kabul, Kushner introduces Milton Ceiling, a repressed British computer specialist, and the Homebody's distant husband. He arrives in Kabul with their twenty-something daughter, Priscilla, a deeply troubled young woman; both hope to find the Homebody or to claim her remains. Milton, paralyzed with fear at being in the midst of this dangerous, unstable place, accepts the official explanation that a brutally-mangled body of a woman recently found is that of his wife. He sinks into an alcohol and drug-induced daze with the assistance of Quango Twistleton, an unofficial liaison for the British government, who has remained in the rubble of Kabul because it provides him easy access to a steady flow of the drugs to which he is profoundly addicted.

In short order, Milton and Priscilla learn that the Homebody courted disaster. Appearing on the public streets without a burka and wearing a Walkman to listen to her favorite Frank Sinatra records, "It's Nice to Go Trav'ling" and "Come Fly with Me," she has outraged the Taliban. Priscilla refuses to accept this scenario and the whole story. Donning a burka, she slips into the dangerous, exotic environs of the Taliban's Kabul on a journey to find her mother.

In depicting the Taliban, Kushner examines the disturbing face of religious fanaticism, revealing his aversion to fundamentalism of any kind and the inherent intolerance of the fundamentalist. He assails the Taliban for their misogyny and brutality, but he humanizes other Afghani characters trapped within the Taliban's oppressions. Priscilla finds herself a guide, an old poet (in the original New York production the poet was played as an old man, in the revised version and later productions the character was played by a young man), who shows her the world her mother has either embraced or been destroyed by; a city, Kushner suggests, cursed by the myth that the Biblical Cain's grave may be within its city limits. Ironically, the purported location of Cain's grave is now a Taliban minefield, a symbol that hardly needs further explanation. Priscilla, wandering the figurative minefield that is Kabul, receives the startling news that her mother may be alive and living as the wife of a well-to-do Muslim. This character is never seen, but his Afghani wife, Mahala, is, and her rage at both the Taliban and the West is total. In this character, Kushner's bittersweet globalism takes on an acidic edge. Mahala is a former librarian who, like the Homebody, reveres language and books; a woman of intellect and dignity, she is obliged to beg for Priscilla's help in escaping Afghanistan. The position of women under the Taliban's regime, and the constant terror and isolation are, she reveals, causing her to forget the alphabet — a loss she finds insupportable. She spews rage in various dialects demonstrating Kushner's facile manipulation of and appreciation for language.

Mahala wants to shed the literal and figurative burka she is forced to wear as a citizen of Afghanistan, but the seeming impossibility of doing so enrages her. Priscilla ruefully notes that Mahala "isn't mad, she's fucking furious. It isn't at all the same" (*Homebody/Kabul* 80). If oppressions are severe enough, she suggests, they inevitably lead to the defeat of total resignation or to an unending fury true survivors require in order to endure the unendurable.

Whether or not the Homebody is dead or alive is never confirmed, but this is not the point engaging Kushner's interest. The collision of cultures, as the Homebody explains, is what matters: "Ours is a time of connection; the private, and we must accept this, and it's a hard thing to accept, the private is gone. All must be touched. All touch corrupts. All must be corrupted" (*Homebody/Kabul* 2). This corrupting touch may eventually inspire greater understanding, but in the short term it seems to have nearly demolished Kabul and shattered the lives of both the citizenry of that city and the visiting Westerners. Only Priscilla and Mahala seem to profit from this corruption. Priscilla has lost a mother (and become further estranged from her distant, judgmental father), but she has matured on her individual journey into the dark, surreal recesses of Kabul, taking responsibility for saving Mahala's sanity and probably her life. The Homebody's mantra, Sinatra's "It's Nice to Go Trav'ling," has now become Priscilla's. Having spent her life stuck in the stasis resulting from her desire to be everything her parents are not, Priscilla is now prepared to progress toward the future, looking back, like Walter Benjamin's description of Paul Klee's painting, "Angelus Novus," gazing at the rubble of her own dysfunctional family history. Mahala is on a journey to a new future, too; she ends up in London living in the Homebody's home and with the Homebody's husband, enjoying first-hand the luxuries of the West, but appearing not to have succumbed to them.

The corrupting touch, as Kushner sees it, is immersion in another world and another life; it is a leap into a culture at once alien, inviting, and appalling. Priscilla's yearning, desperate search for her missing mother (and perhaps a connection with the distracted Homebody she never felt at home), expands into a deeper comprehension of difference and the need to search for the connection the Homebody has described as essential. Sinatra's "Come Fly with Me" is a central metaphor — a musical motif representing the varied journeys of its characters. The Homebody, as Mahala explains, has made the complete journey, choosing what no Afghani woman would, to become a suffering, endangered citizen of a suffering, endangered country. As John Heilpern explains, *Homebody/Kabul* depicts a "journey without maps to the ravaged, symbolic center of a fucked-up universe," and he describes the play as a towering drama about

> lost civilizations and unsolvable paradoxes, furious differences and opposites and disintegrating, rotting pidgin cultures. It's about desolation and love in land-mined places, child murderers and fanatics, tranquilized existence and opium highs, travel in the largest sense of the word — travel of the mind and soul. To where? An unknowable mystery, perhaps, where all confusion is banished [Heilpern 1].

Homebody/Kabul's haunting timeliness generally impressed its first critics and audiences, but Kushner eschews the label of prophet. His mission remains two-fold: first, to prod a vigorous discussion of strategies for navigating the political, social, and intellectual minefields of our time, and secondly, to incite an emotional, humanizing response from his audience to the harrowing, existential impulse toward survival — even of the most unthinkable horrors. Whereas Bertolt Brecht's alienation effect means to distance his audience from an emotional response, thereby liberating a rational view of the play's action, Kushner, a disciple of Brecht's work, departs from the master by retaining the intellectual and political focus, but courting the audience's emotional response. In this, Kushner is a thoroughly American playwright — despite his leanings toward the uncompromising rationality of the Brechtian style, he combines it with an equally potent strand of character-driven American lyric realism. *Homebody/Kabul* is much more than merely a dramatic response to a terrible moment in contemporary history, it is a plea for creating a process for humanizing an alien "enemy" and, at the same time, perhaps understanding, or redeeming, our own sins and errors.

Kushner's themes are most effectively delivered through his characteristically voluptuous language; The Homebody basks in language, it is her only friend: "I can't help myself," she says, "I blame it on books, how else to explain it? My parents don't speak like this; no one I know does; no one does. It's an alien influence, and my borders have only been broached by books. Sad to say" (*Homebody/Kabul* 12). Until she flees to Afghanistan, that is. The comparatively inarticulate Priscilla rejects the torrents of language within which her mother finds refuge; for the Homebody, words are tickets for an imaginary safe passage from her comfortably unhappy life. Priscilla's Afghan guide, the poet, writes what may either be poetry or, more likely, intelligence for the Northern Alliance in Esperanto, the universal language Kushner describes as one free of the baggage of cultural history. It is a blameless mode of expression by which to communicate without the inherent cultural oppressions and the burdens of the past soaking every other language in blood. Mahala's anger cannot be fully expressed even through the range of dialects she utilizes to vent her rage against the Taliban and the West, both of which, in her view, have visited so much misery on Afghanistan and its citizens. Mahala, comfortably ensconced in London, admits "We're people of terrible luxuries. Sometimes I think they're what Afghanistan needs, the Taliban. Anything anything for certainty. I get the appeal of fascism now. Uncertainty kills" (139).

Homebody/Kabul, like much of Kushner's dramatic output, teeters on the brink of an abyss of despair, tentatively balanced on the edge of a hard-won hopefulness. No cockeyed optimist, Kushner is instead a clear-eyed one. He hopes for a world willing to save itself even at this most hopeless of times; Kushner's *Homebody/Kabul* is an excoriating visit to a world that those succumbing to luxury in the West generally prefer to know little about. Such a luxury, Kushner argues, is no longer possible, as Priscilla learns on her grim journey into a once mysteriously beautiful world engulfed in evil, violence, and despair. Personal losses have been endured and the inevitable wrench of change has altered the lives of all of the play's characters as their individual journeys continue beyond the play's end.

Curiously, despite the overall grimness of the play, Kushner opts for an optimistic longing as *Homebody/Kabul* ends. Mahala, reflecting on the future, exclaims to Priscilla, "I am gardening now! To a Kabuli woman, how shall I express what these English gardens mean? Your mother is a strange lady; to neglect a garden. A garden shows us what may await us in Paradise" (139). A garden also symbolizes a faith in a future; however difficult that future may be — the garden must be tended. A garden may also be a memorial, as Mahala sadly concludes, "In the garden outside, I have planted all my dead" (139).

Kushner raises questions about compassion and connection, war, guilt, displacement, and the complex maze of history as he questions our options in the present moment and illuminates the hard lessons of the past. Such questions address a need in his audience, as he explained in a recent interview:

> I think that people do go to art in general as a way of addressing very deep, very intimate, very mercurial and elusive, ineffable things in a communal setting. It ends a certain kind of inner loneliness. Or it joins one's own loneliness with the inner loneliness of many other people. And I think that that can be healing [Barrett 230].

Kushner, dramatic healer, continues his distinctly individual dramatic journey in *Homebody/Kabul* by raising the great, unanswerable questions and entering fantastic worlds to provide his audience with strategies for living past old hopes and imagining new ones.

Works Cited

Barrett, Amy. "The Way We Live Now: 10–07–01: Questions for Tony Kushner." *New York Times* 7 October 2001, sec. 6.

Fisher, James. *The Theater of Tony Kushner: Living Past Hope.* New York: Routledge, 2002.

Heilpern, John. "Zounds! Kushner's *Homebody/Kabul* Is Our Best Play in Last 10 Years." *New York Observer* 5 January 2002.

Kushner, Tony. *Angels in America, Part Two: Perestroika.* New York: Theatre Communications Group, Inc., 1994.

_____. "Afterword," *A Bright Room Called Day.* New York: Theatre Communications Group, Inc., 1994.

_____. E-mail to James Fisher, March 25, 2002.

_____. "Fighting the Arts Bullies." *The Nation* 29 November 1999.

_____. *Homebody/Kabul.* New York: Theatre Communications Group, Inc., 2002.

_____. "Only We Who Guard the Mystery Shall Be Unhappy." *The Nation* 24 March 2003.

Peyser, Marc. "Tales From Behind Enemy Lines." *Newsweek* 17 December 2001.

Phillips, Michael. "After the Attack: Media/Culture; Tony Kushner: 'It's No Time for Silence.'" *Los Angeles Times* 22 September 2001, part VI.

Poniewozik, James. "What's Entertainment Now?" *Time* 1 October 2001.

Reston, James, Jr. "A Prophet in His Time." *American Theatre* March 2002.

12

The Therapy of Desire

BERT STERN

Philosophy heals human diseases, diseases produced by false beliefs. Its arguments are to the soul as the doctor's remedies are to the body. They can heal, and they are to be evaluated in terms of their power to heal. — Martha Nussbaum, *The Therapy of Desire*

Caroline, or Change began with invitation from the San Francisco Opera for Tony Kushner to write a libretto. Himself an ardent lover of opera and raised in a musical family, Kushner was tickled by the possibilities: "Since I would be writing lyrics, I had permission to write ... well, lyrically, to use a loosely rhythmic, loosely rhymed verse instead of prose." (xi) [all quotations from the text of *Caroline, or Change* are taken from Tony Kushner's libretto, published by the Theatre Communications Group, Inc., 2004]. As he continually does in other ways, Kushner would renew himself as a writer by taking on this new form that involved both words and music.

But the idea of an opera (later to become a "musical theater piece") also attracted Kushner in a more personal way. He'd been thinking about the story of Caroline for many years. It is about the South during the Civil Rights movement. But it is also the story of Kushner's boyhood, captured with lyrical intensity by the compression of theater. By drawing these public and personal strands together, Kushner "wanted to tell to music a central component of my childhood, and perhaps the missing key to my memory of these characters, these incidents, that time" (xi).

Obviously, this is a large order — to illuminate an essence of the writer's roots in an eight-year-old boy caught between his private world and the still largely mysterious adult world that he is leaning to join. Clearly, lyric material.

Kushner's task was made easier by his working in collaboration with the equally renowned director George C. Wolfe and the composer Jeanine

Tesori. The wonder of the direction includes the choric realization of the basement appliances and the paradoxically epic space opened by them and by the Moon as *deus ex machina* character. Tesori's music allowed Kushner more deeply to fathom "the relationship of sound and sense, the emotional and the rational" (xiii). Between them, writer and composer made music aimed at "the place inside us only song can reach" (xiii). Music, in Kushner's words, "is a blessing that enters the soul through the ear" (xiv).

Though I believe, and will try to show at the end of this essay, Kushner means blessing in its full sense, the marriage of word and song and simple staging is a sure vehicle for that blessing. That melding helps account for the depths of sorrow and hunger and joy achieved in a setting deliberately cage-like. But *Caroline is* also a story, and often story is something that follows just after feeling, in the way you might look back at a vivid experience after you have stepped out of it. Anyway, in the naked text, as Kushner puts it in his preface to the published libretto, "*Caroline* returns ... to something resembling its nascent condition — silence" (xv).

Much brews in the silence, even without performance.

One of Kushner's direct aims was to write a show "about race relations, the civil rights movement, and African Americans and southern Jews in the early 1960, a time of protean change sweeping the country — and to write about those things from the perspective of a small, somewhat isolated southern town" (xi). That silence, as I understand, includes the hidden heart, where the man looks back at the boy and gives him nurture. It is the silence of the creative heart carrying out its action. I'd say it is in that silence that the show has its greatest astonishments, in the recreation of a past with all its wounds and hungers.

Much of the action of *Caroline* takes place in the basement and living room of one house. The show does step out into the streets a few times (Caroline's talk with Dotty Moffett, the bus's herald's cry that the President is dead), but in neither case does the text support a widened world. Extreme contraction, close to what Blake meant by "the limits of contraction," is the alembic in which *Caroline* is distilled. There is a sense of claustrophobia everywhere, life driven down into basements and odd corners, a picture that has its counterparts in the public and private lives of our time. Only in the children does the prospect of new growth appear.

Caroline is a tale of two families. Caroline is locked both in her poverty and in sorrow and anger over a lost husband and a lost son (the father emotionally wrecked by one war and the son killed by another.) Her present family consists of two sons, eight and ten, and a daughter, Emmie, in her mid-adolescence and rebellious both personally and politically. Emmie is already an avid follower of Dr. Martin Luther King's movement.

By Carolyn's lights, Emmy is already dangerously regardless of racist conventions, though for all that, Caroline wishes Emmie not to yield to the reins Caroline herself tries to impose.

The Gellman family is caught in change and losses of their own. Stuart Gellman, like his first wife, who recently died of lung cancer, is a musician. He has recently moved to Lake Charles, Louisiana from New York City with Noah and a new wife, Rose Stopnick Gellman. Gellman is almost completely distracted, and what's human in him finds expression only in his clarinet. "My father's a clarinet," Noah says, until Rose teaches him that the proper form is "My father plays a clarinet" (20). But Noah is right. As to Rose, she is a strong-willed and ignorant woman struggling to find her balance in the new family and the new culture. There is a poignant distance between the boy and these guardians—a father who is absent (Gellman doesn't know what grade Noah is in or even how old he is) and a wife who is over-intended,

The loss of his true mother casts a thick shadow over Noah. He has no interest in school, and mopes around the house. His parents want him to wake up, understand hard facts, and become a good citizen of the household. But until late in the play, when Noah's relationship with Rose begins to improve, he finds no place in this family. The only occasion his father has to talk with him is the delivery of cold facts. Face it, he tells the boy, "Your mother is dead" (22). Rose simply tries to improve him, to wake him up. Against that, Noah's only sanctuary is the basement, which is underwater,

> ... planted in the swampy soil,
> sunk in the mud and the marsh and the mire,
> down with the snakes and the snails and the bracken,
> root to the bayou,
> root to the ooze ... [13].

Yet the basement that is hell for Caroline is heaven for the boy.

While Noah is less important to Caroline than she is in him, they serve one another's purposes. Without Noah, Caroline is half-drowned by her memories and the often harsh voices (however musical) of the appliances. The Radio, for instance, as Caroline does the laundry:

> Time's come to perspire!
> Turn on the electric dryer!
> Sucking moisture out the air,
> melt the hairspray in your hair!
> Turn it on, turn on despair [15–16].

The dryer, playing an aged James Brown against the Radio's Supremes, is especially full of hell's damnation, and the washing machine is the dull repetition of Caroline's work. But in Noah's company, Caroline can hold court, and even find a touch of Nat King Cole, her playfully imagined soul-comforting lover.

To add to the torment of what she endures in the basement, Caroline must contend with Rose herself, who tries to force some cooked cabbage on Caroline to take home to her kids, a charity Caroline firmly refuses. Rose is part of an old lefty family, but she's caught up in the implacable contradictions: she wishes to exploit Caroline (she pays her *bupkes*) and at the same time to keep her conscience sweet. She has no imagination at all for Caroline herself. Their non-communication is important as a foil to Noah's own relationship with Caroline.

That relationship offers to Caroline the occasional pleasure of mock courtship. Noah adores her. Her anger and grief, he sees accurately, are part of her strength, and Noah sees the almost powerless woman as "stronger than my dad," and, indeed, as having powers equivalent to those of "The President of the United States" (14). So he courts her for a favor, in the medieval sense: in this case, the favor of lighting her daily cigarette for her and then, when she can free herself sufficiently from her sorrows, smoke rings. The ritual of cigarette lighting is mock-erotic, and Noah and Caroline both know that Mr. Gellman mustn't know about it. Eros here is like gossamer. Yet for both of them, the ritual comes close to the border of transgression, and is part of what makes the visits and their relationship so precious to both of them, though Caroline would deny it.

While Noah adores her, many aspects of her he can't see: her bondage and her poverty. But he *does* recognize the rich, complex soul that gives her a fuller humanity than anyone else in his world. Caroline is more than the directly presented figure. She is also her music, the music of her words and of her memory, without which she wouldn't carry the stature she does.

Caroline's memory has become a kind of steel trap for her, encompassing everything in her except her hope and concern for her children and her scattered moments with Noah. She is frozen in poverty, frozen in memories of the husband she loved who came back from Korea to find that he couldn't get a job, and started drinking. Caroline still loves the man, before the war destroyed him, but when he took up hitting her, after his return she "beat his face in" (74) and kicked him out of the house. Their first child, Larry, was killed in Vietnam, and her heart is with him as well. It is Caroline's attachment to the two dead men that so strongly holds her to the past. She is part of history's collateral damage.

When the play opens, after we've heard Caroline's deep moan and taken in her hell, we see that the relationship between Caroline and Noah, while something like a courtship, is something else as well. Noah releases in Caroline an awakening of the heart, as in her song, "Gonna Pass Me a Law," in which, while her laws are the wishes that she know more than she does and that her dead son come home, she also passes a law that

> say Nat King Cole
> gotta come over my house
> come over every night
> and stroke my soul [45].

In the meantime, Noah is as close to that fantasy as she can get. Later, after Noah seriously offends her, she ends the secret cigarette rituals they share.

Caroline's future is carried historically by her daughter Emmie, who breathes new hope through her active involvement in the new Civil Rights movement. Caroline is both proud and uneasy about her, hoping she "don't never get hurt / nor learn how to mind me" (45).

But Caroline herself is, as she says, one of Lot's daughters. She can no longer change her life or circumstance. Like Leah in *The Dybbuk*, she's possessed by ghosts and phantom lovers, including Nat King Cole. In the present and actual, she can only continue to scrape by so long as she is able. She will "endure," like Faulkner's Dilsey. Hope lies in the children — in her own daughter but also in Noah. Their fates and their values are the only possible positive transmutations of her sorrow.

Noah's connection with Kushner is a kind of teaser. They both moved to Lake Charles with their families when they were children, but, unlike Noah, Kushner did not lose his mother in childhood. He was working on the second part of *Angels in America* when she died. Whether Kushner himself or only Noah had a passion for Barbie dolls, Noah's passion points to his homosexual identity down the road. As if to make the separation of real and imagined worlds more equivocal, at Kushner's invitation the real Caroline attended the premiere performance of the show. All this points to a reading of Noah's role as a kind of portrait of the artist as a young boy. What goes on between them is at the root of Kushner's soul.

* * *

Noah's story, then, is a *Bildungsroman*. How he grows up, the kind of adult he will grow up to be, is what's at stake. What's at stake, we could say, is whether Noah can escape, as Caroline cannot, from the narrow bonds imposed on him.

One of Kushner's most brilliant achievements in *Caroline, or Change* is the way he allows us intimacy with Noah's innerness, and in this way recover our own childhood consciousness, at a point when Noah's life hangs in the balance between true understanding and yielding to a social reality driven largely by greed. The boy, with his clear appealing voice, resembles the conventional ingénue. He is open to everything, but especially to Caroline, who strokes his soul in the manner of a tough Zen teacher. Noah projects onto Caroline's family the common humanity he doesn't get from his own. He wants them to be his community. He's drawn to blackness itself for the depth of soul he doesn't find in his own family. In his imagination, the Thibodeaux

> ... talk about how my mama died
> they talk about my tragedy
> they wish that they could take me in
> and I could live with Caroline
> and Emmie Jackie Larry Joe.
> Each evening I could up and go
> home to be a Thibodeaux.
> Emmie Jackie Larry Joe
> and Noah
> Noah Thibodeaux [63].

And in one of the most touching moments of the play, Noah sings and plays with Emmie and Jackie and Joe in a choric dance that takes place not so much in *his* imagination as in that of the show itself. Noah's hunger for Black culture seems to point to Kushner's own debt to it, the way it shapes his poetry and his heart, a debt acknowledge by his invitation of the historical Caroline to the play's premiere.

While Noah is drawn to the family's Black soul, he is too young to see their physical poverty, to understand that they can't afford meat and that Jackie has bad teeth Caroline hasn't the money to attend to. Indeed, an important movement in Noah's story is that it opens him to the politics of money and to the ties of cruelty and hypocrisy that bind oppressor and oppressed. The oppressor (witness Rose Stopnick Gellman) is intent on having her cake and eating it. Daughter of a lefty family and herself a New York liberal, she is nonetheless willing to use Caroline as not quite a slave. (Not to pick on Rose, her dilemma is in some sense the dilemma of all of us who know the ways that we stand on the backs of the poor.)

2

While change in *Caroline* includes changes within the family and locale, as well as political change, through John Kennedy's assassination, it is also small change and exchange, coins in the pocket, and, for Caroline, lack of change is a poverty that keeps her from buying sweets for her children, or much of anything beyond bare necessities. Her anguish over the lack of money is one of the many elements of Caroline's sorrow. Caroline's need, along with Noah's cold-eyed curiosity about money, leads to the unpleasant cat-and-mouse game the two get into over the change Noah leaves in the pockets of pants he throw on the dirty laundry pile.

Through that carelessness, Noah learns the brutality possible when one holds the power of change, however spare. Against his father and new mother trying to initiate Noah into the realities of money, Kushner tracks a line that exposes raw capitalism as what it aspires to be— the sole arbitrator of what it means to be human. Kushner's line leads to the heart's high truth and wider sky.

* * *

Other than Caroline, the adults who work to shape Noah are his father and Rose, who want the boy to "grow up," to be responsible for his things, to help out a little around the house, to be a good citizen, and to put his grief behind him. They want him, in short, to act like a grown up, the models for which are in short supply, except in Caroline.

Rose is especially troubled by Noah's carelessness with money. For her, for the world, money is a serious thing. Money also lets us see the tortured form that Rose's social sensitivity takes. After explaining to Noah that Caroline works "all day in this horrible basement" not because she likes it but because she is poor, Rose adds:

> She's poor, it's embarrassing
> to have her find money
> just left in the laundry:
> think of the things she could do with these quarters,
> these nickels and pennies—[37].

Rose's blindness marks that of others— particularly, her father. Father and daughter see the injustice of money, but to do something about it in real life, in praxis, is beyond them.

Still, by Rose's lights and Mr. Stopnick's, Noah's path is to be toward understanding money and its importance: "You've got to learn. / Money's important, / a cause for concern" (38).

Through this part of the action, the Gellmans illustrate the very principle they preach: the power of money. Between them, while they believe they are helping the boy, in fact they impose on him the corruptive power of money, and even, for a while, transforming his relationship with Caroline to something purely monetary. Mr. Gellman makes a rule that, from now on, in exchange for carrying out a few chores, like picking up his own room, Noah will receive $1.50 a week, and in this way be initiated into consumerism. No doubt of the early success of this experiment: Noah is made an immediate consumer, "Buy, buy, / buy buy buy!" (52) his only cry — buy everything, including dresses for his secret Barbie doll.

Rose Stopnick, in turn, proposes to break Noah's sloppy habits by *her* new rule: any change Noah leaves in his pockets when he throws his pants into the dirty laundry basket belongs to Caroline. Thus Rose shapes the win-win in her win-win edict: either Noah will become responsible, or Caroline will receive a backdoor raise, a sop to Rose's conscience.

These new rules awaken Noah's greed, but his greed operates against a vision even colder. Mr. Gellman is a strict Darwinian determinist and materialist, with its emotional legacy of our being lost in the stars, in a realm where faith hope and charity sound like empty wind. From that early modernist sense of our having been abandoned by the death of God, and our desolation projects a universe of ice:

> There is no God, Noah,
> we don't believe in God,
> In all that corny stuff.
> We're scientific people!
> Space is infinite and empty and cold,
> people are descended from apes, actually and usually act worse than apes,
> and a boy your age should sleep without a light on,
> and your mother is dead
> and there is no God [22].

Gellman's naturalist vision leaves no room for sentiment or, for that matter, for anything else that might relieve us from the dead weight of reality. We are scientific people, who must refuse to live in a world of illusion. (Mr. Gellman wants Noah to buy a chemistry set with his soon to be earned *gelt.*) Scientific people don't use opiates. When we look out at the stars we are looking not for heaven or even the wonder of our being in largeness, but for a space "infinite and empty and cold." Scientific people believe that we "are descended from apes / and usually act worse than apes." Noah must be a man and "sleep without a light on." Noah's mother is dead, there is no more to say. Such a view casts a long shadow over Noah, and, for an interval, makes his heart cold.

* * *

Caroline herself welcomes the new rule. True, she doesn't like "taking candy from a baby," (53) but she deeply needs the change. It could mean as much as a dollar a week raise, to help with the overdue rent, get the children to the dentist, feed them meat instead of meat-flavored bread, even get them some sweets and "shiny junk" (52). In short, it could end the life of neediness.

For both characters, the exchange that begins between them represents a nadir: for Caroline, it means giving up her pride and dignity, and for Noah, it means experimenting with his father's vision of humanity. Once Caroline actually walks off with the change she finds, Noah begins an experiment: he will leave a quarter, to see what will happen, then two quarters, a dollar bill. In all this, Noah, as experimenter, can't foresee consequences, but we do. Caroline takes the quarter and the two quarters, but when Noah leaves a dollar bill in his pocket, she returns it to Noah, with a warning:

> Left this dollar
> in your pocket!
> Mind your money!
> Lucky for you I didn't take it [54].

But when Noah asks Caroline to light her cigarette, Caroline turns away from him:

> No you can't! Now go on get!
> You ain't lighting no more cigarettes
> never again and if I catch you
> playing with matches I tell your mama [55].

Noah's response to the new coolness between them, a response that might make his father glad, is to continue his experiment. He drops back a notch, this time working up to only 75 cents, and Caroline takes it. Noah has a sentimentalized fantasy about what his money has bought him:

> Now I know what they talk about,
> at the Thibodeaux house, at suppertime.
> Before it was a mystery.
> Now they count my quarters and
> they talk about me! [56].

At this level, the intended end of the game for Noah is not just to resume the old relationship with Caroline but to have a new one, as savior and member of her family. For the time being, "at least now at supper, they talk about me." Although Noah's motive is misguided and cruel, we see its deep sources in his hunger to be Black, to be in the bosom of a Black family rather than a white Jewish one. In the Thibodeaux world, Noah feels, he can be something other than a scientific person. In their world it's all right to have feeling.

For Caroline the game soon gets old. She sees through its core illusion, so she resigns from the game. From now on, she will leave the change in the bleach cup, and the Gellman's can do whatever they want with it. And so the matter rests, Rose trying to make it right with Caroline, in blind, bland, cruelty, by explaining that it was only a game.

3

Channukah comes to the Gellmans, the *mishpuchah*, including the Gellman and Stopnick grandparents, all gathered. In this picture of festivity there's a bow to Dickens, but also, more deeply, to Joyce. The air is rich with cooking smells from the kitchen, where Caroline, with the help of Emmy and Dotty Moffett, is turning out a feast, including sizzling latkes and roast goose. The grandparents dance a *hora* while Noah explains the symbols and non-symbols of the occasion (chicken fat is symbolic of the temple oil, but the goose is just food. The general mood is harmonious and exultant:

> America America God shed His
> grace on thee,
> where every Jew's a Maccabee
> and crown'd thy good with
> brotherhood...
> and bade our blessings multiply:
> Mi kamocha ba-eilim Adonai? ... [82].

the Hebrew being the words inscribed on the Maccabean battle banner: "Who is like thee, O Lord!"

On the one hand, the riches and festivity, on the other, the cruel tensions that lie just below. For both Kushner and Joyce, the festivity stops when politics breaks in. Rose's father begins it:

> The South is in a might frenzy, ...
> The old world's ending!
> Negroes marching!
> Change is coming!
> Down with the filthy capitalist chazzerim! [84].

For the elder Stopnick, the "Negro" becomes the Maccabees: "Now the Negro leads the way! Comes at last the freedom day!" (89). He believes that the "Negroes" must stop the non-violence plan, non-violence "will get you burned" (90). Stopnick has been waiting for this moment since the 1930s.

Emmie, defined by her outspokenness as against her mother's pru-
dent taciturnity, gets into an argument with Stopnick, which he much
enjoys. But to Emmy, this is no game. The stakes are too big:

> I'd like to know how you come to feel
> you know so much about what is real,
> sitting safe and high and pretty,
> way up North in New York City? [90].

Caroline ends the argument: "CHILD, YOU HEAR ME? HUSH YOUR
MOUTH!" (91) and, back in the kitchen, Emma explodes: "I'll never be a
queen, that's true, but I'm a damn sight bettern' prouder'n you!" (92). So
mother and daughter fall out, in the inevitable poor communication
between generations about the meaning of change.
    All this sets up another level of tension. Back in the dining room,
Mr. Stopnick's commands everyone's attention with his announcement
that he has a gift, Channukah gelt, for Noah: a twenty dollar bill. It is as
if Eres, the Greek goddess of discord and dark sister of Eros, has thrown
her golden apple into the room. Because the gift comes with a caveat.
Before handing the bill to Noah, Stopnick explains the laws of money to
Noah:

> What means this money, Noah boychick?
> You won't learn this in Arithmetic!
> Money follows certain laws,
> it's worth how much it's worth because
> somewhere, something's valued less,
> it's how our blessings come, I guess.
> Golden, shiny, but never pure.
> Think from whence your riches stem.
> Think of someone who is poor:
> And know you stole this gold from them.
> Especially here in the Devil's South!
> You'd rip you gold from a starving man's mouth [94].

The last line perfectly sets up the following scene, called "The Twenty Dollar Bill."
    In the gospel according to Stopnick, a fantasy of revolution will
resolve the guilty and cruel realities of money, and, as he puts it with a
dramatic irony, bring down "the filthy chazzerim." (A chazzer is one who
eats like an animal, one who is wildly greedy.)

* * *

Noah, this time by accident, leaves the $20 dollar bill in his pants, and, when he realizes what he has done, he has the whole day to brood about it in school. As soon as he's home, he rushes into the basement to find Caroline: "Did you find...?" She answers him, "with little pause," according to the stage directions,

> Yup.
> I did.
> (Silence, then:)
> And now its mine [102].

The raw quarrel that follows could have been scripted by the devil. Noah starts it:

> NO! GIVE IT BACK!
> CAROLINE!
> I HATE YOU! I HATE YOU! I HATE YOU!
> There's a bomb!
> President Johnson has built a bomb
> special made to kill all Negroes!
> I hate you, hate you, kill all Negroes! Really! For
> true!
> I hope he drops this bomb on you! [104].

Caroline's reply is more coolly delivered but just as lethal:

> Noah, hell is like this basement,
> only hotter than this, hotter than August
> with the washer and the dryer and the boiler
> full blast, hell's hotter than goose fat,
> much hotter than that.
> Hell's so hot it makes flesh fry.
> (Little pause)
> And hell's where Jews go when they die.
> (She gives Noah the twenty)
> Take your twenty dollars baby.
> So long, Noah, good-bye [104].

The moment is the moral nadir of the show. It is like love betrayed. The relationship appears to end with curses, as Caroline she walks out of the Gellman's lives, leaving the washing machine, still running, behind her.

When, after five days, Rose calls Dotty to find out what has happened to Caroline, the conversation ends in anger, and, after she hangs up, Rose, innocently, cries out:

> You can all go to hell!
> I'm not the enemy! [109].

Yet her own father thinks differently and says so:

> Given the givens, she in
> perfect position
> for the boy to adore her.
> She's competition [110].

Stopnick's accusation is unfair on the face of it, yet the first tender moment between Rose and Noah occurs when Noah lets her kiss him good night. So it is that Jewish and African American relations come to a full stop in Lake Charles, Louisiana, at a time when the Civil Rights Movement is just hitting that city.

At the core, what's most at stake here is the soul of the boy. Though he's only eight, Noah has already enacted with Caroline a struggle between races and between classes that ends with hurt and bitterness all around. For Noah the loss is enormous. He sings his lament, which ends with the lines:

> And the fourth day day day Caroline stayed away-way-way
> and she didn't come back back back and she didn't come back
> back back.
> (*Little pause*)
> I did it. I killed her. I did it she died [108].

Then Caroline comes back, in the scene called "How Long Has This Been Going On?" It's been going on a long time, these cruel struggles we raise between us. Yet in *Caroline*, it ends with a boy's plain words: Caroline, "Sorry I hid from you" (123).

He had hidden in a world where Rose can believe that she is not the enemy, and where the cold emptiness of space and determinism chills us to the bone. He had hidden in the world of "Buy! Buy! Buy!" We don't know what Noah has been saved for, but we know that it was Caroline who redeemed him and who initiated him into the hard lessons of suffering and into the heart's loyalties.

I like to think that Noah has also been saved to become Kushner, at a moment when he might have become another slave of appetite, self-deception and betrayal.

*　*　*

After the matinee performance of his ART production of *The Children*

of Herakles, Peter Sellars spoke of the public theater as the Greeks understood it, as not only as a place like the senate, where people can say anything, but also as a place where everyone is accountable and no one has
the last word. All citizens of Athens were required to go to the theater. If
they couldn't pay, the state paid for them. The theater was a place where
even one who has no voice is heard.

Kushner's theater is like that and, like that, aspires to keep our final
judgments at bay for as long as possible, and it's meant to stroke our soul —
that is, to heal. What's important, in the end, is not so much what the characters end up with, in loss or gain asd how they submitted themselves to
the test. We could say that Caroline ends up both crushed and non-crushed,
as before, and Noah in more or less the position he began with, but worse,
since for the while Caroline refuses to return to their old relationship, and
Noah seems to turn now to Rose as he would turn to a mother.

But Noah will be all right. He has struggled for a truer conscience,
and gained it. He is, in that sense, cured and ready to become the artist
whose identification with the voiceless gives his show wings.

* * *

"Moon change" and "consequences unforeseen," are both a leit motif
and an embodiment, in the figure of the Moon herself, shiny, in a Josephine
Baker gown. She's present at the death of the assassinated President, but
she enters when Caroline and Dotty are having their quarrel — Caroline
considering Dotty a fast lady because she's going to college, and Dotty
replying that Caroline is "getting pinched and pruney / like them ladies in
your church." The Moon speaks, often beautifully, of the universal principle, but also to specific subplots of change, like Caroline's: "Change come
fast and change come slow / but change come, Caroline Thibodeaux" (33).

Yet Caroline is a rebel against change, in her situation, in the formality
with which she must address the uncomprehending people whom she works
for, and in her specific connections in the future vested in her own Emmie
and in Noah. Change is everywhere — only Caroline is unmoving, in her sad
understanding of white people, in her need, in the strength she brings to the
necessary and nearly crushing tasks she faces, in her way of living with loss.
Hope, for Caroline, is at one remove, as she passes a law and prays that her
"heathen daughter / don't never get hurt / nor learn how to mind me" (45).

Caroline is unmoving, yet she's given wings to Noah. He has learned the
heart's deep secret: in Auden's words, that "we must love one another or die."

In a time when faith, hope and charity are dying species, Kushner
keeps hope alive. In this piece of musical theater, he achieves what Goethe
said the stage was for — containing heaven, hell and earth in the relation
between an unhappy woman and a small, lost boy.

Contributors

Paula T. Alekson is a Visiting Instructor in Theatre Arts at Mount Holyoke College. She has received degrees from Brandeis University (playwriting) and from Mount Holyoke, and is currently completing her doctoral work in Drama at Tufts University where she was awarded the Professor Kalman A. Burnim Prize for Scholarly Excellence in Drama (2001) and the Student Award for Outstanding Contributions to Undergraduate Education (2000). Her dissertation examines the construction of the popular persona and image of Madame Vestris.

James Fisher (Editor) is Professor of Theater at Wabash College. He has been the McLain/McTurnan/Arnold Research Scholar and the LaFollette Lecturer at Wabash, and has twice held a six-month fellowship at Chicago's Newberry Library in 1991 and 2001 and was named 1996 "Indiana Theatre Person of the Year" by the Indiana Theatre Association, the year he directed the Indiana premiere of Tony Kushner's *Angels in America*. He has received fellowships and grants from the Society for Theatre Research and the Western European Center at Indiana University. Fisher is the author of five books, including *The Theater of Tony Kushner. Living Past Hope* (Routledge, 2002), *The Theater of Yesterday and Tomorrow: Commedia dell'arte on the Modern Stage* (The Edwin Mellen Press, 1992), and Greenwood Press bio-bibliographies of Al Jolson, Spencer Tracy, and Eddie Cantor. He is at work on a book examining fools and clowns in the plays of Luigi Pirandello, Eduardo de Filippo, and Dario Fo, as well as another book on gay drama post–*The Boys in the Band*. In collaboration with Felicia Hardison Londré he is also co-authoring the *Historical Dictionary of American Theatre: Modernism, 1880–1930*. He is editor of the *Puppetry Yearbook* and has published on theater and film in a wide variety of publications.

Atsushi Fujita received his MA at the Graduate School of Languages and Culture, Nagoya University, and finished a Ph.D program at the same school in March 2005. He enrolled in the Ph.D program in Theatre at the Graduate Center, City University of New York in 2003. His research interests are contemporary American gay theatre and queer theory. He is now an instructor at Aichi Gakuin University, Nihon Fukushi University and Nagoya Sangyo University. His published essays include "Response to The Boys in the Band: The Discourses of Minoritizing and Universalizing Views," published in *Chubu America Bungaku*, 2005,and "Dumb Type: Toward Unification of Art and Politics," published in *Tagenbunka*, 2003.

David Garrett Izzo has published nine books and over forty articles of literary scholarship concerning twentieth century literature including *The Writings of Richard Stern, W. H. Auden Encyclopedia, Christopher Isherwood Encyclopedia*, and *Stephen Vincent Benet: His Life and Work* (co-editor with Lincoln Konkle. He has also published two novels and two plays. He has a Ph.D. from Temple University and is a professor at Fayetteville State University in North Carolina, where he continues his work as a prolific scholar. David's website is: www.davidgarrettizzo.com.

Jeff Johnson is Professor of English at Brevard Community College. He is the author of several books, including *William Inge and the Subversion of Gender* (2005) and *Pervert in the Pulpit: Morality in the Works of David Lynch* (2004). He received an MFA in Creative Writing from Goddard College, an MA in English from the University of Central Florida, as has done postgraduate study at Columbia University and Harvard University. He is the winner of the 2001 Florida New Playwright Award, has directed his own work as well as plays by Marsha Norman, Sam Shepard, and Shakespeare, and has published in a wide range of publications.

Jacob Juntunen (Northwestern University) is currently a Ph.D candidate in Northwestern University's Interdisciplinary Program in Theatre and Drama. His dissertation focuses on Larry Kramer and Tony Kushner and asks how popular theatre in the late-twentieth century does political work. He has presented papers at numerous conferences and Jacob's original plays have been produced by Edward Albee and the Northwest Dramatists Guild, among others. Most recently, his play *A Kind of Surrender* was produced in Chicago by Infamous Commonwealth Theatre, where he is an ensemble member.

David Krasner teaches theatre, drama, and performance at Yale University. He has twice received the Errol Hill Award from the American Society of Theatre Research, and his book, *A Beautiful Pageant: African*

American Theatre, Drama, and Performance in the Harlem Renaissance, 1910–1927, was a 2002 finalist for the George Freedley Award of the Theatre Library Association. He recently edited Blackwell's *Companion to Twentieth-Century American Drama* (2005), and is currently co-editing *Staging Philosophy: New Approaches to Theater and Performance* (Michigan), editing an anthology *Theatre in Theory: 1900–2000* (Blackwell), and writing *American Drama, 1945–2000: An Introduction* (Blackwell). He is additionally working on his third installment of *African American Theatre and Performance History from 1927 to 1947.*

Felicia Hardison Londré is Curators' Professor of Theatre at the University of Missouri-Kansas City, Honorary Co-Founder of the Heart of America Shakespeare Festival, and dramaturge for the Nebraska Shakespeare Festival. In 2001 she received the Outstanding Teacher of Theatre in Higher Education award presented by the Association for Theatre in Higher Education. In 1998 she received a University of Montana Distinguished Alumna Award, having earned her B.A. there. After Fulbright studies at the Université de Caen, she earned her M.A. in Romance Languages at the University of Washington, and her Ph.D. at the University of Wisconsin. She has held visiting professorships at Hosei University in Tokyo and Marquette University in Milwaukee as well as invited lecture tours in Hungary and France, including the Sorbonne. In 1999 she was inducted into the College of Fellows of the American Theatre at the Kennedy Center in Washington, D.C., and has served as secretary of the board. She was the founding secretary of the Shakespeare Theatre Association of America, and has served as president of the American Theatre and Drama Society. She is currently president of the Kansas City-Westport branch of the League of American Pen Women. Winner of the 2003 National Amy & Eric Burger Essays on Theatre Competition, Felicia's ten books include *The History of North American Theater: The United States, Canada, and Mexico* (with Daniel J. Watermeier, Continuum, 1998), *Love's Labours Lost: Critical Essays* (Garland, 1997), *Shakespeare Companies and Festivals: An International Guide* (Greenwood, 1995), and *Words at Play: Creative Writing and Dramaturgy* (Southern Illinois University Press, 2005).

Stefka Mihaylova holds degrees in English from Sofia University (Bulgaria) and in Gender Studies from the Central European University in Hungary. Currently, she is a Ph.D. Candidate in the Theatre and Drama Program at Northwestern University. Her research focuses on late twentieth-century British and American feminist theatre, theatre semiotics and issues of reception. Stefka wishes to gratefully acknowledge the assistance of Juliette Caron, archivist at the Theatre of Europe at the Odeon, for providing documents from Giorgio Strehler's 1984 production of Corneille's *L'Illusion Comique.*

Bert Stern is Milligan Professor of English, Emeritus at Wabash College, and has taught at the Aristotle University of Thessaloniki as Fulbright Professor of American Literature and at Peking University as an exchange professor. He is also Vice President and Editor-in-Chief Emeritus at Hilton Publishing. At present, he teaches in a program for probationers called "Changing Lives Through Literature." Bert's essays have appeared in anthologies and, among others, *The New Republic, The Columbia Teacher's College Record, Southern Review, Sewanee Review, the Wallace Stevens Journal,* and *China Daily.* His poems have appeared in *Poetry, The Beloit Poetry Journal, New Letters, Indiana Review, The American Poetry Review, Off the Coast,* and elsewhere. His book on Wallace Stevens was published by The University of Michigan Press in 1965, and his chapbook, *Silk/The Ragpicker's Grandson,* was published by Red Dust in 1998.

Robert Vorlicky is Associate Professor of Drama (and coordinator of the Honors Program) at Tisch School of the Arts, New York University. He is the author of *Act Like a Man: Challenging Masculinities in American Drama* (1995) and editor of *Tony Kushner in Conversation* (1998) and *From Inner Worlds to Outer Space: The Multimedia Performances of Dan Kwong* (2004), all published by the University of Michigan Press. Prior to joining the Tisch faculty, he taught at Marymount Manhattan College. He is currently editor of performance and film reviews for *The David Mamet Review* and has served as president of The American Theatre and Drama Society (1999–2002). He has received fellowships from the NEH, Fulbright Foundation, Karolyi Foundation in Creative Writing, Wisconsin Arts Board grant for playwriting, and a Senior Research Fellowship from TSOA (1998).

Index

Access Hollywood 59, 72
ACT UP 17, 153
Actor's Equity Association 159
The Advocate 153
Age of Anxiety 74
AIDS 3, 16, 17, 18, 19, 21, 23, 25, 34, 38, 46, 47, 52, 53, 60, 90, 91, 94, 104, 109, 112–126, 153, 168
Albee, Edward 1, 9, 10, 16, 29, 38
Aleichem, Sholem 154
Alekson, Paula T. 3, 149–170, 215
All the Conspirators 67
Allen, Tim 174
al Qaeda 176
Altman, Nathan 151
The America Play 44
"America the Beautiful" 175
American Theatre 186
And the Band Played On 114
Anderson, Robert 8
Angels in America 1, 2, 3, 5–25, 28–53, 63, 66, 67, 70, 75, 77, 83, 90, 91, 92, 94, 95, 98–110, 112–126, 153, 160, 166, 172, 174, 179, 191, 194, 195, 205
"Angelus Novus" 66, 123, 194, 197
Animal Farm 58, 60
Ansky, S. 90, 93, 149–170
Arena Stage 152
Arizona Theatre Company 157
Armelina 130
Army-McCarthy hearings 108, 113, 115
ART (American Repertory Theatre) 213
As Is 112
The Ascent of F6, 65, 77, 78, 80, 82, 83, 84, 87, 88
Assassins 174
Auden, W.H. 4, 56–95
The Auden Generation 63
Auschwitz 192
AZT 24, 108, 118

Balaganchik 131
Baraka, Amiri *see* Jones, LeRoi
Beck, John 172

Beckett, Samuel 41, 42, 49
Benjamin, Walter 48, 66, 68, 69, 89, 91, 92, 93, 95, 101, 123, 194, 197
Bennett, Susan 173, 176, 177, 179
Bent 16
The Berkeley Repertory Theatre 176
Bernard Telsey Casting 160
Bersani, Leo 124, 125
Bethesda Fountain 109, 125
Bialik, Hayyim Nahman 151
The Bible 196
bin Laden, Osama 174, 175, 180
Blake, William 202
Bleuler, Eugen 75
Blok, Alexandr 131
Blood Wedding 43
Bloom, Harold 109, 149, 194
Bobbitt, Myra Hope 160, 161, 162, 163
Böhme-Kuby, Susanna 142
Boleyn, Anne 45
Bond, Edward 43
Bonner, Stephen Eric 100
Booth, Shirley 28, 33
Bornstein, Lisa 172
Borreca, Art 99
The Boston Globe 166
The Boston Herald 166
The Boy in the Basement 9
The Boys in the Band 16
Brady, Owen 64, 65
Brando, Marlon 12
Brantley, Ben 161, 166, 167, 169, 170
Brave New World 80
Brecht, Bertolt 2, 3, 17, 18, 22, 41, 43, 57, 69, 78, 91, 92, 95, 135–146, 152, 198
Brenton, Howard 43
A Bright Room Called Day 2, 57, 60, 61, 62, 63, 66, 91, 94, 153, 190
British Union of Fascists 57, 65
Broadway 8, 18, 113, 152, 157, 160, 166, 174
Brook, Peter 152
Brooklyn Academy of Music 161, 191
Brothers Grimm 152
The Brothers Karamazov 193

The Brown Book of Nazi Terror 62, 63
Brustein, Robert 22, 37, 38, 185
Budries, David 158, 159, 165
Bullins, Ed 41
Bush, George W. 57, 59, 60, 63, 73, 90, 174,
    175, 176, 180, 181, 184, 185, 186, 187, 191,
    192, 193
Bush, Laura 2, 193
Butler, Judith 121

Cabaret 64
Cadden, Michael 116
La Cage aux Folles 16
Calderón de la Barca, Pedro 130
California Shakespearean Festival 157
Camino Real 10, 12–13, 25, 44
Carey, James 182, 183
Carlson, Marvin 173, 177, 178, 183
Caroline, or Change 1, 2, 3, 201–214
Carousel 160, 166, 167
Cat on a Hot Tin Roof 13–14, 92
Cavett, Dick 21
Celestina 131
Central Park 109, 125
Chagall, Marc 151, 159
Chaiken, Joseph 152
Chaucer, Geoffrey 45
Chayefsky, Paddy 152
Chekhov, Anton 16, 41, 154
Chelsea Theatre Centre 190
Cheney, Richard 57
The Chicago Tribune 175, 186
The Children of Herakles 213–214
The Children's Hour 8
The Christian Science Monitor 184
Christiansen, Richard 186
Christopher and His Kind 64
The Chronicle of Higher Education 186
Churchill, Caryl 41, 43, 92
CIA (Central Intelligence Agency) 60, 193
Le Cid 128, 129, 142
Civil Rights 58, 201, 213
Clitandre 129
CNN (Cable News Network) 187
Cocteau, Jean 65
Cohn, Roy 2, 20, 21–22, 23, 24, 46, 47, 67,
    75, 83, 91, 106, 107, 112–126
The Cold War 72, 113, 181
Cole, Nat King 204, 205
Collins, Pat 158, 159
Columbia University 91
Come Back, Little Sheba 28–39
"Come Fly with Me" 196, 197
commedia dell'arte 131
Communist Party 63
Conklin, John 158, 159, 161, 162
Corneille, Pierre 8, 95, 127–134, 135–146,
    149–170
Corpus Christi 195
Coward, Noel 177

The Creation of the World and Other Business
    157
Crowley, Mart 16

The Dance of Death 65, 77
Dante 82, 84
Darwin, Charles 208
Dean, Phillip Hayes 41
Death of a Salesman 43
*The Death of the Last Black Man in the
    Whole Entire World* 44
DeGeneres, Ellen 63
DeLillo, Don 72
Democracy in America 99
Dendy, Michael 162
The Depression 66, 78
Desarthe, Gérard 140
Dickens, Charles 210
Disney World 186
The Dog Beneath the Skin 64, 65, 70, 77, 78,
    80, 94
Doone, Rupert 65, 77
Dorfman, Ariel 95, 152
Dorfman, Robert 170
Dort, Bernard 139, 140
Dostoyevsky, Fyodor 193
Doudai, Naomi 143
Down There on a Visit 64
The Drag 8
Drama Desk Award 153
Dretzin, Julie 160, 161, 162, 165, 166
A Dybbuk, or Between Two Worlds 3, 90, 93,
    95, 149–170, 205
Dyer, Richard 166

Early Auden 94
Edgar, David 43
Edwardes, Jane 1
Eisenhower, Dwight D. 37
Elder, Lonne, III 41
Eliot, T.S. 66, 73, 77, 78, 87
The Emperor Jones 44
The End of the Day 154
Endgame 49
Entertainment Tonight 72
Esperanto 198
Etheridge, Melissa 63
Eureka Theatre Company 160
Eustis, Oscar 105
Everything in the Garden 16

Faber & Faber 77–78
Fajrajsl, Diana 143
Fanger, Iris 166, 167, 184
Faulkner, William 205
FDA (Food and Drug Administration) 118
Feingold, Michael 42, 169, 170, 185, 186
Fierstein, Harvey 17, 92, 112
Finkle, David 160
Finnish IKL 59

Fischer, Ernst 17
Fisher, James 3, 4, 5–27, 38, 90, 91, 92, 94, 105, 127, 133, 137, 152, 168, 174, 190–200, 215
Foreman, Richard 41, 91, 92
Fornes, Maria Irene 41, 43
Franco, Francisco 76
Franklin, Nancy 112
Freud, Sigmund 69, 73, 76
Frost, David 6
Fuchs, Elinor 42
Fujita, Atsushi 3, 112–126, 215–216
Fulbright Scholar Program 128
Funnyhouse of a Negro 42, 43, 44, 45, 48, 49, 50, 53

Galati, Frank 191
La Galerie du Palais 129
García Lorca, Federico 43, 44
Gardner, Elysa 185
Garland, Judy 105
Geertz, Clifford 180, 183
Gender Trouble 121
Genet, Jean 31
Gibson, Mel 59
Gilbert, W.S. 78
Giuliani, Rudolph 172
The Glass Menagerie 10–11, 16, 19, 42, 44
Glimmer Glass Opera 154
Goethe, Johann Wolfgang von 95, 152, 214
Golder, John 138
Goldstein, Jess 158, 159, 162
"The Good Life" 69
The Good Person of Setzuan 95, 152, 153
Gorbachev, Mikhail 109
"The Grand Inquisitor" 193
Granovsky Theatre 151
Gray, Sam 163, 165, 167
Greenglass, David 115
Greenspan, David 43
Griffin, Roger 58, 59
Grim(m) 152
"The Group Movement of the Middle Class" 69
The Group Theatre (British) 65
Guare, John 17, 41, 43
Gussow, Mel 160
Guthrie, Tyrone 157, 158
Guthrie Theatre 157
Guzmán de Alfarache 130

Habimah Theatre 150, 151, 152, 153
The Hairy Ape 44
Hall, Howard 172
Halle, Randall 101
Halperin, David M. 122
Hamlet 87
Hammerstein, Oscar 160
Hardy, Alexandre 128
Hare, David 43, 92

Harries, Martin 99
Hartford Stage Company 135, 149–170
Hartigan, Patti 172
Hayden, Michael 160, 161, 162, 165, 166, 169
HBO (Home Box Office) 2, 77, 99, 112, 191
Hegel, Georg Wilhelm Friedrich 3, 33, 98–110
Hegel's Idea of Freedom 104
Heilpern, John 172, 198
Hellman, Lillian 8, 115
Hemingway, Ernest 35
Henry Box Brown 2
Herbert, Bob 56
Hinkle, Marin 170
Hirsch, John 152, 153
Hitler, Adolf 58, 60, 61, 65, 74, 76
HIV *see* AIDS
Hoffman, William 112
Hollywood 59, 92
Holocaust 61, 153, 167
Homebody/Kabul 2, 3, 44, 160, 172–188, 190–200
Homos 124
Hotel de Bourgogne 138
HUAC (House Un-American Activities Committee) 46
Hughes, Holly 43
Hughie 44
Hurwitt, Robert 172
Hussein, Saddam 191
Huxley, Aldous 66, 73, 80
Hwang, David Henry 41
Hydriotaphia, or The Death of Dr. Browne 95
Hynes, Samuel 63

The Illusion 3, 95, 127–134, 135–146
L'Illusion comique see *The Illusion*
Imperceptible Mutabilities of the Third Kingdom 44
"In Defense of Gossip" 68
Independence Day 180
Industrial Revolution 71
Inferno 42, 82
Inge, William 3, 9, 28–39
Ionesco, Eugene 41
Iraq War 2, 3, 191, 193
Isherwood, Charles 169
Isherwood, Christopher 4, 56–95
Israeli National Theatre 151
"It's Nice to Go Trav'ling" 196, 197
Izzo, David Garrett 4, 56–95, 216

Jackson, Janet 59
James, Henry 86, 87
Jeffrey 113
Johnson, Jeff 3, 28–39, 216
Johnson, Lyndon B. 212
Jones, LeRoi 16, 41
Jones, Robert Emmet 12, 13

Jones, Therese 112
Joseph Papp Public Theatre 149, 152, 157,
    167, 169, 170, 191
Joyce, James 210
Juntunen, Jacob 3, 172–188, 216

Kafka, Franz 154
Kant, Immanuel 101
Karzai, Hamid 176
Kauffmann, Stanley 9, 29–36
Kaufman, Moisés 7
Kazin, Alfred 6
Kennedy, Adrienne 4, 41–53
Kennedy, John F. 206
Kerr, Cynthia 141
Kerr, Walter 14
Kershaw, Baz 137, 143, 146
Kierkegaard, Soren 34, 66, 69, 71
King, Martin Luther 202
Kirkpatrick, Jeane 106
Klee, Paul 66, 123, 194, 197
Klein, Julia M. 186
Kleist, Heinrich von 95, 152
The Klezmatics 159
Knowles, Ric 173, 178
Korean War 204
Körner, Stephen 101
Kramer, Larry 16, 17, 90, 92, 112, 114
Krasner, David 3, 98–110, 216–217
Krebs, Albin 117
Kulick, Brian 167, 168, 169, 170
Kunitz, Stanley 92
Kushner, Tony (British historian) 57

Lahr, John 18
Lamkin, Marguerite 92
Lamos, Mark 3, 149–170
Lancaster, Burt 28
Lane, Nathan 63
Lang, Jack 136
Langham, Michael 157
Lawrence, D.H. 80, 87
Lawrence, T.E. 74, 75, 81, 83
League of American Theaters and Producers
    174
Leland, John 181
A Lesson in Dead Language 44
Letter to Lord Byron 71
Liam 65
Liebman, Ron 168
A Life of William Inge: The Strains of Tri-
    umph 36–37
Lincoln Center 160
Linney, Romulus 157
Lions and Shadows 62, 74, 75
Lips Together, Teeth Apart 113
Lloyd, Matthew 143
London, Frank 159
Londré, Felicia Hardison 3, 127–134, 217
Long Day's Journey into Night 42, 44

Lope de Rueda 130
LORT (League of Resident Theatres) 159
Los Angeles Drama Critics Circle Award 153
The Los Angeles Times 175, 186
Love-Suicide at Schofield Barracks 157
Love! Valour! Compassion!, 113
"The Loved One" 63
Love's Labours Lost 131
Ludlam, Charles 16, 92
Lumet, Sidney 152
Lumumba, Patrice 45, 47, 49

Maeterlinck, Maurice 42
Mallinson, G.J. 129
Mamet, David 41, 43
Manitoba Theatre Center 152, 153
Mann, Thomas 154
Manson, Charles 170
Mark Taper Forum 152, 153, 160
Markham, Kika 190
Marks, Peter 160, 181
Marley, Lord 63
Marx, Karl 68, 70, 76, 91, 92
McAuley, Gay 139
McCarthy, Joseph 9, 19, 36, 108, 113, 114,
    115, 118
McGovern, George 17
McKinley, Jesse 172
McLaughlin, Ellen 43
McNally, Terrence 92, 113, 195
Mee, Charles 41
Mélite 128
The Memorial 78
Mendelson, Edward 65
Le Menteur 130
Merlo, Frank 92
The Metropolitan Opera 154
Mihaylova, Stefka 3, 135–146, 217–218
Millennium Approaches see Angels in Amer-
    ica
Miller, Arthur 1, 22, 43, 56, 157
Miller, Dennis 170
Milner, Ron 41
Mitterand, François 136
Modern Humorist 175
Moise and the World of Reason 7
Molière 127
Mondory 129
Morrissett, Paul 159
Mosley, Oswald 57, 58, 59, 61, 65
Mother Courage and Her Children 91, 142
Ms. Magazine 114
Munich Biennale 154
Munich Olympics 2
Munsterberg, Willi 63
"Musée des Beaux Arts" 88
Mussolini, Benito 61, 63, 65, 74, 76
Myers, Bruce 152

The Nation 114, 117, 186

The National Endowment for the Arts 176, 177
National Lawyers Guild 115
The National Theatre of the Deaf 152
Nazis 57, 59, 61, 63, 65, 91, 152
The Necessity of Art 17
Nederlander Theatre 154
Neighborhood Playhouse 152
Neugroschel, Joachim 154, 155, 169
The New Criterion 184
The New Deal 63
The New Republic 185
The New York Post 183
New York Shakespeare Festival 62
The New York Theatre Workshop 160, 172–188, 190, 191
The New York Times 9, 117, 160, 161, 166, 181
New York University 172
Newsday 167, 168, 181
Newsweek 117, 120, 175, 176, 177
Nichols, Mike 99
Nicola, Jim 174, 175, 177
Nietzsche, Friedrich 61
The Night of the Iguana 20, 44
9/11 3, 172–188, 190–200
1984 58
Nixon, Richard M. 17
The Normal Heart 112
Northern Alliance 198
Northwestern University 157
The Notebook of Trigorin 16
Nussbaum, Martha 201

Obie Award 190
Off Broadway 149, 154, 156, 167, 168, 173
On the Frontier 65, 78
One Arm 7, 13
O'Neill, Eugene 1, 17, 18, 42, 43, 44, 90
Only We Who Guard the Mystery Shall Be Unhappy 2, 193
The Orators 76, 78
O'Regan, Michael 138
Orpheus Descending 13
Orwell, George 58, 60
Othello 114
Our Country's Good 154
Our Town 8
Owen, Wilfred 73
The Owl Answers 44, 45, 48, 50–51
Oxford University 92

Pacheco, Patrick 167
Palais Cardinal 138
Palais Royal 138
Parks, Suzan-Lori 43, 44, 51
The Passion of the Christ 59
The Patriot Act 181
Patten, Alan 104
PBS (Public Broadcasting System) 43, 152
The People Who Led to My Plays 41, 42

Perestroika see *Angels in America*
Phenomenology of Spirit 100
Phillips, Michael 172, 186, 187
The Philosophy of History 100
Pinter, Harold 41
Pirandello, Luigi 131
La Place Royal 129
The Play of the Week 152
Playwrights Horizons 154
Plummer, Christopher 157
Pochodo, Elizabeth 186
Podhoretz, John 183, 184
Portland Opera 154
Presley, Delma Eugene 16
Proust, Marcel 13
"Psychology and Art Today" 69
"Psychology and Criticism" 69
Pulitzer Prize 149, 153, 160
Pullman Car Hiawatha 94

Queen Victoria 45, 47, 49
Queer Nation 17
Queer Social Philosophy: Critical Readings from Kant to Adorno 101
Quintero, Fernando 60

Rafalowicz, Mira 152
Reagan, Ronald W. 2, 18, 22, 24, 59, 60, 70, 72, 90, 91, 94, 114
Redgrave, Vanessa 153
Reinelt, Janelle 141
Reports from the Holocaust 114
Reston, James, Jr. 186, 187, 195
Rilke, Rainer Maria 5, 92
The Rise and Fall of the City of Mahagonny 78
Roberts, Sam 115
Rodgers, Richard 160
Romanian Iron Guard 59
The Rose Tattoo 92
Rosenberg, Ethel 23, 24, 46, 47, 48, 113, 114, 115, 118, 119
Rosenberg, Julius 113, 114, 115, 118
Rostand, Edmond 157
Rousseau, Jean-Jacques 101
Rudnick, Paul 113
Ruíz de Alarcón, Juan 130
Rumsfeld, Donald 185

Safe Sex 112
St. Cecilia, or The Power of Music 2, 95, 152
Saint = Foucault 122
St. Patrick's Cathedral 153
San Francisco Opera 201
Sanchez, Sonia 41
Scarry, Elaine 108
Schechner, Richard 91
Schine, G. David 115
Schwarzenegger, Arnold 174
Schweitzer, Albert 154

Science of Logic 106
The Seagull 16
Seattle Opera 154
Sellars, Peter 214
Shakespeare, William 45, 47, 70, 114, 131, 157, 158
Shange, Ntozake 41
Shepard, Sam 41
Sherman, Martin 16
Sherrill, Robert 117, 120
Shilts, Randy 114
Simon, John 18
Sinatra, Frank 196, 197
The Sisters Rosensweig 160
The Skin of Our Teeth 66, 94
Sklamberg, Lorin 159
Sklepowich, Edward A. 6
Slavs! Thinking About the Longstanding Problems of Virtue and Happiness 2, 95, 153
Small Craft Warnings 14–16, 18, 21
Smith, Anna Deavere 41
Solomon, Alisa 99
Something Cloudy, Something Clear 16
Sondheim, Stephen 174
"Song of Songs" 165
Spanish Civil War 75
Spanish Falange 59
Spellman, Cardinal Francis 113
Spender, Stephen 73, 75, 76, 86, 87
Spielberg, Steven 2
Spoto, Donald 7
Springsteen, Bruce 77
Stalin, Josef 74, 153
Stanislavski, Constantin 142, 150
Stein, Gertrude 41, 42
Stella, a Play for Lovers 95, 152
Steppenwolf Theatre 191
Stern, Bert 3, 201–214, 218
Stern, Howard 59
Stevens, Amy 158, 161, 162
Stewart, Jon 175
Steyn, Mark 184
Stonewall riot 3, 17, 98, 99, 105, 106, 121
Strancar, Nada 140
A Streetcar Named Desire 11–12, 17, 19, 44
Strehler, Giorgio 135, 136, 137, 140, 141, 146
Strindberg, August 10, 42
Stuhlberg, Michael 169, 170
Suddenly Last Summer 14, 19, 20
La Suivante 129
Sullivan, Arthur 78
Summer and Smoke 11
Svigals, Alicia 159
Sweet Bird of Youth 13

Taliban 174, 176, 177, 181, 184, 186, 187, 191, 196, 199
Taylor, Charles 101
Taylor, Markland 166
Tea and Sympathy 8, 9

The Tempest 131, 132
The Tenth Man 152
Tesori, Jeanine 201–202
The Theater of Tony Kushner: Living Past Hope 94, 127, 152
Théâtre de l'Europe 135, 136, 140
Théâtre de Marais 138
"The Theatre of the Fabulous" 123
Theatre of the Ridiculous 16
TheatreMania.com 160
"Theses on the Philosophy of History" 66, 91, 123
Thinking About the Longstanding Problems of Virtue and Happiness 154
Thomas, Norman 17
The Threepenny Opera 78, 91, 136, 139
The Tiny Closet 9
The Toilet 16
Tony Award 149, 153, 154
Tony Kushner in Conversation 3
Torch Song Trilogy 16, 112
Traveling Jewish Theatre 152
Trotsky, Leon 92
"Troubling the Waters: Visions of Apocalypse in Wilder's *The Skin of Our Teeth* and Kushner's *Angels in America*" 94
Trump, Donald 113
Turville-Petre, Francis 64
"The Two Journeymen" 152

Understanding Brecht 91
Underworld 72
Université de Caen 128
USA Today 185

Vakhtangov, Evgeny 150, 151, 152
Vandergrift, Deborah 160, 161, 162, 163
Variety 166, 169
La Verdad sospechosa 130
La Veuve 129
La Vida es sueño 130
Vidal, Gore 7, 10
Vietnam War 17, 63, 191, 204
Vilar, Jean 142
The Village Voice 7, 169, 185
The Virgin Mary 48
Vogel, Paula 41, 92
Vorlicky, Robert 3, 41–55, 218
Voss, Ralph 36, 37

Wainwright, Jeffrey 143
"Walking Backwards into the Future" 91
War on Terror 3, 173, 176, 180, 181, 183, 185, 186, 190
Warhol, Andy 113
The Washington Post 160
Wasserstein, Wendy 160
The Waste Land 73
Webster, John 130
The Weekly Standard 183

Weimar Republic 59
Welch, Joseph 115, 116
Wellman, Mac 41
Wertheim, Albert 36
West, Mae 8
"Whispers of Immortality" 78
The White Devil 130
Who's Afraid of Virginia Woolf?, 9, 38
Widows 95, 152
Wilde, Oscar 62
Wilder, Thornton 8, 41, 66, 70, 78, 94
William the Conqueror 45, 47
Williams, Raymond 68, 69, 70, 91, 181, 194
Williams, Tennessee 1, 3, 5–27, 29, 38, 41, 42, 43, 44, 90, 92
Wilson, August 41
Windham, Donald 6

Winer, Linda 168, 170, 181
Wolcott, James 39
Wolfe, George C. 201
A Woman Killed with Kindness, or The Tragedy of Jane Shore 132
Wood, Allen W. 103
The World in the Evening 64
World Trade Center 172–188
World War II 89

Yale University 63
Yeats, William Butler 87
Yiddish Art Theatre 151
Yiddish theatre 3

Zion, Sydney 113

DATE DUE
